Egypt & Nasser

Volume 2

1957-66

Egypt & Nasser

Volume 2

1957-66

Edited by Dan Hofstadter

FACTS ON FILE, INC. NEW YORK, N.Y.

Egypt & Nasser

Volume 2

1957-66

Published by Facts on File, Inc.,
119 West 57th Street, New York, N.Y. 10019.

Library of Congress Catalog Card No. 74-154632
ISBN 0-87196-204-7

9 8 7 6 5 4 3 2 1
PRINTED IN
THE UNITED STATES OF AMERICA

CONTENTS

Page

INTRODUCTION 1

NASSER'S GROWING PRESTIGE AMONG ARABS (1957) 3
- U.S. Proposes Eisenhower Doctrine 3
- Wafdists Jailed 14
- Nasser Sponsors Elections 15
- Egyptian-Jordanian Strain 16
- Egypt Shuns West 18

FEDERATION WITH SYRIA (1957–8)............ 23
- Communists & Baathists Struggle for Syria 23
- Syrian-Turkish Crisis 26
- Egyptian-Syrian Economic Unity Steps 28
- USSR Vs. Turkish Buildup Against Syria......... 30
- Egyptian Troops in Syria 33
- Egypt & Syria Form UAR 35
- Syrian Communist Party Smashed 38
- Syria Alleges Plot by Saud 39
- UAR Federates with Yemen 41

THE UAR, ITS NEIGHBORS AND RUSSIA (1958–61)...................... 45
- Lebanese Insurrection & Iraqi Revolution 45
- Nile Waters Agreement....................... 53
- Nasser Quarrels with Kassem & Khrushchev....... 54
- 2d Soviet Loan for Aswan Dam 63
- Soviet-UAR Quarrel Renewed 65
- Nasser Bars Israeli Cargoes from Suez............ 66
- Attempt to Normalize UAR-Jordanian Ties....... 70

Page

EGYPTIAN-SYRIAN UNION'S FINAL YEARS (1959–61) 73
Domestic Developments 73
Foreign Relations 74
U.S. Labor Union Boycotts Egyptian Vessel 77
Syria Secedes from UAR 82
Yemeni Ties Cut 88

UAR: '3D WORLD' CHAMPION (1961–6) 91
Nasser's Blueprint for the Future 91
Egyptian-Israeli Missile Race 100
Syrian-Egyptian Relations Further Strained 102
Nasser Fails to Unite Egypt, Syria & Iraq 105
Arab Summit Meeting 116
UAR & Iraq Form Joint Command 119
Khrushchev Visits UAR 122
Other Developments 126
New Government, Parliament & Constitution 127
Cypriot Seeks Nasser's Support 137
Nasser Vs. Tshombé 139
U.S.-UAR Friction 145
Cairo-Bonn-Pankow-Jerusalem Dispute 147
Nasser Seeks Stronger Foreign Ties 157
Egyptian Editor Convicted as U.S. Spy 161
Opposition to the U.S. 162
Tunisia Ends Ties 165
Internal Developments 166
UAR & Arab League Boycott 3 U.S. Firms 168

ADVENTURE IN YEMEN (1959–66) 171
Crisis in Yemen 171
Civil War in Yemen 174
UAR Expands Military Role 183
Armistice 195
Fresh Clashes & New Negotiations 199
UAR Bogged Down in Yemen 203

Page

UAR Wages Gas Warfare 205
Egypt Withdraws from Yemen 210

INDEX 215

Wide World

Gamal Abdel Nasser

INTRODUCTION

THIS 2D VOLUME OF THE FACTS ON FILE record of *Egypt & Nasser* resumes the chronicle in early 1957. It takes up Egyptian Pres. Gamal Abdel Nasser's consolidation of power within Egypt and his emergence as a world figure. The resolution of the 1956 Suez crisis has been dealt with in the final section of the first volume.

In this volume the title United Arab Republic (UAR) is used frequently. This name was first given to a short-lived union of Egypt and Syria (1958-61). After this union dissolved, Egypt retained this supranational political designation as its official title. Reference works often list Egypt as United Arab Republic under the letter U for the entire period 1958-71. In the world of Arab journalism and diplomacy, Egypt was often referred to as *al-Gumhuriya al-Arabiya al-Muttahida* (United Arab Republic); but privately, Egyptians themselves preferred the simpler and more evocative *Misr* (Egypt).

Egypt proper is a nearly rainless expanse of desert in the northeast corner of Africa. The ribbon-like Nile valley, fanning into a broad delta as it approaches the Mediterranean, provides virtually all of the country's irrigation. In this valley, only 3½% of the nation's area, about 31 million people dwelt in 1966. In the 1960s the annual rate of population increase was about 3%—one of the world's highest. This factor, along with high life expectancy (about 53 years) and low emigration, accounts for a serious imbalance between resources and population. All domestic government policy is generally regarded as a direct or indirect attempt to resolve this pressing problem.

More than 92% of Egypt is Sunni (orthodox) Moslem; about 7% is Coptic Christian. Arabic is the universal language. Almost 35% of the population is illiterate.

Egypt was ruled by foreigners almost constantly from the time of Alexander the Great (4th century BC) until recently. The last period of foreign rule began in 1882, when the British occupied the country. Egypt became independent in 1922, but Britain retained paramount influence until the end of World War II. Under the reign of King Farouk (1936–52), the British diplomatic and military presence jockeyed for power with the palace and the country's major political party, the Wafd. Then a clandestine junta of military officers (the "Free Officers") seized power July 26, 1952. The junta proclaimed a republic June 18, 1953; by mid-Apr. 1954, after a series of struggles, their leader, Lt. Col. Gamal Abdel Nasser ('Abd-ul-Nasser), established himself as premier and virtual dictator of Egypt.

The first volume of this FACTS ON FILE treatment of Nasser's Egypt records the strongman's overthrow of Farouk, his elimination of his major domestic enemies, his negotiation of the withdrawal of British troops from Egyptian soil, his unsuccessful bid for American credits to finance a new Nile dam at Aswan, his subsequent break with the U.S., his nationalization of the Suez Canal, leading to the Suez crisis of 1956, and the aftermath of this crisis, including certain events of 1957. This volume records the story of Egypt from Jan. 1957 to Dec. 1966.

The period 1957–66 was a unique one in Egyptian history: Falling mainly between the 2d and 3d Egyptian-Israeli wars (the Sinai campaign of Nov. 1956 and the June war of 1967), it was a decade in which no foreign troops occupied Egyptian soil and its territorial integrity went unchallenged. This period of domestic peace also saw a rise in economic development unequalled since the 1920s, relative social order and unprecedented foreign prestige. But during this era of extensive influence abroad there were 2 major catastrophes in Egypt's Arab policy, each with far-reaching domestic and foreign consequences: the ill-fated union with Syria (1958–61) and the disastrous military intervention in the Yemeni civil war (1962–7).

NASSER'S GROWING PRESTIGE AMONG ARABS (1957)

U.S. Proposes Eisenhower Doctrine

The Suez crisis of 1956 brought both American and Soviet influence into the Mideast on an unprecedented scale. While welcoming its own new role, the U.S. was wary of the favor that the USSR had gained among many Arabs as a result of its pro-Egyptian stand.

The Eisenhower Doctrine was the major American response to the growth of Soviet influence in the Middle East after the onset of the Suez crisis. Pres. Dwight D. Eisenhower made his proposals before a special joint session of Congress Jan. 5, 1957, and these were incorporated in a joint Congressional resolution introduced a few minutes later by Rep. Thomas S. Gordon (D., Ill.), chairman of the House Foreign Affairs Committee. The resolution authorized the President (a) to employ U.S. armed forces to safeguard the independence of any country or group of countries in the Middle East requesting aid against aggression from a country controlled by international communism; and (b) to offer military and economic assistance to such lands.

Eisenhower had asked Congress to authorize him to commit the U.S., at his discretion, to cooperate with any Mideastern country in developing that country's economic strength as part of a new program designed to prevent Communist penetration of the area. Eisenhower requested $400 million in economic aid funds to carry out his Middle Eastern program over the next 2 years.

Explaining that his proposal "is primarily designed to deal with the possibility of Communist aggression, direct and indirect," Eisenhower told Congress that "it would, first of all, authorize the United States to cooperate with and assist any nation or group of nations in the Middle East in the development of economic strength dedicated to the maintenance of national independence." He asked Congress to let him finance the new economic and military programs with money "available under the Mutual Security Act of 1954, as amended, without regard to existing limitations." He said he did not ask for new money immediately because he thought "presently appropriated funds will be adequate for the balance of the present fiscal year [fiscal 1957] ending June 30." He said he would request "the authorization of $200 million to be available during each of the fiscal years 1958 and 1959 for discretionary use in the area."

The U.S. State Department seemed primarily concerned that the NATO bulwark in Turkey might be outflanked by Soviet penetration into Syria and eventually Egypt. Eisenhower, therefore, also requested authority to undertake "programs of military assistance and cooperation with any nation or group of nations [in the middle east] which desires such aid." This, he said, should "include the employment of the armed forces of the United States to secure and protect the territorial integrity and political independence of such nations requesting such aid against overt armed aggression from any nation controlled by international communism." Eisenhower said that such measures "would have to be consonant" with U.S. "treaty obligations," including the UN Charter, and with any UN "action or recommendation." "They would also, if armed attack occurs, be subject to the overriding authority of the United Nations Security Council in accordance with the Charter," he said.

The fact that Eisenhower and State Secy. John Foster Dulles were considering this plan—which Dulles was said to have originated—had already been made known to *N.Y. Times* writer James Reston by an unnamed "reliable source" Dec. 27, 1956. The President, it was reported, had discussed it with Dulles that day and intended to broach it to Congressional leaders Jan. 1, 1957. Observers labeled this and subsequent "leaks" to the press a "trial balloon" to test reaction in the U.S. and abroad. By Dec. 29, it was reported, the Administration had adopted the plan. Dulles and U.S. Amb.-

to-UN Henry Cabot Lodge conferred with UN Secy. Gen. Dag Hammarskjöld in New York Dec. 31 and were said to have discussed the new U.S. plan. Dulles Dec. 31 issued a statement saying U.S. policies had not "yet been finalized" and must "reinforce and fit into United Nations policies." A 2d Dulles statement Dec. 31 asserted that the U.S. "has a major responsibility to help prevent the spread to the Middle East of Soviet imperialism" and would "have to accept" during 1957 "an increasing responsibility to assist the free nations of the Middle East, and elsewhere, to maintain their freedom and to develop their welfare."

Eisenhower promised Congress Jan. 5 that if military action seemed "called for," he "would, of course, maintain hour-by-hour contact with the Congress if it were in session" or, if Congress were not in session and "the situation had grave implications, I would at once call the Congress into special session." Eisenhower warned that "in the situation now existing, the greatest risk . . . is that ambitious despots may miscalculate." If they "estimate that the Middle East is inadequately defended, they might be tempted to use open measures of armed attack," he predicted, and "that would start a chain of circumstances which would almost surely involve the United States in great military action." He said he was "convinced that the best insurance against this dangerous contingency is to make clear now our readiness to cooperate fully and freely with our friends of the Middle East in ways consonant with the purposes and principles of the United Nations."

Eisenhower announced that in his Jan. 5 message he would "send a special mission to the Middle East to explain the cooperation we are prepared to give." Eisenhower Jan. 7 appointed ex-Rep. James P. Richards (D., S.C.), 62, a former House Foreign Affairs Committee chairman, as $20,000-a-year head of the new mission. Richards, sworn in the same day, received the rank of ambassador and of special assistant to the President on Middle East problems. Dulles told the House Foreign Affairs Committee that Richards would be the "primary figure" in running the program.

The President said in his Jan. 5 message that his authority to use U.S. forces in the Middle East "would not be exercised except at the desire of the nation attacked" and that he hoped "this authority would never have to be exercised at all. Nothing is more necessary to assure this than that our policy with respect to the defense of the area be promptly and clearly determined and declared." "Experience shows," he said, "that indirect aggression rarely if ever succeeds where there is reasonable security against direct aggression, where the government possesses loyal security forces and where economic conditions are such as not to make communism seem an attractive alternative."

Eisenhower said there was an "imperative need that any lack of power in the area should be made good, not by external or alien force, but by the increased vigor and security of the independent nations of the area." Explaining the need for his program, Eisenhower told Congress that the UN "can always be helpful, but it cannot be a wholly dependable protector of freedom when the ambitions of the Soviet Union are involved." He cited the USSR's "callous indifference" to the UN General Assembly's "recommendations, even censure," over Hungary. He contrasted this with the UN's success in bringing about "a cease-fire and withdrawal of hostile forces from Egypt" by "governments and peoples who had a decent respect for the opinions of mankind as reflected in the United Nations General Assembly."

Eisenhower listed 3 "simple and indisputable facts" with which he said the world was confronted: (1) "The Middle East, which has always been coveted by Russia, would today be prized more than ever by international communism"; Russia needed "a recognizable success" to offset its failure in Hungary, and addition of the Mideast to its sphere would be an important step in achieving its "announced purpose of communizing the world." (2) "The Soviet rulers continue to show that they do not scruple to use any means to gain their ends." (3) "The free nations of the Mideast need, and for the most part want, added strength to assure their continued independence."

Eisenhower said he deemed it "necessary to seek the cooperation of the Congress" because "only with that cooperation can we give the reassurance needed to deter aggression, to give courage and confidence to those who are dedicated to freedom and thus prevent a chain of events which would gravely endanger all of the free world." He said that "our joint resolve should be so couched as to make it apparent that if need be our words will be backed by action." The President conceded that his plan "will not solve" or even "deal directly" with "the problems of Palestine and relations between Israel and the Arab states, and the future of the Arab refugees" or "the future status of the Suez Canal."

The joint resolution introduced by Rep. Gordon Jan. 5 was worded so as to authorize the President to use U.S. forces "as he deems necessary to secure and protect the territorial integrity and political independence" of Middle Eastern nations "requesting such aid against overt armed aggression from any nation controlled by international communism." It also provided that: (a) such action "shall be consonant" with U.S. treaty obligations, the UN Charter and UN actions and recommendations; (b) such measures "shall be immediately reported to the Security Council and shall not . . . affect the authority and the responsibility of the Security Council" to restore peace and security; (c) the President might use up to $200 million from any existing mutual security appropriations "without regard to the provisions of any other law or regulation"; (d) he must report his actions under the program to Congress every January.

The new Eisenhower Doctrine was criticized by Democratic leaders in the U.S. Senate, but many Republicans seemed ready to support it. Foreign diplomats gave it a mixed reception. Sen. Alexander Wiley (Wis.), ranking Republican of the Senate Foreign Relations Committee, had said Dec. 28, 1956 that Congress would act "in the interest of peace" if it gave the President standby authority to use U.S. forces in the Middle East. He said he considered the situation similar to one in 1955, when Congress gave Eisenhower such authority in the case of Taiwan (Formosa). But Sen. Mike Mansfield (D., Mont.) of the Senate Foreign Relations Committee said he saw no parallel. He pointed out Dec. 28 that before Congress had acted in 1955, Eisenhower had "committed" the U.S. "to defend Formosa against any major assault," and there was "an already negotiated American-Nationalist Chinese security pact." But, he said, in the Middle East "we have already gone to the UN with the matter. Why . . . authorize the President to get us, alone, stuck out there?" Wiley denied Dec. 30 that the plan meant a break in the Eisenhower policy of working through the UN. He said he was sure the President would not use the authority requested "except in conjunction" with the UN. Sen. Hubert H. Humphrey (D., Minn.) of the Senate Foreign Relations Committee charged Dec. 30 that the Eisenhower Administration had proposed an "adolescent and shocking" shift in position after, "in effect," it had "renounced the use of force." He said it would be wiser to come out for a strong UN police force for the Middle East. Humphrey also accused the Administration of "insulting" Democratic Senators by telling the press about its plans before informing any members of the Senate majority. He called it "a rather peculiar and unorthodox way of announcing a new policy." Sen. John J. Sparkman (D., Ala.) of the Senate Foreign Relations Committee said Dec. 30 that he saw no need to give Eisenhower "advance authority" since Congress would be in session and immediately available if emergency action were required.

Eisenhower's request for authority to use U.S. military force to repel Communist aggression in the middle east was rejected Feb. 13 by the Senate Foreign Relations and Armed

Services Committees. The committees, by vote of 15 Democrats to 13 Republicans, adopted a substitute announcing that the U.S. "is prepared to use armed forces to assist any nation or group of nations requesting assistance against armed aggression from any country controlled by international communism; provided, that such employment shall be consonant" with U.S. "treaty obligations" and the UN Charter.

The negative reaction on the part of the Soviets to the Eisenhower Doctrine was predictable, but an anti-U.S. response was reported among many Arabs too—even in pro-American Jordan. The Soviet Communist Party newspaper *Pravda* denounced the Eisenhower Doctrine Jan. 1, 1957 as a plan "for the further enslavement of Middle Eastern peoples" that would turn the area "into a permanent hotbed of military conflict." *Pravda* called it a "plan to strengthen American colonial domination" in the Middle East and charged that one aim "is to grab the riches of the Middle East region, which are slipping out of the hands of the British colonialists." The unofficial Soviet government newspaper *Izvestia* Jan. 4 labeled the proposal an effort to "rekindle the flames of war in the Middle East."

Jordan's National Front Party warned in a cable to Eisenhower Jan. 6 that a threat of military intervention would increase Arab hatred of the U.S. It assailed the Eisenhower Doctrine as a violation of the UN Charter.

A deadlock in negotiations over Egyptian assets in the U.S., frozen during the Suez crisis, was a further setback for American-Egyptian relations. Egyptian Amb.-to-U.S. Ahmed Hussein met Jan. 14 with William Rountree, Assistant State Secretary for Mideast affairs, in a vain attempt to secure the release of an estimated $40–$60 million in Egyptian assets.

State Department News Division chief Lincoln White Jan. 14 denied reports that the U.S. had refused Egypt permission to buy U.S. surplus wheat. Egyptian wheat purchases in the U.S. were reported Jan. 14 to have totaled 280,000 tons (worth $19.6 million) since 1955. (The U.S. Agriculture Department Jan. 15 authorized Israel to buy $1.9 million worth of surplus corn under an agreement made before Israel invaded Egypt).

Egyptian Pres. Gamal Abdel Nasser said Jan. 16 that he had asked the U.S. for an explanation of "the vague parts" of the Eisenhower Doctrine. Nasser, interviewed by the evening *Ethnos* of Athens on his 39th birthday, asserted that he was not "pro-East or pro-West" but that, "while Russia helped us" during the Suez crisis, "America froze $50 million" in Egyptian assets.

The Eisenhower Doctrine apparently brought Syria even closer to the USSR. Syrian Foreign Min. Salah el-Bitar declared Jan. 4 that 2 elements must be added to the U.S. plan for it to win Arab support: (a) "It should not restrict the use of force . . . [to] aggression by just one side . . . [but] should mention that force will be used against all aggression from, whatever direction it comes"; (b) "all countries agreeing with the United States in opposing aggression should participate with her in using force against an aggressor."

The *N.Y. Times* reported Jan. 15 that Syria had recently received 10 MiG-17 jet fighters and was scheduled to receive Soviet pilots and technicians to train Syrians to use the aircraft.

In a joint statement issued Jan. 21 following talks in New Delhi Jan. 17-19, Indian Prime Min. Jawaharlal Nehru and Syrian Pres. Shukri al-Kuwatly said that "a military approach" to the problems of the Mideast would "only serve to create further disharmony" and endanger world peace. The statement denounced "intervention by big powers in the form of military pacts and alliances" as "detrimental" to the Mideast. "The Baghdad Pact," it noted, "has caused bitter conflicts and divisions in the Arab world and has greatly increased international tensions."

Syria, Egypt, Saudi Arabia and Jordan, in a statement

issued Jan. 19 following talks in Cairo, rejected the Eisenhower Doctrine's "vacuum theory" of Mideastern politics and said that Arab nationalism was "the sole basis on which Arab policy could be formulated." Leaders of the 4 Arab countries agreed "never to allow their countries to become a sphere of influence for any foreign power."

After attending the Arab meeting, King Saud of Saudi Arabia met Jan. 30-Feb. 1 with Pres. Eisenhower and State Secy. John Foster Dulles in Washington for talks centering on the Eisenhower Doctrine and Middle East politics. Dulles told newsmen Feb. 1 that the talks had "gone extremely well" and that "a good many misunderstandings" about U.S. Mideast policy had been "cleared up." Eisenhower said at his news conference Feb. 6 that his talks with Saud had cleared away "much of the underbrush of misunderstanding" and had resulted in progress toward "a peaceful and maybe even eventually a united Middle East."

Saud, in a *N.Y. Herald Tribune* interview Feb. 3, had said that the Arab states would accept the Eisenhower Doctrine if "the points I raised here could be clarified to them as they have been to me." Saudi Arabian officials said Feb. 4 that the king hoped to "open the door" for rebuilding of Egypt's and Syria's ties with the West through his talks with Eisenhower. Saud had remained in Washington for further talks with the President after the close of his formal visit Feb. 1. The king told newsmen Feb. 6 that the Eisenhower Doctrine was "a good one . . . , entitled to consideration and appreciation" by Arab states. Saud ended his visit to the U.S. Feb. 9. In a communiqué issued jointly with Saud Feb. 8, Eisenhower expressed U.S. willingness to "provide assistance for the strengthening of the Saudi Arabian armed forces within the constitutional processes" of the U.S. Saud pledged a 5-year extension of the agreement governing U.S. use of the Dhahran air base.

The 4 Moslem states of the Baghdad Pact–Turkey, Pakistan, Iran and Iraq—declared their full support of the Eisenhower Doctrine Jan. 21 as "best designed to maintain peace" in the Mideast and to "advance the economic well-being of [its] peoples." A communiqué issued following meetings of leaders of the 4 states in Ankara Jan. 19–20 "noted with satisfaction" that the U.S. plan "recognizes the threat posed by Communist aggression and subversion in countries of the Middle East." The communiqué also (a) called for "early settlement of the Palestine question through the UN," (b) "expressed the hope" that "freedom of navigation in the Suez Canal consistent with Egyptian sovereignty" would be insured "in accordance with the [Constantinople] Convention of 1888" and "that the Canal should be insulated from the politics of any one power," and (c) "deplored the destruction of pipelines in Syria" and urged their "early restoration." The Ankara talks, presided over by Turkish Pres. Celâl Bayar, involved Turkish Premier Adnan Menderes, Iraqi Premier Nuri as-Said, Pakistani Premier Hussein Suhrawardy and Iranian Premier Hussein Ala and were attended by Iraqi Crown Prince Abdul Illah.

Pres. Nasser of Egypt, King Saud of Saudi Arabia, Pres. Shukri al-Kuwatly of Syria and King Hussein of Jordan met in Cairo with their defense ministers Feb. 25–27 to coordinate Arab political and military strategy. Saud, en route home from the U.S., briefed the conference Feb. 25–26 on the Eisenhower Doctrine and U.S. mideastern policy. He was reported to have failed in an effort to persuade the conferees to adopt a strong statement opposing Soviet infiltration of the Mideast. A communiqué issued Feb. 27 reaffirmed the 4 Arab states' policies of "positive neutrality" and said that the rulers were determined to "protect the Arab nations from the harms of the cold war." Without mentioning the Eisenhower Doctrine, they declared that "the defense of the Arab world should emanate from the Arab nation in the light of its real security and outside the scope of foreign pacts." The communiqué also: demanded Israeli withdrawals from Egypt and compensation of Egypt by Israel, Britain and France for invasion damage; upheld Egypt's "sovereignty" over the Suez Canal; and condemned alleged British "aggression" against Yemen.

Sudanese Foreign Min. Muhammad Ahmed Mahgoub told the Sudanese parliament May 28 that Sudan would neither reply to nor announce a policy toward Eisenhower-Doctrine aid offers for the time being.

Lebanese Foreign Min. Charles Malik told the Lebanese parliament Nov. 26 that the U.S. had pledged "unlimited" economic and military assistance to Lebanon in return for Lebanese adherence to the Eisenhower Doctrine. Malik, defending the pro-Western policies of Premier Sami es-Solh, said that U.S. aid offers had been limited only by Lebanon's capacity to absorb such aid. He said that the U.S. had given "clarification" that Lebanon was not committed under the Eisenhower Doctrine to involvement in U.S. military actions or Arab-Israeli peace efforts. He indicated that the U.S. had agreed to ease requirements for "counterpart funds" and would supply missile equipment for the Lebanese army.

U.S. State Secy. Dulles, testifying Jan. 7 before the House Foreign Affairs Committee on Eisenhower's new Mideast program, had said that under the new plan "it would be entirely possible" for the U.S. to resume the shipment of military aid to Israel. Dulles said that the U.S. had limited all arms shipments to the Middle East to "relatively small amounts."

The Israeli government May 21 announced its adherence to the Eisenhower Doctrine despite threats by left-wing Mapam and Ahdut Avodah cabinet members to resign from Premier David Ben-Gurion's government and oppose the issue in the Knesset (parliament).

(The Libyan government, in an announcement disclosing that U.S. aid was scheduled at $23 million during fiscal

1957–8, revealed that $7 million of the amount had been pledged from Eisenhower-Doctrine funds.)

Wafdists Jailed

In July 1957, apparently relying on his new popularity, Nasser, who was believed to still fear the influence of the old Wafd party, especially in the Delta area, staged a new attack on the Wafd's already decimated cadres.

The Egyptian government confirmed July 18 that ex-Foreign Min. Muhammad Salah el-Din and other Wafdist politicians and army officers had been arrested in Apr. 1957 for plotting against the Nasser regime. The government said July 19 that a supreme military court had been created to try the group, reported to have been led by Ahmed Atf Nassar, a former Egyptian army brigadier. The reports stated that Egyptian security police had arrested 12 former cabinet ministers and other politicians and 70 Egyptian army officers of the Alexandria garrison on charges of plotting to restore Maj. Gen. Muhammad Naguib, former Egyptian president and premier. Among those reported held were Salah el-Din, last Wafdist foreign minister under the Farouk monarchy; Abdel Fattah Hassan, Wafdist ex-war and social affairs minister; and Ahmed el-Sakka, ex-aide to former Wafdist Premier Mustafa Nahas.

The trial of the accused opened before the special military court Aug. 12. Salah el-Din, Hassan and Sakka were found guilty and imprisoned Oct. 20.

Egyptian officials Aug. 30 had announced the arrest of 18 persons charged with being members of an underground Communist Party pledged to overthrow the Nasser regime. 13 members of the party were tried *in camera* Oct. 21–24. They were sentenced Oct. 31 to imprisonment on charges of conspiring to overthrow the government. Shortly thereafter the property of all Communist-front organizations was confiscated by the Egyptian government.

Nasser Sponsors Elections

Nasser May 27, 1957 decreed himself chairman of a newly formed National Union, which was created to be Egypt's sole political party.

The Egyptian government announced June 17 a list of 1,142 officially approved National Union candidates for 350 seats in Egypt's proposed unicameral Majlis al-Umma (National Parliament). The announcement said that approved candidates had been selected by Nasser and 3 cabinet members from a list of 2,469 prospective candidates. (51 candidates permitted to campaign unopposed included all 16 members of the Nasser cabinet.) 1,210 candidates were rejected as "unworthy"; they included all the candidates presented in 5 entire constituencies.

The elections took place July 3, and 5 million Egyptians voted for candidates to Egypt's first post-revolution national parliament. The voting, limited to 270 constituencies permitted to put up approved opposition candidates, was repeated July 14 in 168 districts where candidates had failed to win a majority. 2 women candidates, Mrs. Rawia Attia, 34, a captain in a women's commando unit, and Mrs. Amina Shoukri, 40, an Alexandria welfare leader, were elected July 14 as the first known female members of any Arab parliament. 16 persons were killed July 3 and 2 more July 14 in election disorders.

Nasser opened the new Majlis (parliament) July 22, asserting that Egypt had won its "war of independence" against the "imperialists." Nasser outlined the government's economic plans, which were aimed at reducing poverty in Egypt. He said that the government had established an atomic energy commission and would submit bills to provide for the first stage of construction of the Aswan High Dam at an estimated cost of E£60 million ($172.8 million).

Nasser told the Majlis July 22 that Egypt had broken the West's monopoly on Mideast arms by turning to the Soviet bloc for equipment. He reviewed Soviet and Czechoslovak-equipped Egyptian troops in Cairo July 23 in celebrations marking the 5th anniversary of Egypt's military revolution against the Farouk monarchy. Arms shown July 23 included Soviet mobile rocket launchers, howitzers, multiple machine guns and flights of Ilyushin and MiG jets.

Nasser Aug. 2 named Wing Commander Ali Sabry, his chief political aide, to the cabinet-rank post of state minister for presidential affairs.

Egyptian-Jordanian Strain

The resolution of the 1956 Suez crisis in Egypt's favor gave Nasser great prestige in an Arab world in which tensions were rising between traditionally pro-Western Arabs and pro-Nasser Arabs more favorable to the Eastern bloc. Nasserite factions appeared in all the so-called "moderate" Arab states.

The clash between pro-Western elements and Nasserites was especially severe in Jordan, ruled by the Western-educated Hashemite King Hussein, linked until Mar. 13, 1957 by a military treaty to Britain but also inhabited by large numbers of Palestinians who felt especially attracted to Nasser's "anti-imperialist" foreign policy. Jordan protested in June 1957 against allegedly illicit activities of the Egyptian embassy and Nasserite "agents" in Amman, the Jordanian capital, and Egypt retaliated.

The Jordanian and Egyptian governments June 10, 1957 demanded the recall of high diplomatic and military representatives in Amman and Cairo but made no move to sever diplomatic relations. Jordan demanded the withdrawal of Lt. Col. Fuad Hillal, Egyptian military attaché in Amman, and Muhammad Abdul Aziz, Egyptian consul general in Jerusalem, charging that Hillal had plotted to assassinate several "official personalities" during the current visit of Saudi Arabian King Saud. (Saud had arrived in Jordan June 8 for talks with King Hussein, reportedly on the formation of an anti-Soviet bloc of Arab states.) Egypt demanded the recall of Jordanian Amb.-to-Egypt Abdel Moneim el-Rifai. Egypt denied the assassination charges against Hillal and asserted that he was the victim of a Jordanian frame-up.

A Jordanian government statement June 11 derided the Egyptian charges and noted a series of complaints and expulsions directed against Egyptian military attachés by the governments of Libya, Tunisia, Sudan, Iraq, Lebanon and Saudi Arabia. Jordan also reportedly demanded the withdrawal of the Egyptian delegate to the joint Arab military command in Amman June 10 and of Col. Jawdat al-Attassi, Syrian military attaché in Amman, June 11.

Egypt's semi-official Middle East News Agency, in what observers termed a major propaganda barrage against Jordan, charged June 23 that Jordanian Deputy Premier and Foreign Min. Samir el-Rifai and Israeli Premier David Ben-Gurion had met at U.S. instigation "with a view to reaching agreement . . . [on the] conclusion of a peace agreement between the 2 countries." The news agency claimed that an agreement already had been reached between Israel and "the representatives of pro-West Arab countries on the forcible transfer of Palestinian refugees to . . . the desert between Jordan and Iraq."

King Hussein visited his cousin King Feisal of Iraq (also of the Hashemite dynasty) June 22–24. A joint communiqué issued June 24 stressed the "brotherly atmosphere" of the discussions and announced the reactivation of the Iraqi-Jordanian treaty of 1947, which entailed a certain amount of military cooperation. In what was widely interpreted to be an implicit reference to Egypt, the communiqué stated: "No Arab country should interfere in the internal affairs of any other Arab country." The statement was considered a rebuff to Nasser.

A 2d critical point in Egypt-Jordan relations occurred in November, when Nasser initiated a press and radio "war" against King Hussein. Details of the propaganda campaign and Hussein's reaction:

Nov. 3—The Cairo newspaper *Al-Shaab* accused Hussein of negotiating with Israel in exchange for a $30 million U.S. bribe.

Nov. 4—A Jordanian government statement accused "responsible Egyptians" of "carrying out secret communications and contacts with the Israelis." It denounced Nasser as a "little dictator," a "slave of Moscow," a "Don Quixote hitting only himself."

Nov. 4-14—The Egyptian press and radio "war" was intensified. Egyptian propagandists accused Jordan of becoming a "base of American imperialism." The Jordanian press attacked the Egyptian press and accused Egyptian journalists of "ignoring the ethics of journalism and prostituting their profession."

Nov. 9—Hussein thanked the Jordanian people for their demonstrations of loyalty.

Nov. 13—Hussein attacked Nasser as a "tool of international communism."

Nov. 14—King Saud of Saudi Arabia and King Feisal of Iraq called on Egypt to cease the propaganda attack.

The press and radio "war" subsided after mid-November. Many observers described it as an unprecedented attempt to foment revolution through the use of the news media.

Egypt Shuns West

Because of Egypt's poor relations with the West, the result of the Suez crisis and the nationalization policy that followed it, Nasser turned Eastward in search of loans and armaments.

The Soviet Union had flaunted in front of the Western Big 3, in mid-February and in mid-April 1957, its new diplomatic penetration of the Middle East via Egypt and Syria. The U.S., Britain and France, in similar notes June 11, rejected Soviet proposals for a Big-4 declaration of a "hands off" policy in the Middle East. The U.S. note, made public in

Washington June 12, said that the USSR's Feb. 11 bid for talks on a Big-4 declaration of joint Mideastern policy was unacceptable. Such a declaration would limit the sovereignty of Middle Eastern states, the U.S. said. It also rejected a Soviet proposal of Apr. 19 for a Big-4 declaration against the use of force in the Mideast, asserting that opposition to the use of force already was a "cardinal element" of U.S. foreign policy.

In turning down what were considered Soviet bids for Western recognition of a Communist role in Mideastern matters, the U.S. advised the USSR that it could best bolster peace in the Middle East by "working constructively within the . . . [UN] for the solution of fundamental problems in the area, among which the Arab-Israeli dispute is outstanding." The U.S. noted, however, that the USSR, instead, had carried out "subversive intervention" against several Middle Eastern states. The British note specifically rejected Soviet charges that the Baghdad Pact had been used for Western intervention against Mideastern governments.

With closer ties to the USSR, Nasser became more stridently anti-Western and anti-U.S. in his public utterances. He charged July 26 that the U.S. had tried to isolate and ruin Egypt after Britain and France had failed in military attempts to force Egypt into submission to the West. Nasser, addressing Alexandrians on the first anniversary of his nationalization of the Suez Canal, said that, "in league with imperialists and world Zionism," the U.S. had abandoned its initial support of Egypt in the UN and had brought "pressure against Egypt by stopping the sale of wheat and oil." "This plan," he charged, "was to realize by peaceful means what the aggressors had failed to realize by force."

Asserting that a Soviet ultimatum of Nov. 5, 1956 had "scared the British and French out of their wits" and had halted fighting in the Canal Zone, Nasser argued that Western "hatred" of Egypt had then grown great enough for Western leaders to devise a divisive scheme for renewed Western penetration. Thus the U.S. had used the Eisenhower Doctrine to "isolate Egypt from the rest of the Arab states and to try to work from within these Arab states" on the pretext of combatting communism. The U.S., he charged, had attempted to force Egyptian participation in the Eisenhower Doctrine by freezing Egypt's funds in the U.S.

Nasser asserted that all these efforts to dominate Egypt had failed. He said: "We had to fight 2 big nations, as well as Israel, and finally the American dollar. But we emerged victorious. . . . We now know who are our friends and who are our enemies."

Nasser, in a filmed interview broadcast July 1 by Britain's Independent Television Authority (ITV), had said he was "sorry about the period of bad relations between Britain and Egypt" but had denounced U.S. Middle Eastern policies for forcing Arab nationalists to turn to communism. Nasser, speaking in English, described Egypt's foreign policy as one of "nonalignment" with the East or West. He defended Egypt's acquisition, in mid-June, of 3 Soviet submarines—2 of them with a range of 20,000 miles and a maximum submerged speed of 16 knots, the 3d a short-range or coastal craft with a 3,400-mile range and submerged speed of 3 knots—as necessary for building up the Egyptian navy.

Nasser, accompanied by Maj. Gen. Abdel Hakim Amer, the Egyptian defense minister, observed naval maneuvers off Alexandria July 27 by Egyptian fleet units including the 3 Soviet subs.

A spokesman for the Israeli Foreign Ministry had said after an emergency meeting of the Israeli cabinet June 19 that Israel intended to ask the Western Big 3 to restore the balance of arms in the Middle East following the latest Soviet move. Radio Israel had warned Egypt later June 19 not to use the new submarines to block Israeli shipping in the Gulf of Aqaba and declared that such a blockade would "light the fires" again and would be suicidal for Egypt.

These totals for post-World War II U.S. and Soviet aid pledges to Egypt, Syria and Yemen had been listed Feb. 8 by the *N.Y. Times* (U.S. figures not including surplus farm commodity sales or military aid pledged through the Defense Department): *To Egypt*—U.S. $61,678,000, Soviet bloc $480 million. *To Syria*—U.S. nothing, Soviet bloc $280 million. *To Yemen*—U.S. nothing, Soviet bloc $26.4 million (including a $16.4 million Communist Chinese loan agreement signed Jan. 13).

Nasser, in a message to the 6th annual meeting of the Organization of Arab Students, held in Berkley, Calif., warned Sept. 2 that the Arab world was ready for "a long struggle" and, if necessary, war against the "imperialist nations."

Official Cairo pronouncements late in 1957 indicated increasingly bad relations with the USSR.

An agreement on Soviet-Egyptian cultural cooperation was signed in Cairo Oct. 19. Maj. Gen. Abdel Hakim Amer, Egypt's war minister and army chief, went to Moscow Nov. 1 as the guest of Soviet Defense Min. Rodion Malinovsky. Amer attended the military parade commemorating the 40th anniversary of the Great October Bolshevik Revolution; he watched maneuvers and inspected Soviet military camps.

It was confirmed in Cairo Nov. 25 that the Czechoslovak government had granted Egypt about $60 million dollars in credits for the supply of capital equipment for Egypt's new industrialization program.

Early in 1958, Egypt signed a major loan agreement with the USSR. Egyptian Industry Min. Aziz Sidky and Chairman Mikhail G. Pervukhin of the Soviet State Committee for Economic Relations with Foreign Countries, meeting in Moscow Jan. 29, signed agreements providing for a reported 700 million-ruble ($175 million at official rates), 12-year loan at 2½% and for increased technical assistance to Egypt. The loan was to be repayed in cotton and other farm products and "freely convertible currencies." The accord reportedly was to bring many Soviet technicians to Egypt for work on projects planned under a 5-year, $750 million Egyptian development program. The agreement was approved by the Egyptian Majlis (parliament) Feb. 10, 1958.

FEDERATION WITH SYRIA (1957-8)

There was precedent for an attempt to unite Egypt and Syria. Egyptian forces had seized Syria from the Turks and occupied it from 1831 to 1839. Mehmet Ali, the Egyptian *pasha*, had centralized government over Aleppo, Damascus, Homs, Jezire, Latakia and Lebanon before the European powers intervened on the sultan's behalf. Under Nasser, Egypt and Syria, both independent of Turkey for about 40 years, were united again—for more than 3½ years, from Feb. 1, 1958 to Sept. 28, 1961—as the United Arab Republic.

Communists & Baathists Struggle for Syria

In 1955 Syria had only 2 political parties with effective organization: the pro-Moscow Communist Party and the Arab Socialist *Baath* (Ba'th, or Resurrection) Party. The latter was a merger of the Arab Socialist Party and al-Baath, founded in 1940 by 2 Syrian teachers in Paris, Michel Aflaq, a Greek Orthodox Christian native of Damascus, and Salah el-Din el-Bitar (Salah-ul-Din Bitar), a Damascene Moslem, later Syria's foreign minister (in 1956–7). The chief tenet of Baath doctrine is a militant and radical espousal of Pan-Arab unity. Its slogan is "Unity, Freedom, Socialism—One Arab Nation, the Bearer of an Eternal Mission." Hence, unlike communism, Baathism is nationalist or supranationalist—not internationalist; it is also Socialist and anti-Zionist.

Bitar and another Baathist were included in the Syrian cabinet in July 1956, and later that year a leading Baathist was elected chairman of the Syrian legislature. The post of chief of army intelligence also went to a Baathist, Col. Abdul Hamid al-Serraj, who ruthlessly rooted out political opponents.

The Suez crisis of 1956 was considered a boon to Syrian leftists—to the Baathists because of the similarity of their views to those of the triumphant Nasser, and to the Communists because of the pro-Egyptian stand adopted by the Soviet Union.

A close cooperation developed between the Baathists and the Communists early in 1957. Conservative candidates suffered a severe defeat in the May by-elections; in the following months, prominent moderates were ousted from power, many by Col. al-Serraj. Maj. Gen. Afif Bizri, a pro-Communist with close Baathist connections, was appointed army chief of staff in August, and moderates failed in efforts to dislodge him.

Nonetheless, a progressive coalition including moderates continued to dominate the legislature. The Syrian government under Premier Shukri al-Kuwatly, a political conservative, pursued a policy of pro-Egyptian neutralism with support for the Soviet's Mideast policies. Between 1954 and 1957, several economic and military aid programs had been implemented with Soviet cooperation. Kuwatly firmly advocated Syrian union with Egypt.

Largely as a consequence of Russia's post-Suez crisis popularity among the Arabs, the Syrian armed forces had developed close ties with the USSR by Sept. 1957, were using extensive quantities of Soviet arms and were heavily infiltrated with pro-Communist officers.

But Syria was surrounded by pro-Western countries: Turkey to the north (a NATO and METO member), Iraq to the east (also a METO member) and pro-British Jordan and pro-French Israel to the south. As the Communist Party and pro-Communist elements gained ascendency in Damascus, these surrounding states became alarmed, as did the Western allies.

Reports from Damascus in Sept. 1957 indicated a growing power struggle in Syria between the internationalistic and pro-Soviet Communists and the supranationalistic Pan-Arab Baathists. Arab reactions to Syrian governmental instability and Western anxiety over a possible Communist takeover precipitated a Syrian crisis of international dimensions late in 1957.

In a statement issued through U.S. State Secy. John Foster Dulles, Pres. Dwight D. Eisenhower reaffirmed Sept. 7 "his intention to carry out the national policy, expressed in the Congressional Middle East resolution" (Eisenhower Doctrine), to "help the nations of the area to defend their independence." Dulles said that Eisenhower had "authorized the accelerated delivery to the countries of the area of economic and other defensive items which have been programmed for their use." Eisenhower "expressed the hope that the international Communists would not push Syria into any acts of aggression against her neighbors and that the people of Syria would act to allay the anxiety caused by recent events," Dulles said.

Dulles told newsmen that, at a conference earlier Sept. 7 among himself, Eisenhower and William M. Rountree, Assistant State Secretary for Mideastern affairs, Deputy State Undersecy. Loy Henderson had reported finding during a visit "in the Near East deep concern at the apparently growing Soviet Communist domination of Syria and the large build-up there of Soviet-bloc arms." Henderson told of anxieties arising in the area over "border incidents and subversive activities directed toward the overthrow of the . . . governments of Syria's Arab neighbors." He also expressed "deep concern lest Syria should become a victim of international communism."

8 USAF transport planes arrived in Amman, Jordan Sept. 9, 1957 with the first U.S. military aid to be expedited to the Middle East under a program to counteract Soviet arms shipments to the Syrian government. The Jordanian shipment—recoilless rifles, machine guns, jeeps and ammunition—was drawn from U.S. and west European arms stocks. It was to be charged against the $10 million U.S. military-aid grant made available to Jordan June 29.

In announcing the Mideast arms program, the State Department had said Sept. 5 that American arms shipments to Lebanon, Turkey and Iraq would be accelerated under orders issued after Deputy State Undersecy. Henderson (ex-U.S. ambassador to Iran) had returned from his Mideast tour.

Dulles indicated Sept. 10 that he had tempered his earlier evaluation of the seriousness of the Syrian situation. He told newsmen that he did not "think it likely" that the Syrian crisis would demand or permit "direct armed intervention" by the U.S. as authorized by the Eisenhower Doctrine. He asserted that he did not believe there would be any "aggression" which "could not be dealt with by the states involved." He said that the Jordanian arms airlift had been ordered at the specific request of the Jordanian government. Warning that the situation was still "in the borderline, grey area," Dulles said: "There has been as yet no [U.S.] determination that Syria is dominated by international communism within the meaning of the Middle East resolution" (Eisenhower Doctrine). "The very fact" that the Syrian crisis "is being taken seriously affords the greatest likelihood that a peaceful solution will be found."

Jordanian Foreign Min. Samir el-Rifai declared Sept. 10 that Jordan would take no action to intervene in Syria despite the "unfortunate" impression created by the arrival of American arms in Jordan. Asserting that Syria was "independent and entitled to do what she likes," Rifai said that "we do not want the Middle East to become a battleground in the cold war." Rifai said that the U.S. arms shipments would be used solely for Jordanian defense and internal security. He reportedly told newsmen that the weapons "will be used against Israel or any country that tries to attack us." "No Arab country would ever be prepared to fight another Arab country," he declared.

Syrian-Turkish Crisis

Reports circulated in early Sept. 1957 of a military buildup in Turkey, a NATO power sandwiched between Syria and the USSR. It was reported Sept. 17 that Nasser had offered to send to Syria Egyptian technicians trained in the use of Soviet weapons in order to allow Syria to limit the influx of Soviet technicians. By mid-October Cairo acknowledged that the Egyptian "technicians" were troops.

A Syrian government statement, issued in Damascus Sept. 7, said that "Syria does not intend to attack anybody" but would "not tolerate any action against her security." Syrian Pres. Shukri al-Kuwatly, in an interview for Egypt's semi-official Middle East News Agency, warned Sept. 7 that Syria would not "allow anyone to interfere in our home affairs or split our home front." He said that, if provoked, Syria would "tear up the belt" being wrapped around it. Kuwatly added: "We are not Communists. . . . We are nationalists and do not substitute our Arab nationalism for any other principles."

A 2d Syrian government declaration, issued after the Syrian cabinet had met Sept. 8 to consider alleged U.S. "aggressive intentions against Syria," charged Sept. 9 that "provocative acts against Syria have begun." The government statement said that American ships and aircraft had been sent close to Syria in an "open challenge" to its independence. Syrian Defense Min. Khaled el-Azm contradicted the anti-U.S. charges Sept. 11 and told newsmen that he had "no desire to damage relations with" the U.S. Premier Sabri el-Assali, however, thanked Soviet Foreign Min. Gromyko Sept. 11 for his "firm attitude toward [U.S.] attempts to break Syrian independence."

Soviet Foreign Min. Andrei A. Gromyko had charged Sept. 10 that special U.S. Mideast envoy Loy Henderson had gone to Turkey to advance Western plans to set "certain Arab countries on Syria—for example, Iraq, Jordan and Lebanon." Gromyko warned that, at the U.S.' instigation, "Turkish troops are concentrating on the borders of Syria" to further "political pressure and attempts to organize an economic blockade" and an "armed intervention in the affairs of Syria."

Gromyko charged that the "conspiracy" was aimed at an eventual blockade of Syria by the U.S. 6th Fleet in the interests of "the oil kings."

Egyptian-Syrian Economic Unity Steps

Egypt and Syria had already taken their first steps toward political union. In Damascus Sept. 4, Egyptian Finance Min. Abdel Moneim el-Kaissouni and Syrian Economy Min. Khalil el-Kallas had signed an agreement "to develop commercial exchanges between the 2 countries and consolidate their economic collaboration" while preparing a specially established joint committee to report in 90 days on what "concrete measures" would most facilitate Syria and Egypt's final economic unification. The 2 countries agreed:

- To revise the current bilateral trade agreement in such a way as to further to the maximum the 2 countries' trade exchanges.
- To revise and expand accordingly the 2 states' current payments agreement.
- To permit the free movement between Egypt and Syria of both countries' nationals, enjoying reciprocal rights of domicile, work, trade and enterprise.
- To encourage the establishment of joint commercial and industrial enterprises, particularly industrial and commercial banks and joint concerns for insurance, shipping and air transport, and the prospects for the reciprocal sharing of technical advances.

Radio Cairo Sept. 9 broadcast an interview-statement from Egyptian Pres. Nasser to *Al Ahram* of Cairo expressing Egypt's "unconditional support" for Syria and attacking the U.S. "Syria's only sin in the eyes of American policy was that she did not dance to the American tune and obey American orders," Nasser said. He asserted that the U.S. had seized on the "Communist threat" in Syria in an effort "to create artificial dangers to break up Arab unity and dissipate its strength." The U.S. also sought "to relieve the pressure on Israel, to draw attention away from her and to divert it to other channels in line with American policy." Nasser said that he had perceived 3 main aims in U.S. Mideastern policy:

- To "get the Arabs to line up behind American policy on all international questions, thus converting the Arab countries into a U.S. sphere of influence."
- To "impose a defense agreement that would serve American interests alone."
- To "liquidate the Israel question on the basis of the *status quo*, which means converting the [1949] armistice lines into permanent borders and repudiating the rights of the Palestine Arabs."

Since the Eisenhower Doctrine was enunciated, Nasser said, the current phase of U.S. policy had moved toward "putting some Arab countries in one sphere together with Israel, a sphere in which the United States would play the role of conciliator and coordinator in all military fields. Thus Israel would no longer be the enemy of those Arab states but their partner in an alliance."

Nasser denounced the U.S. airlift of supplies to Jordan as part of "a large-scale intimidation campaign designed to put the wind up some kings and premiers." The U.S. had already known that Syria had not joined the "Communist camp," Nasser declared. The weapons were sent "to control the interior and to stamp out Arab nationalism if this should prove possible." Egypt would "stand at Syria's side unconditionally and unreservedly," Nasser pledged. "All of Egypt's political, economic and military potentialities are behind Syria in her battle, which is our battle and the battle of Arab nationalism."

Maj. Gen. Afif Bizri, Syria's military commander, and Col. Abdul Hamid al-Serraj, the Syrian army intelligence chief, visited Nasser and Gen. Abdel Hakim Amer, the Egyptian military commander, in Cairo Sept. 11-12. Before leaving Cairo, Bizri declared that the Syrian and Egyptian forces were "one army under one command." Both countries would henceforth consider an attack on one to be an attack on both, he said.

USSR Vs. Turkish Buildup Against Syria

Soviet Premier Nikolai Bulganin, in a letter to Turkish Premier Adnan Menderes Sept. 10, expressed Soviet "concern" at "reports of Turkish troop concentrations on Syria's frontiers and shipments of American arms to Turkey to carry out an attack on Syria."

Menderes, in a reply published by the Turkish government Oct. 5, said that subversive activities in Syria had "reached the maximum limit," and he charged that Syria was "hastily arming beyond the limit of any defense needs" and becoming "an arms depot that probably will be used by others in case of need." Menderes continued:

> It is noteworthy that although we have not received any complaint from our neighbour Syria, your message . . . proves that, as the matter stands today, Soviet Russia has adopted Syria and the Syrian question. Analysis of the facts will suffice to bring out in bold relief the contrast between the policy pursued by your country in the Middle East and your expressions of desire to establish real friendship between Turkey and the USSR. If it is desired to establish relations of genuine friendship with Turkey based upon mutual confidence, abandonment of the policy pursued in the Middle East, particularly in Syria, will certainly have a positive effect.
>
> We wish to emphasize that we do not in the least entertain aggressive designs on any of our neighbors and that there will never be such designs. On the contrary, we desire the inviolability of the independence and territorial integrity of Syria, as well as its happiness and prosperity. As such, we follow with anxiety the events taking place in Syria. . . .
>
> Moved by this sense of uneasiness, and following a joint request together with our friends, the U.S.A. sent Mr. Loy Henderson to Turkey to examine the situation. The talks with Mr. Henderson were not intended for any aggressive purpose but were designed for countries which felt anxiety from the standpoint of their own security as a result of the developments described above. It is the anxiety of losing their independence and freedom in the face of a probable threat which encouraged the peace-loving states of the Middle East to effect a defen-

> sive arrangment among themselves, and to enlist the aid of the U.S.A. and the UK to strengthen it. In the circumstances it is not in the least in accord with the facts to look for an aggressive aim in the Baghdad Pact and to brand the Western powers which joined it with 'colonialism.' . . . The Baghdad Pact, like other defensive pacts, is the product of the anxiety felt by nations which desire to be free . . . .

(The *N. Y. Times* reported Oct. 7 that the Syrian government had accepted a Soviet offer to build a deepwater naval base in Syria north of Latakia, Syria's largest sheltered seaport but then only capable of accommodating light-draft seagoing vessels. The offer reportedly had been made by Soviet Vice Adm. V. F. Kotov during the 10-day visit to the port of 2 Soviet naval vessels, the cruiser *Zhdanov* and the destroyer *Svobodny*, which had sailed Oct. 1.)

Soviet Communist Party First Secy. Nikita S. Khrushchev accused U.S. State Secy. John Foster Dulles of having "turned the pressure on Turkey" and of "pushing Turkey into war with Syria." He challenged the U.S. Senate to investigate his charges. Khrushchev made these assertions in an interview in Moscow with James Reston of the *N. Y. Times*. When Reston asked the Soviet Communist leader to document the charges, Khrushchev replied: "I advise you to ask Mr. Dulles. As a man who often appeals to God, let him swear that he did not give such instructions to Henderson" before sending Henderson in August on a fact-finding mission to the Middle East. The interview appeared in the *Times*' Oct. 8-10 editions, and the official Soviet text–differing somewhat from Reston's notes–appeared Oct. 10.

"In moving their troops" to the Syrian frontier, Khrushchev said, "the Turks are laying bare parts of their frontier with us" in the Soviet Union. "They should not do that," he added. "They are very weak. Turkey would not last one day in case of war. . . . If war breaks out, we are near Turkey and you [in the U.S.] are not. When the guns begin to fire the rockets can begin flying, and then it will be too late to think about it."

Khrushchev told Reston that the Soviet Union was quite

aware that Egyptian Pres. Nasser had imprisioned Egyptian Communists but that the Soviet Union still cooperated with Egypt against "all kinds of colonialism, including American," for the sake of "practical coexistence." He scoffed at the notions of a "Soviet provocation" in Syria and of any Communist menace to the Middle East, whose Arabs were not Communists but nationalists, he said. Although he admitted that the USSR had sold arms to Syria, he emphasized that "not one of our soldiers" was currently in the country.

The Syrian government Oct. 9 formally accused Turkey of concentrating its troops on the Syro-Turkish border and of making unauthorized flights over Syrian territory. Syria demanded in its note to Ankara that all such activities "should cease" immediately. The Turkish government replied Oct. 17, denying these allegations and Syria's charge that Turkish frontier guards had fired on Syrian civilians. Turkey attributed the current mutual tension to the Soviet Union's efforts to turn Syria into an "arms dump" to be used against Turkey. It described its troop movements as normal seasonal maneuvers.

Gunfire had been exchanged between Syrian and Turkish border guards for about 45 minutes Oct. 8 near the Syrian town of Jerablus after Turkish railroad workmen were shot at by Syrian gendarmes as they sought to labor in a "free zone" area of the Istanbul-Baghdad railroad's border crossing point.

Turkish UN delegation chief Seyfullah Esin had denied Oct. 15 as "entirely false" Syrian allegations of a Turkish border provocation and of plans for an invasion of Syria. Esin told the UN General Assembly that Turkey had "valid reasons" for concern over Syria, a country "with which we have a long common frontier." Turkish Defense Min. Shemi Ergim had warned Oct. 14 that any aggressor moving against Turkey would be "broken into pieces by Turkey's strong army." He said that Turkey would take "all precautions" to defend its territory. Turkish Foreign Ministry spokesmen had insisted Oct. 9 that "Turkey has no aggressive designs against any country."

Egyptian Troops in Syria

The Egyptian government announced Oct. 13, 1957 that "basic elements" of Egypt's armed forces had been landing in Syria since mid-September. A communiqué said that additional units had landed in Latakia Oct. 13 under escort of Egyptian and Syrian air and naval units. It said that the troop movements, intended "to reinforce [Syria's] forces and strengthen her defensive capacities," had been agreed on at the Cairo meeting Sept. 11 of Egyptian Pres. Gamal Abdel Nasser, War Min. Abdel Hakim Amer and Maj. Gen. Afif Bizri, Syrian army chief of staff. Damascus radio reported Oct. 14 that the Egyptian troops, estimated by U.S. sources to number from 1,000 to 1,600 men, had reached Aleppo, 30 miles from the Turkish frontier.

Lebanese sources said Oct. 15 that King Saud of Saudi Arabia, visiting Lebanon since Oct. 10, had expressed anger at Egypt's shipment of troops to Syria. Informants termed the Egyptian move "outright sabotage" and a blow at Saudi Arabian efforts to moderate disputes among Arab states. Acting Lebanese Foreign Min. Jamil Mekkaoui, welcoming Saud Oct. 11, said that Lebanon would consider any attack against Syria an attack against itself. The Lebanese parliament's foreign affairs committee was revealed Oct. 9 to have asked Foreign Min. Charles Malik to seek U.S. agreement to a "clarification" of Lebanese commitments under the U.S.-Lebanese Eisenhower Doctrine agreement.

King Hussein of Jordan warned Oct. 15 that "non-Arab hands" were attempting to "subvert" and control Syria, but he said he was certain "Syrian Arabs will . . . never allow their subversive regime to use arms against any brother Arab country." (Hussein had met with King Feisal of Iraq Oct. 13, reportedly in an effort to secure aid for Jordan's $20 million military deficit. A 2d shipment of U.S. tanks and artillery was turned over to Jordan Oct. 6.)

The Egyptian-owned Middle East News Agency reported Oct. 16 that the Syrian army had declared a state of emergency and had canceled all leaves. Syrian military authorities were said to be arming civilian volunteers in Homs and Aleppo.

U.S. State Secy. Dulles warned the Soviet Union Oct. 16 that it would face armed American retaliation against Soviet territory in the event of a Russian attack on Turkey. Speaking at a news conference in Washington, Dulles stressed that "in case of attack and aggression" against Turkey, the U.S. would be bound by its NATO ties and the Eisenhower Doctrine to react in Turkey's defense. "Certainly, if there is an attack on Turkey by the Soviet Union, it would not mean a purely defensive operation by the [U.S.], with the Soviet Union as a privileged sanctuary," Dulles asserted.

Asked by reporters if his policy implied a reemphasis on policies of "brinkmanship"—a hostile characterization of Dulles' anti-Communist international defense policies—Dulles observed that, historically, "the world has been always on the brink of war." The U.S., he said, would "wage peace" more effectively by bearing in mind that "war is an ever-present danger." Dulles said he saw "some resemblance" in the current Turkish-Syrian-Soviet situation "to the period of the Korean War." He warned that behind the "smokescreen" of Soviet charges, "something more serious . . . may be taking place." He asserted, however, "that is is unlikely that there will be an outbreak of war."

Soviet Foreign Min. Andrei A. Gromyko charged Oct. 16 that the "Turkish general staff, together with American advisers," had made "detailed plans for an attack by Turkey on Syria" "immediately after the elections in Turkey" Oct. 27. In a letter to Sir Leslie Munro, UN General Assembly president, Gromyko demanded that the UN "immediately render Syria the armed assistance necessary to put a stop to aggression" if it occurred. Gromyko declared that "the Soviet Union is prepared to take part with its forces in suppressing aggression" against Syria.

Syrian Foreign Min. Salah el-Bitar urged Oct. 16 that the General Assembly set up a commission to "make an impartial and international investigation" of the Syrian-Turkish border situation. Writing to UN Secy. Gen. Dag Hammarskjöld, Bitar asked for the inclusion on the Assembly agenda of Syria's "complaint about threats to the security of Syria and to international peace." Bitar said that foreign states had intervened in Syrian affairs "to sway its policies or overthrow its government."

The U.S. delegation Oct. 16 announced its support for Syria's request for an Assembly investigation, which, it said, would "clarify who it is [that] threatens peace in the area."

Radio Mecca announced Oct. 21 that Saudi Arabian King Saud had offered his good offices as mediator to Turkey and Syria and that Turkish and Syrian delegations would meet Saud in Damman, Saudi Arabia, within 2 days. Both Turkey and Syria at first confirmed the Saudi Arabian statement, but the Syrian Foreign Ministry announced later Oct. 21 that Syria had rejected Saud's offer and would keep the matter before the UN. After Turkey agreed Oct. 18 to a UN debate on the "fictitious situation," the crisis subsided.

Egypt & Syria Form UAR

In the face of mounting Communist power within Syria, non-Communist elements—in particular the radical nationalists of the Baath Party—sought to counter this power by allying themselves with Egyptian Pres. Gamal Abdel Nasser. Nasser, an Arab hero since the Suez crisis of 1956, was popular with most sections of the Syrian population and also acceptable to the Soviet Union. The arrival of Egyptian troops in Syria in Sept.–Oct. 1957—and the increased prestige for Nasser that accompanied them—suited both Egypt and the Soviet Union. Egypt seemed at last to be realizing its longed-for leadership in the Arab world. The USSR, for its part, had already established its reputation as Egypt's friend and had in any case just about abandoned its support of local Communist parties in the Middle East in preference to better ties with recognized neutral Arab governments.

The Syrian Chamber of Deputies and the Egyptian National Assembly (Majlis) agreed Nov. 18, 1957 on the establishment of some form of Syro-Egyptian federal union.

Nasser and Syrian Pres. Shukri al-Kuwatly Feb. 1, 1958 formally proclaimed the union of Egypt and Syria in a new entity entitled the United Arab Republic. Meeting in Cairo, the 2 leaders termed the union the first step toward an eventual federation embracing all Arab nations. The proclamation asserted that "this unity, which is the fruit of Arab nationalism," would remain open "to any Arab state desirous of joining . . . in a union or federation." The proclamation of the new state, reportedly hastened at Kuwatly's request to counter increasing communist penetration of the Syrian government and army, was made before the Syrian and Egyptian cabinets, meeting in Cairo, had agreed on details of the merger. The proclamation stated, however, that the new republic would be based on "the presidential democratic system of government" with executive "authority vested in the head of state, assisted by ministers appointed by [and] responsible to him." The proclamation and announcements made Feb. 2 (after a meeting of the unified Egypt-Syrian cabinets) called for:

- The nomination of the republic's first president in separate sessions of the Egyptian and Syrian parliaments.
- An Egyptian-Syrian plebiscite Feb. 21 to approve the presidential nomination and unity proclamation.
- The appointment by the president of an interim 20-man cabinet and of a governor general to rule Syria during the preparation of a constitution.
- The dissolution of Syrian political parties to form an Egyptian-type unitary national political front.

• The merger of Syrian and Egyptian governmental, economic, legal, commercial and military services, with diplomatic missions in Damascus to be reduced to consular status.

The new United Arab Republic had an estimated Arab population of 27,266,000 (23,410,000 Egyptian), a geographic area of 458,432 square miles (386,198 Egyptian), an army of 200,000, a jet air force of 300 MiG fighters and 60 Ilyushin bombers, and 4 or 5 Soviet-built submarines.

Egyptian Pres. Nasser was formally nominated Feb. 5 by the Egyptian Majlis and by Syrian Pres. Kuwatly (as head of the Syrian parliament in Damascus) to serve as first president of the United Arab Republic. Nasser, speaking before the Egyptian Majlis, outlined a 17-point plan for a "presidential democracy," to be approved together with his candidacy by an Egypto-Syrian plebiscite Feb. 21.

Nasser's program for the UAR:

• Legislative powers would be exercised in a 400-seat assembly appointed by the president, half of its members to be named from the current Syrian and Egyptian parliaments.
• Executive powers would be vested in the president.
• The judiciary would remain an independent branch with all existing Syrian and Egyptian laws remaining in force until voided or superseded.
• The Republic would consist of Syrian and Egyptian regions, each with an executive council with powers, functions and membership determined by the president.

Nasser Mar. 6 made public his first United Arab Republican cabinet and simultaneously named 2 Egyptian and 2 Syrian UAR vice presidents. He placed foreign affairs, defense and other key ministries in Egyptian hands. He dropped or downgraded Syrian and Egyptian cabinets, among them Syrian Defense Min. Khaled el-Azm and Egyptian Commerce Min. Muhammad Abu Nosseir. Syrian ex-Pres. Kuwatly, said to be in ill health, was not listed in the UAR cabinet and was believed to have retired from active political life.

Appointed Mar. 6 as UAR vice presidents were: Egyptian Field Marshal Abdel Hakim Amer, UAR war minister; Abdel Latif el-Boghdadi, speaker of the last Egyptian National Assembly; Sabri al-Assali, last premier of Syria; Akram Hourani, Socialist leader and speaker of the final Syrian National Assembly.

Appointed Mar. 6 to 8 joint Egypto-Syrian ministries were: *Foreign Affairs*—Dr. Mahmoud Fawzi of Egypt; *War*—Field Marshal Amer of Egypt; *Industry*—Aziz Sidky of Egypt; *Religion*—Ahmed Hassan al-Bakoury of Egypt; *Presidential Affairs*—Ali Sabry of Egypt; *State Minister for Arab Affairs*—Salah el-Bitar of Syria.

Named to UAR ministries with separate Egyptian and Syrian departments were: *Finance*—Hassan Abbas Zaky (Egypt), Fakher el-Kayali (Syria); *Interior*—Zakaria Mohieddin (Egypt), Abdul Hamid al-Serraj (Syria); *Health*—Nurreddin Tarraf (Egypt), Shawkhat el-Kanawati (Syria); *Justice*—Ahmad Hosni (Egypt), Abdel Wahab Homad (Syria); *Public Works*—Ahmed Abdul el-Sharabasi (Egypt), Nureddin Kuhala (Syria); *Rural Affairs*—Muhammad Abu Nosseir (Egypt), Ahmad Abdel Kerim (Syria); *Trade & Economy*—Abdel Moneim el-Kaissouni (Egypt), Khalil el-Kallas (Syria); *Agriculture*—Sayed Marei (Egypt), Ahmad Elhag Yunis (Syria); *Communications*—Mustafa Khalil (Egypt), Ain Nakuri (Syria); *Planning and Social Affairs for Egypt*—Hussein Shafei; *Planning for Syria*—Hassan Jabarrah; *Social Affairs for Syria*—Mustafa Hamdoun.

Syrian Communist Party Smashed

The establishment of the UAR was immediately followed by an attack on powerful Syrian Communist figures. Khaled Bagdash, the Syrian Communist leader, left Damascus for Moscow with his family Feb. 5, 1958 amid reports that the Syrian Communist Party would be suppressed in a projected formation of a "national front of all Syrian parties."

The UAR announced in Cairo Mar. 22 the resignation of

Field Marshal Afif Bizri, pro-Soviet former Syrian Army chief of staff. Bizri's dismissal with the rank of lieutenant general was considered to have consolidated Nasser's control over the Syrian army. UAR spokesmen said Mar. 23 that Bizri had been fired because Nasser "did not like to have officers in the joint Syrian-Egyptian army mixed up in politics."

Khaled el-Azm, pro-Soviet former Syrian defense minister, crossed into Lebanon Mar. 22, reportedly en route to exile in Europe. Col. Abdul Hamid al-Serraj, UAR interior minister for Syria, ordered all Syrian Communist Party assets seized Mar. 18 after the Communist Party failed to comply with decrees ordering all Syrian parties to dissolve and turn their funds over to a government agency.

Syria Alleges Plot by Saud

Lt. Col. Serraj, leftist Syrian army intelligence chief, charged Mar. 5, 1958 that King Saud of Saudi Arabia had plotted to stop the formation of the UAR by inspiring a Syrian army coup and the assassination of Nasser. Serraj told newsmen that Assad Ibrahim, one of Saud's fathers-in-law, had assured him (Serraj) of U.S. and Western recognition for a new Syrian regime with Serraj as president. He said that Ibrahim had given him 3 checks totaling £1,900,000 ($5,320,000) as a bribe to carry out the plot. Serraj said also that he had informed Field Marshal Abdel Hakim Amer of the planned coup and had cashed the checks for use by the UAR.

Nasser said in a broadcast Mar. 5 that the plot had been financed by "imperialists and oil interests" and that the funds would be used for UAR industrial development.

Serraj quoted Ibrahim as having said: "King Saud has described the Egypto-Syrian union as Egyptian imperialism and has sworn . . . that this union shall not take place and that he places all his power, moral and financial, at your disposal, offering you the Syrian presidency."

A Saudi Arabian communiqué issued in Jidda Mar. 1 said

that Saud had confirmed his readiness "to cooperate with all Arab states within the commitments he has already undertaken." It stressed Saud's support for "every effort" at Arab unity, whether through the UAR or the Arab Federation of Jordan & Iraq. The Saudi Arabian government Mar. 7 formally denied that King Saud had plotted the assassination of Nasser in an effort to halt the formation of the UAR.

Syrian army headquarters in Damascus charged Mar. 5 that a Jordanian patrol had shelled Syrian border positions the previous night. In a message to King Hussein of Jordan, Saud declared Mar. 8 that the Arab nations should "get together to serve the interests of the Arab world and resist the enemies lying in wait for us."

Nasser charged in Damascus Mar. 9 that "imperialist" nations and Israel "want to take Jordan, Lebanon and parts of Syria and Iraq." Nasser warned that only "the path of nonalignment and positive neutrality between East and West" could defend Arab interests. UAR officials had announced in Cairo Mar. 8 that Nasser had withdrawn the Egyptian military mission that had been training Saudi Arabian armed forces under the currently dormant joint Egypto-Syro-Saudi-Jordanian army command. Mid-March dispatches from Saudi Arabia said that Egyptian embassy guards in Riyadh had been increased Mar. 13 after attacks by anti-Egyptian rioters.

Saudi Arabian Amb.-to-Lebanon Sheikh Abdul Aziz Kuheimy protested formally to Lebanese Premier-Interior Min. Sami es-Solh Mar. 18 against Lebanese press attacks on King Saud. The king Mar. 23 relinquished to his brother, the Emir Faisal, control over the country's foreign, internal and fiscal policies. A connection between this move and the Saud-Nasser dispute was reported internationally. This elicited this commentary Apr. 10 by the diplomatic correspondent of the London *Times:* "In spite of conflicting reports, it now seems possible to assess the position of the Saudi Arabian government since the establishment of the United

Arab Republic of Egypt and Syria and since the Emir Faisal . . . took over the Ministries of Finance and Interior. The Emir Faisal, while in Cairo for medical treatment, saw Pres. Nasser and [Syrian ex-Pres.] Shukry Kuwatly a few days before they announced the creation of the United Arab Republic, but neither of them informed him of their intentions and he was affronted by this treatment. When he returned to Saudi Arabia his pro-Egyptian attitude had modified, and King Saud chose the moment to make clear that differences with his brother, if, in fact, they existed before, were now at an end. On this view King Saud still retains ultimate control and Saudi Arabia is likely to remain poised between the United Arab Republic and the [Arab] Federation of Iraq & Jordan."

As premier of Saudi Arabia, Faisal visited UAR Pres. Nasser in Cairo Aug. 15-17, 1958. Before leaving, the emir told Cairenes that all of the 2 countries' misunderstandings had been cleared up and all previous differences "ironed out." In a brief communiqué, Faisal and Nasser stated that their talks had "resulted in complete agreement as well as in the reaffirmation of brotherhood and friendship between the 2 countries." Both leaders expressed their opposition to "the presence of foreign forces on the territory of any Arab state" and condemned "any interference in the affairs of others on the part of any foreign state or states that puts the peace and security of the world in danger."

UAR Federates with Yemen

Shortly after the creation of the United Arab Republic the new republic federated with Yemen. The Imam Ahmad, ruler of the south Arabian kingdom of Yemen, had proposed a loose federation that would involve no alienation of the Yemeni sovereign's absolute powers but enable him to deal more efficiently with his chief enemies, the British colony of Aden and internal anti-monarchist agitators.

Egyptian officials announced Feb. 11, 1958 that Yemen

would federate with the UAR after the expected approval of the new state by the Syro-Egyptian plebiscite Feb. 21. The federation accord was reached in Cairo talks Feb. 5-11 among Egyptian Foreign Min. Mahmoud Fawzi and State Min. Ali Sabry, Yemeni Crown Prince Seif al-Islam Muhammad al-Badr and Deputy Foreign Min. Hassan bin Ibrahim, and Abdulah el-Samahy, adviser to the Imam Ahmad of Yemen. The agreement reportedly provided for Egyptian military and economic aid to Yemen and Yeman's continuation as a monarchy.

UAR Pres. Nasser and Crown Prince Muhammad al-Badr of Yemen announced in Cairo Mar. 2 that Yemen would federate with the UAR but would remain an absolutist monarchy under the Imam Ahmad. Badr, who had joined Nasser in Damascus Mar. 1 after stopping en route from Yemen to confer with King Saud of Saudi Arabia, told Cairo demonstrators Mar. 2 that the new federation would work "to liberate Palestine and clear colonialism out of occupied areas [presumably Aden] south of Yemen."

The Cairo newspaper *Al-Shaab* reported Mar. 2 that Nasser and Ahmad planned to form a supreme council empowered to veto federation policies. A federal council, composed of equal numbers of Yemeni and UAR delegates, would formulate joint economic, foreign, defense and cultural policies for submission to the supreme council. Yemen and the UAR would retain their separate governments, armies (under joint command), currencies and diplomatic corps.

An accord signed in Damascus Mar. 8 by Nasser and Crown Prince Badr of Yemen formally linked the UAR and Yemen in a federation to be known as the United Arab States. The accord, which permitted Imam Ahmad to retain his Yemeni throne and absolute powers, provided for the establishment of "unified armed forces" and foreign policies. A supreme federal council of the UAR and Yemeni chiefs of state would, however, retain veto powers over lower federal bodies charged with forming common policies. The agreement linked 4½ million Yemenis with 23½ million Egyptians and 4 million Syrians in a federation that had no common frontiers.

(A Presidential decree issued by Nasser Oct. 21, 1959 gave Field Marshal Abdel Hakim Amer, UAR vice president, full powers over the Syrian Region cabinet to carry out Nasser's reportedly lagging program of political, industrial and land reforms in Syria. Syrian Interior Min. Abdul Hamid al-Serraj was put in control of Syrian news and propaganda.)

THE UAR, ITS NEIGHBORS AND RUSSIA (1958-61)

Lebanese Insurrection & Iraqi Revolution

Following the formation of the United Arab Republic, UAR Pres. Gamal Abdel Nasser played an increasingly strong if clandestine role in the affairs of non-UAR Arab countries—including traditionally pro-Western Lebanon. In May 1958 an insurrection broke out in Lebanon. The rebel forces were a loose coalition of Moslem, Druze and Socialist dissidents. A virtual civil war continued throughout June and July. The government, backed largely by conservative Christian elements of the population, was headed Premier Sami es-Solh, a Moslem, and the state by Pres. Camille Chamoun, a Maronite Catholic. The opposition was led by Saeb Salem (from the Moslem quarter of Beirut), Rashid Karame (from the Moslem quarter of Tripoli) and Kemal Jumblatt (from the Druze hills southeast of Beirut).

The UN Security Council June 6, 10 and 11 debated a Lebanese complaint against UAR interference in its internal affairs. Swedish Amb.-to-UN Gunnar Jarring June 10 submitted a resolution reporting that Lebanon had presented "strong and precise allegations tending to show that foreign interference has in fact taken place," but the UAR was not expressly specified.

At a news conference in Beirut June 25, Pres. Chamoun charged "massive interference" by the UAR on the side of the insurgents. He said: "The situation now developing in Lebanon is far from being a domestic issue. It involves the stability and peace of the middle east. Interference by the UAR is but one milestone of its desire to dominate the Arab world. An earlier milestone was in Apr. 1957, when an attempt was made to overthrow the legal authority in Jordan. We knew then that Lebanon would be the next victim of a similar attempt. As a matter of fact, the smuggling of military equipment on a large scale and the infiltration of 'volunteers' and terrorists—Syrians, Egyptians, Palestinians—began at that time. 3 or 4 months ago the smuggling of arms and men began to accelerate to the extent that the present armed rebellion became possible. . . . ."

The overthrow of the Iraqi government in an armed coup July 14 emphasized the apparent danger in which, it was said, the UAR's clandestine activities placed Lebanon. Lebanon was generally regarded as being within the "Western sphere of influence." In response to an urgent appeal from Pres. Chamoun, U.S. Pres. Dwight D. Eisenhower announced July 15 that U.S. Marines were being landed in Lebanon. It was understood that the Marines' intervention was "legitimate" because of the UAR's alleged intervention on the side of the rebels.

Eisenhower's statement said:

Yesterday morning [July 14] I received from Pres. Chamoun an urgent plea that some U.S. forces be stationed in Lebanon to help maintain security and to evidence the concern of the United States for the integrity and independence of Lebanon. Pres. Chamoun's appeal was made with the concurrence of all the members of the Lebanese cabinet.

Pres. Chamoun made clear that he considered an immediate U.S. response imperative if Lebanon's independence, already menaced from without, were to be preserved in the face of the grave developments which occurred yesterday in Baghdad, whereby the lawful government was violently overthrown and many of its members martyred.

In response to this appeal from the government of Lebanon, the United States has dispatched a contingent of U.S. forces to Lebanon to protect American lives and by their presence there to encourage the Lebanese government in defense of Lebanese sovereignty and integrity. These forces have not been sent as any act of war. They will demonstrate the concern of the United States for the independence and integrity of Lebanon, which we deem vital to the national interest and world peace. Our concern will also be shown by economic assistance. We shall act in accordance with these legitimate concerns.

The United States, this morning, will report its action to an emergency meeting of the UN Security Council. As the UN Charter recognizes, there is an inherent right of collective self-defense. In conformity with the spirit of the Charter, the United States is reporting the measures taken by it to the Security Council, making clear that these measures will be terminated as soon as the Security Council has itself taken the measures necessary to maintain international peace and security.

The United States believes that the UN can and should take measures which are adequate to preserve the independence and integrity of Lebanon. It is apparent, however, that in the face of the tragic and shocking events that are occurring nearby, more will be required than the team of UN observers now in Lebanon. Therefore, the United States will support in the UN measures which seem to be adequate to meet the new situation and which will enable the U.S. forces promptly to be withdrawn.

Lebanon is a small peace-loving state with which the United States has traditionally had the most friendly relations. There are in Lebanon about 2,500 Americans and we cannot, consistently with our historic relations and with the principles of the United Nations, stand idly by when Lebanon appeals for evidence of our concern, and when Lebanon may not be able to preserve internal order and defend itself against indirect aggression.

Eisenhower late July 15 said in a special message to the U.S. Congress:

On July 14 I received an urgent request from the president of the Lebanon that some U.S. forces be stationed in Lebanon. Pres. Chamoun stated that without an immediate showing of U.S. support, the government of Lebanon would be unable to survive. This request was made with the concurrence of all the members of the Lebanese cabinet. I have replied that we would do this, and a contingent of U.S. Marines has now arrived in Lebanon. This initial dispatch of troops will be augmented as required. United States forces will be withdrawn as rapidly as circumstances permit.

Simultaneously, I requested that an urgent meeting of the UN Security Council be held on July 15. At that meeting, the permanent representative of the United States reported to the Council the action which this government has taken. He also expressed the hope that the United Nations could soon take further effective measures to meet more fully the situation in Lebanon. . . .

U.S. forces are being sent to the Lebanon to protect American lives and by their presence to assist the government of Lebanon in the preservation of Lebanon's territorial integrity and independence, which have been deemed vital to U.S. national interests and world peace.

About 2 months ago a violent insurrection broke out in Lebanon, particularly along the border with Syria, which, with Egypt, forms the United Arab Republic. This revolt was encouraged and strongly backed by the official Cairo, Damascus and Soviet radios, which broadcast to Lebanon in the Arabic language. The insurrection was further supported by sizeable amounts of arms, ammunition and money and by personnel infiltrated from Syria to fight against the lawful authorities. The avowed purpose of these activities was to overthrow the legally constituted government of Lebanon and to install by violence a government which would subordinate the independence of Lebanon to the policies of the United Arab Republic.

Lebanon referred this situation to the Security Council. In view of the international implications of what was occurring in Lebanon, the Security Council . . . decided to send observers into Lebanon for the purpose of ensuring that further outside assistance to the insurrection would cease. The UN Secretary General subsequently undertook a mission to the area to reinforce the work of the observers.

It was our belief that the efforts of the Secretary General and of the UN observers were helpful in reducing further aid in terms of personnel and military equipment from across the frontiers of Lebanon. There was a basis for hope that the situation might be moving towards a peaceful solution, consonant with the continuing integrity of Lebanon, and that the aspect of indirect aggression from without was being brought under control.

The situation was radically changed, however, on July 14, when there was a violent outbreak in Baghdad, in nearby Iraq. Elements of Iraq strongly sympathetic to the United Arab Republic seem to have murdered or driven from office individuals comprising the lawful government of that country. . . .

We share with the government of Lebanon the view that these events in Iraq demonstrate a ruthlessness of aggressive purpose which tiny Lebanon cannot combat without further evidence of support from other friendly nations.

After the most detailed consideration, I have concluded that, given the developments in Iraq, the measures thus far taken by the Security Council are not sufficient to preserve the independence and integrity of Lebanon. I have considered, furthermore, the question of our responsibility to protect and safeguard American citizens in Lebanon, of whom there are about 2,500. Pending the taking of adequate measures by the United Nations, the United States will be acting pursuant to what the UN Charter recognizes as an inherent right—the right of all nations to work together and to seek help where necessary to preserve their independence. I repeat that we wish to withdraw our forces as soon as the UN has taken further effective steps designed to safeguard Lebanese independence.

It is clear that the events which have been occurring in Lebanon represent indirect aggression from without, and that such aggression endangers the independence and integrity of Lebanon. . . .

1,500 U.S. Marines landed near Beirut July 15. By July 20, more than 10,000 American troops were stationed in and around the Lebanese capital.

In a speech in Damascus on July 18, Nasser vigorously protested the American action: "The excuses that the imperialists made at the time of Suez are the same as the excuses made today .... by those who want to place us within their spheres of influence.... [The Americans] forget their own history and their own past; they forget that another revolution also took place in the month of July—a revolution in the United States to get rid of British imperialism and achieve freedom. That revolution was victorious. It proclaimed the same principles that our brethren, the free people of Iraq, proclaim today...."

As order returned to Lebanon, however, many observers concluded that the U.S. troop landing had foiled Nasser's ambitions in that country. American troops were surprised to notice a friendly, almost holiday atmosphere on their arrival. Western correspondents tended to attribute Nasser's ultimate lack of success in Lebanon to the small nation's virtual dependence on tourism and on aid from the U.S. and France (which still had no diplomatic ties with the UAR).

The day Pres. Chamoun had appealed to the US for military assistance—July 14, 1958—a violent revolt against the pro-British and pro-Western Iraqi government took place. For 2 days the sole source of information was Baghdad radio, which announced that:

- King Feisal and Crown Prince Abdul Illah of the ruling Hashemite dynasty had been killed.
- Premier Nuri as-Said (al-Sa'id) had been killed.
- A republican cabinet under Brig. Abdul Karim el-Kassem ('Abd-ul-Karim Qassem) had been formed.
- All Iraqi troops in Jordan, numbering some 12,000, had been withdrawn.

Friendship with Nasser and the UAR was declared by the victorious Iraqi rebel regime. For one week officials of the old regime and foreign nationals were attacked in a bloody rampage. 2 Jordanian ministers, Deputy Premier Ibrahim Hashim, 80, and Suleiman Toukan, 66, defense minister of the Federal Arab Union of Jordan & Iraq, were murdered by mobs.

(King Hussein of Jordan, also a Hashemite, had maintained close political ties with Feisal. The 2 Hashemite kingdoms of Jordan and Iraq had shared a pro-British orientation frequently denounced by Arab nationalists, who often had labeled both countries as a "tool of imperialism." 2 weeks after the proclamation of Egypt's fusion with Syria, Hussein and Feisal Feb. 14 had proclaimed in Amman the union of their kingdoms as the Arab Federation, with one parliament, one army, federal ministries of foreign affairs, defense and justice, a unified diplomatic service, a single legal system, a unified educational system and a common customs union. Feisal had become the federation's head of state and Hussein his deputy.)

King Hussein, in a radio broadcast July 14, expressed deep sorrow at the Baghdad revolution, which he termed the work of "hired elements." In a further broadcast the morning of July 14 Hussein made public his request to "friendly states" to send "effective military aid" to Jordan "as a temporary measure to protect our borders from surrounding enemies." By the afternoon of July 18, 2,000 paratroops of the British army's 16th Independent Paratroop Brigade had been airlifted into Amman from Cyprus. More than 50 U.S. jet fighter planes had overflown Jordanian territory July 17 as a gesture of solidarity for the British paratroops.

The Jordanian government had lodged a complaint with the UN Security Council July 17 against alleged UAR interference in internal Jordanian affairs. King Hussein July 20 severed diplomatic relations with the UAR. He had told newsmen in Amman July 19 that he considered it his "high responsibility," as succeeding head of the Federal Arab Union of Jordan & Iraq, "to restore order and peace to the Iraq part of the union." He said that "murderers and rebels in the Iraqi part of the Arab Union had assassinated . . . all members of the [Iraqi] royal family" during the Baghdad bloodbath.

Nasser appeared to have been both surprised and gratified

by the sudden coup in Baghdad. Despite the advantages accruing to the UAR from the Iraqi revolution, no evidence was made public to show that Nasser's reputed penchant for intrigue had played any direct role in it.

Brig. Kassem, then 44 and the chief of the Iraqi rebel regime, had been born in Baghdad, the son of a petty landowner. He was graduated from the Iraq Military Academy in 1934, served in Palestine in 1948 as a battalion commander and was regarded by foreign military attachés as an excellent officer. He commanded an infantry brigade at the outbreak of the revolution. He was a devoutly religious Sunni (orthodox) Moslem.

In an interview July 22 with the Baghdad correspondent of the London *Times*, Kassem declared:

> Our revolution did not happen as a spontaneous event or fortuitous accident but was the outcome of detailed planning by the responsible people in the revolutionary movement. This planning took carefully into account Iraq's position in the Middle East specifically and in the world pattern political generally and also the situation in Iraq itself.
>
> It was fundamental to the thought of the architects of the revolution that Iraq would not oppose the Western powers out of a feeling of resentment but, on the contrary, would cooperate with them, particularly in the oil question. We believe that oil production and distribution should be fully maintained, and we shall do our best to expand both.
>
> One of the charges falsely made by the old régime was that the opposition and the Iraq national movement generally was directed against the West, and that they would do everything possible to harm the West for the sheer pleasure of harming those countries. The truth is the very opposite. As long as the interests of the West are good for both parties, Iraq will not only endeavor to maintain things that are good for both but will increase the extent of her cooperation, especially in oil production. Oil is as important to us as it is to the West and to the world economy.
>
> The revolution has taken place to free the people of Iraq from tyranny and corruption in its domestic affairs. . . . The revolution sprang from internal causes. Responsible people in the West knew what sort of régime Iraq had. Now we are free from that clique we will do our best to improve the lot of the Iraqi people and to ráise their living standards and human dignity. Above all, we intend to establish the rule of law.
>
> Under the old régime there was no law or justice in Iraq. Only the

interests of the governing classes were served by the administration of the law under that régime. Those who have now come to power will place the interests of the people first and last. . . .

Iraq has many sources of wealth besides oil and other minerals. She has 5 rivers—not 2, as is commonly thought—near all of which lies fertile land. The government will do its utmost to develop all these natural resources and to increase the productivity of agriculture and industry for the good of the nation.

. . . Friendship between Iraq and any state anywhere must be based on mutual interest and mutual interest and mutual esteem, not on any form of dependence. Our friendship with the West, therefore, must enjoy this character.

Unfortunately, in the past a limited few claimed Iraq's friendships with foreign countries for themselves and [their own] benefit, considering that it gave them the power and privilege of ignoring the Iraqi people's wishes. But since our government expresses the will of the people, who have full confidence in it, the path is now open to genuine friendship with any government which has good will towards Iraq. It is for the West to make up their minds to accept friendship based on mutual interest and felt by both sides, for on this basis it will endure.

Kassem July 24 spoke of his own role in the uprising. He said at a press conference for foreign correspondents in Baghdad that he had desired a revolution in Iraq ever since he had been a junior officer. He had never had any political ties and had never taken part in any conspiratorial movement, Kassem said, until 1955, when he and Col. Abdel Salam Arif (or Abd-ul-Salam Muhammad Arif), the new deputy premier, had agreed that the only hope of fundamental change in Iraq lay in military action. With other military men and with the people's support, the revolution had been prepared in advance. "The first stage . . . was planned to be completed at 6 a.m. on July 14, and in fact by the time we were in command of the situation," Kassem said. "Perhaps we should thank the foolishness of those who decided to send part of the army to Jordan, for they facilitated the revolution and destroyed themselves."

Nasser flew July 16 to Moscow. He held brief discussions with Soviet Communist Party leader Khrushchev, after which the 2 leaders issued a joint communiqué denouncing "the aggression of the United States and other colonial powers in the Middle East."

Nasser then flew to Damascus. There he met with representatives of the new Iraqi republican government, including Col. Arif. An agreement was signed by the 2 Arab states July 19. It provided for: (a) Full support for the Arab League and the Arab collective security pact (the Arab counterpart to the Baghdad Pact, METO). (b) Mutual defense in case of foreign aggression. (c) Both countries to "cooperate fully in the international field to safeguard . . . [their] rights, support the UN Charter and strengthen peace in the Middle East and the world." (d) Economic and cultural cooperation. (e) "Continuous contact and consultations."

Nile Waters Agreement

Egypt and the Sudan resumed negotiations Oct. 10, 1958 on sharing the Nile waters, and they reached agreement Nov. 4. Bilateral discussions on the matter had been suspended since Jan. 1958, and all previous negotiations had been unsuccessful. The Sudanese delegation was headed by Gen. Muhammad Talaat Farid and the Egyptian by Zakaria Mohieddin (Muhyi-ul-Din).

The Nov. 4 agreement, superseding a 1929 treaty that had antedated Sudanese sovereignty, specified that: (a) The Sudan agreed to the construction of the Aswan Dam. (b) The Sudan would share ⅓ of the total annual flow of the Nile as soon as the dam started to store water. (c) Egypt would pay E£15 million in hard currency to compensate those displaced by the greater Nile inundation in the Wadi Halfa area south of Aswan. (d) There would be a number of technical projects and agreements dealing with Nile exploitation and the leasing of water flow. (e) The new agreement would remain binding for 100 years.

New trade, financial and customs agreements were also initialled Nov. 4.

Nasser Quarrels with Kassem & Khrushchev

Premier Abdul Karim el-Kassem of Iraq emerged in 1959 as Nasser's main rival for influence in the Mideast. Kassem's opposition to Nasser was to a degree a continuation of the policy of his predecessor, Premier Nuri as-Said, who had been killed in the July revolt along with Iraq's last Hashemite monarch, King Feisal. But, whereas the dispute between Nasser and Gen. Nuri had been chiefly ideological, Kassem saw a specific threat in the Nasserite hegemony over Syria. The Soviet Union, meanwhile, had been angered by Nasser's destruction of Khaled Bagdash's disciplined Middle East (Syrian) Communist Party. Hence, Soviet Premier Khrushchev responded favorably to Kassem's request for Soviet aid.

The UAR-Iraqi antagonism was heightened by an uprising in Iraq in Mar. 1959. The Iraqi army garrison of Mosul, an important oil town in the north, revolted against Kassem, and the insurrection was put down after bloody fighting. The Associated Press reported from Mosul, Mar. 17 that the uprising had been backed by Sheik Ahmad Ajil Alldya-war, ruler of 60,000 Shammar tribesmen, and by other wealthy landowners fearful that Kassem-régime land reforms of Sept. 1958 would end their power. Kurdish tribesmen were said to have joined pro-Kassem forces after receiving assurances of greater Kurdish tribal autonomy. Up to 2,000 persons were reported killed in the uprising, which began with clashes during a Mosul rally Mar. 6 of pro-Communist peace partisans. The fighting itself and the charges and countercharges over the instigation of the mutiny (led by Col. Abdel Wahab el-Shawaf, who had asked Kassem to ban the rally) brought the Nasser-Kassem rift into sharp focus, and the USSR entered the propaganda battle on Iraq's side.

Iraqi military planes were reported Mar. 10 to have bombed and strafed the village of Hamoudiya, in the Tel Kotchek area of Syria, 3 miles from the Syrian-Iraqi border. No casualties were reported from the attack, which was believed to be directed against Iraqi rebels retreating toward the Syrian frontier. Radio Damascus charged Mar. 14 that Iraqi fighters had attacked 3 villages in the Tel Kotchek area. UAR army headquarters reported Mar. 15 that 30 armed Iraqis had crossed the Syrian frontier and attacked Syrian border guards in the Talhamar area earlier that day. Leading officials of the UAR embassy in Baghdad had been declared *personae non gratae* by Iraq Mar. 9 and were expelled to Syria Mar. 10.

Nasser declared his opposition to the Kassem regime Mar. 11-15 and made clear that he considered the USSR responsible for a growing rift among Arab nationalists. Nasser, speaking in Damascus, charged Mar. 11 that Kassem and Communist "agents of a foreign power" had tried to divide the Arab peoples and subject them to "foreign influence." In his first public attack on the Kassem regime, Nasser asserted that the UAR had supported Kassem's revolutionary government but had been repaid with hostility by Iraq. Nasser told Damascus demonstrators Mar. 12 that "the [anti-Kassem] Shawaf revolt in Iraq was not inspired by a foreign power or by the United Arab Republic" but was caused by Kassem's effort to introduce "a Communist reign of terror in Iraq."

Addressing a Damascus funeral procession for Col. Muhammad Said Shihab, an Iraqi officer who had participated in the Shawaf revolt and had died of wounds after escaping to Syria, Nasser warned Mar. 13 that "the banner of Arab nationalism will be raised over Baghdad" despite Kassem's opposition. Nasser accused Iraq-based Communists of efforts to detach Syria from the UAR and annex it to Iraq under plans for "a Communist Fertile Crescent" (Syria, Jordan, Iraq and Palestine) in the Middle East. Nasser told a Damascus crowd Mar. 15 that Kassem's repression of the Iraq revolt had been a "massacre of honest Arab nationalists" who fought Iraq's "democracy of blood, gallows and Communist kangaroo courts."

Nasser's public denunciation of the Iraqi and Soviet regimes was backed by organized political and religious demonstrations in Cairo and Damascus in which Kassem and the USSR were reviled as anti-Moslem. UAR Vice Pres. Abdel Hakim Amer said at Cairo memorial services for the Iraqi rebel dead Mar. 16 that Communist agents had provoked the Mosul garrison into its "revolution against . . . dictatorship" to provide excuses for the suppression of Arab nationalists in Iraq. The UAR demonstrations were held in answer to anti-Nasser rallies staged in Baghdad.

Iraqi Foreign Min. Hashim Jawad charged Mar. 15 that the Iraqi rebellion had been "organized by the United Arab Republic" and supplied with weapons by it. He declared that Nasser had inspired 3 conspiracies against the Kassem government within the past 8 months. The rebellion, he said, was "100%" linked to UAR efforts to overthrow the Kassem government. (Iraqi National Guidance Director Gen. Shardi Ahmed, a member of the pro-UAR Istiqlal [Independence] Party, was dismissed Mar. 17 and replaced by Dhummoun Ayyoub, a member of the National Democratic Party.)

Nasser had already taken action against domestic communism in the UAR's Egyptian and Syrian regions. More than 200 Egyptian Communist leaders were reported arrested Jan. 1, 1959 in an anti-Communist crackdown ordered by Nasser. The arrests, which followed similar action in the Syrian Region of the UAR, came after Nasser had denounced Arab Communists Dec. 23, 1958 for attempts to prevent the union of Egypt and Syria. 2 printing firms, the Dar el-Hana and Dar el-Nadim companies, founded with Soviet and Communist Chinese funds to print Communist propaganda for Middle Eastern distribution, were closed by the police. Cairo dispatches said Jan. 1 that street fighting had been reported in Damascus, Aleppo and other Syrian cities between Communists and nationalists loyal to Nasser.

Soviet Premier Khrushchev, meanwhile, had warned Nasser Mar. 16, 1959 that the UAR was "doomed to failure" in its efforts to suppress domestic Communists and to force Iraq into union with Syria and Egypt. Khrushchev, speaking at a Moscow reception marking the signing of a 550 million-ruble ($137 million at official rates) Soviet-Iraqi economic and technical aid agreement, asserted that the USSR considered the new Iraqi regime "more progressive" than the UAR government and would come to its aid in case of any "trouble." Khrushchev asserted that Iraq's rebels were a "clique of conspirators" who were crushed when "the people supported Premier Kassem." Khrushchev conceded that "we were irked over Nasser's latest pronouncements against communism." He warned that "if Nasser continues his attacks against communism, he will not add anything to his laurels but would only win the commendations of the reactionaries." He told the UAR's leaders that the USSR's "sympathies toward Iraq are greater" than those toward the UAR.

Nasser, in a statement issued in Damascus Mar. 16 by the UAR's semi-official Middle East News Agency, denied Khrushchev's charges that the UAR was seeking to annex Iraq. He asserted that the UAR campaign for Arab solidarity had always been based on "unanimous Arab approval," not on coercion. The Middle East News Agency declared Mar. 17 that Khrushchev's attack on Nasser meant that "an open battle between Arab nationalism and Communist imperialism has started."

Khrushchev defended Soviet ties with Iraq Mar. 19 and described Nasser as "a rather hotheaded young man" who "took upon himself more than his stature permitted" in his attacks on communism and the Iraqi government. Khrushchev denied that he had interfered in UAR affairs by criticizing Nasser's suppression of UAR Communists. Khrushchev said that he only "was defending the Communist faith to which I adhere." But Nasser told a Damascus crowd Mar. 20 that Khrushchev's "defense of the Communist minority in our country" was unacceptable "interference in our affairs." He denounced UAR Communists as foreign "agents" allied with Britain in opposition to Arab nationalism. Nasser warned the USSR Mar. 22 that with his "hot-headedness," the UAR would "win against the new agents of communism."

Nasser charged Mar. 22 that Iraq's revolutionary regime had refused to join the UAR in an attack against Israel in 1958. Speaking on Radio Damascus, Nasser said that the UAR had "decided to enter a decisive battle against Israel if aggression continued" in the form of Israeli border raids. Nasser reported that the UAR had "asked Kassem, under the terms of our military agreement, to stand with us against Israel and send Iraqi army units, but Kassem refused." He said that UAR leaders then knew that "we would be alone if we entered a conflict with Israel."

The Iraqi government formally withdrew Mar. 24 from membership in the Baghdad (METO) Pact. Notification of the break with the British-Pakistani-Turkish-Iranian defense alliance was given to the U.S. and British ambassadors in Baghdad. The Baghdad radio announced Mar. 24 that the withdrawal was "effective today" despite treaty provisions requiring 6 months' notification for renunciation. Iraq had not participated in the Baghdad Pact since the overthrow of the Iraqi monarchy in July 1958. Premier Kassem, who announced the METO renunciation publicly, told a group of Iraqi editors Mar. 24 that "we quit the Baghdad Pact in order not to provide pact members with a cause for interference in our internal affairs." He said Iraq's positive neutralist policies excluded membership in any "aggressive grouping." Kassem also advised Iraqi newspapers to "forget Nasser" and halt their attacks on the UAR. He urged them not to "waste time replying to criticism from abroad which doesn't bother us at all."

(The *N. Y. Times* reported Mar. 23 that British Prime Min. Macmillan, in his U.S. talks with Pres. Eisenhower, had expressed British willingness to supply Iraq with Western arms to limit Iraqi dependence on the USSR.)

Nasser, who returned to Cairo Mar. 26 from a month-long visit to the Syrian Region of the UAR, said at an officers' meeting Mar. 30 that the UAR would "crush the Communist agents" as it had "crushed the imperialist agents." "We believed at the beginning of our revolution that the Communists were independent, but they proved to be agents of Moscow," he asserted.

Pres. Nasser Apr. 16 repeated and expanded on his earlier charge that Arab Communists had plotted to seize Iraq, divide Egypt and Syria and establish a "Red Fertile Crescent" in the Middle East with Soviet backing. Nasser gave this version of the Mosul uprising in an interview for the Indian magazine *Blitz:* The "Communist master-plot" had called for a Communist-dominated federation of Iraq, Syria, Jordan, Lebanon and Kuwait, which would insure Soviet access to the Persian Gulf, the Gulf of Aqaba and the Indian Ocean; Arab Communists had discussed the plan at the 21st Soviet Communist Party Congress in Moscow Jan. 27-Feb. 5 and had agreed to use their "iron grip on Iraq" to "organize an all-Arab underground for . . . subversion and sabotage against neighboring Arab countries"; Baghdad was to be the "command post of the Communist counterrevolution against Arab nationalism." Nasser asserted that the "enormous Soviet goodwill built up over 3 years of friendship was lost in less than 3 weeks" with the suppression of the anti-Communist revolt attempted by Iraq's Mosul garrison. He charged that Communists had plotted to prevent the merger of Egypt and Syria but that the plebiscite approving the union had "isolated and repudiated" the Communists. Nasser said that he "personally" had prevented a Communist coup in Syria in Dec. 1958.

Nasser, in an interview in the July 20, 1959 issue of *Life* magazine, portrayed himself as an Arab nationalist opposed both to communism and to Moslem fanaticism. Nasser asserted that the UAR's policy of "positive neutrality" had furthered Arab independence by avoiding compromising entanglements with either the Western or Soviet blocs. He said: "The fact that I criticized the Soviet Union never did mean that I was aligning . . . [the UAR] with the U.S."; "the same is true for the other side."

Nasser asserted July 22 that Kassem had rebuffed UAR efforts to end the rivalry and differences between Iraq and the UAR. Nasser, speaking at a Cairo rally on the eve of the 7th anniversary of the Egyptian revolution, said that Kassem had failed to reply to peace overtures relayed to him by Syrian Interior Min. Abdul Hamid al-Serraj. Nasser said that the Serraj mission had been carried out "at the height of the quarrel" with Iraq. He said Serraj had tried to persuade Kassem that the UAR sought "unity," not political union with Iraq.

Kassem was the target of an unsuccessful assassination attempt Oct. 7. While recovering from wounds suffered in the attack, Kassem said Nov. 1 that "Iraq has nothing against the United Arab Republic, but if they have anything against us, we . . . know how to deal effectively with them." Interviewed in a Baghdad hospital, Kassem warned that if "any other Arab country" attempted to "send an aggressive army against us," it would be defeated. Kassem asserted that the question of his eventual successor had been "worked . . . out" so that it did "not matter whether I live 2 days or 2 . . . years."

Nasser Nov. 4 held the U.S. partly to blame for the growth of communism in Iraq. He asserted that if Kassem "would just give a sign, the people would follow him" against the Iraqi Communists. The UAR leader, interviewed in his Cairo home by the *N.Y. Times*, said that the majority of Iraqis would support a movement to free Iraq from communism. He described them as Arab and Iraqi nationalists and denied that the UAR had opposed them as enemies of the broader Arab nationalist movement led by the UAR. "The question," he said, "is not one of Arab unity or union with us" but of "the independence of the Iraqi people."

Nasser blamed the Communist penetration of Iraq on policies formulated by ex-British Prime Min. Anthony Eden, the late U.S. State Secy. Dulles (who had died May 24) and the late Iraqi Premier Nuri as-Said. He said that Iraq's resistance to communism had been weakened by its membership in the former Baghdad Pact. He asserted that he had "told Mr. Dulles in 1953 that when you pressure governments to follow you, they will be called your agents." Nasser denied that the UAR sought to monopolize leadership of Arab nationalism. He said: "Unity does not mean that you have to have one single Arab country. There will be united countries like Egypt and Syria. Some others will be federated. Others will be independent but in agreement, acting in a spirit of solidarity."

Nasser had met Mar. 25, 1959 with Pres. Fuad Chehab of Lebanon and had pledged that the UAR would respect Lebanon's integrity and indepencence. (Nasser and Chehab, meeting on the Lebanese-Syrian border, reached agreement on unspecified support for Arab nationalist policies and on the elimination of Lebanese-UAR economic disagreements. The economic agreement was believed to involve the ending of Syrian restrictions and taxes on Lebanese transit trade to the Mediterranean.)

In respect to his ideological and political feud with the Soviet Union, Nasser made 3 significant foreign policy statements in his address at the July 22 rally in Cairo: (1) The UAR sought friendship with the U.S., Britain and USSR, but it demanded that all relations be "based on mutual respect." (2) It would continue support for "the 200 million sufferers of imperialist injustice in Africa and Asia." (3) It would continue efforts to impose an economic boycott on Israel, which was "a spearhead by imperialists to enable them to gain a foothold in the newly independent countries in Africa."

Nasser was said to be taking a serious gamble in his propaganda confontation with Moscow, for he was entirely dependent on the Soviet Union for the construction of the Aswan

High Dam. At his news conference Apr. 29, 1959, U.S. Pres. Eisenhower had verified that the U.S. was still unprepared to extend air to the UAR for the Aswan project. Eisenhower also confirmed that the U.S. was "very concerned about Iraq" and was eager to do "anything we can do to promote better relations with this country without making other enemies" in the Middle East. The President said that his policy toward Iraq was based on consistent American efforts "to be friends with everybody in the Middle East." He expressed doubt over whether the Iraqi situation was "the most dangerous" facing the U.S. He acknowledged that U.S. relations with Iraq had been complicated by Iraq's "connections with communism and . . . difficulties with Egypt." Eisenhower said that the U.S. had considered Iraq "one of the most progressive of the countries in the region." He specified that this opinion had been formed "after the revolution . . . that removed the king [Feisal] and the prime minister [Nuri as-Said]." Eisenhower, asked whether the U.S. was rebuilding good relations with Nasser as a result of the Iraqi crisis, replied only that the U.S. was "trying to be fair with everybody" and was "not trying to promote personal quarrels" among Mideastern leaders.

By early autumn 1959, after a lull in the Egypto-Soviet quarrel, it was clear that the Russians had decided to uphold their agreement to help build the Aswan High Dam. The extension of Soviet financial aid from the first phase of the Aswan High Dam to the construction of the entire Aswan project was predicted Oct. 31 by Ahmed Said, Egyptian chief engineer for the dam. Interviewed on his return from Moscow with final plans for the project, Said asserted that (1) E£20 million of the E£32 million pledged in Soviet aid for the project would be left unspent after the completion of the first phase and would have to be spent in the USSR and Soviet bloc; (2) Soviet engineering plans already completed included work on 2d-phase portions of the project. Nevertheless the UAR Public Works Ministry denied Nov. 7 that the

USSR had offered or had been asked to participate in any but the first stage of the 3-part Aswan project.

Outlining the UAR's financial needs, Nasser Nov. 4 had appealed for E£1 billion ($2.85 billion) in foreign aid within the next 5 years, with "another E£300 million" ($855 million) for Syrian development. He said: The USSR had supplied the UAR with E£60 million in credit to buy factories. But it "does not give us all we need," and the UAR was eager for trade and aid from the U.S., he asserted.

Soviet Premier Khrushchev, in an interview published Nov. 10 by Cairo's *Al Goumhouria*, said that the USSR would continue its aid to the UAR despite Nasser's attacks on Arab communism. Khrushchev, who pledged continued Soviet support for the Arab states against Israel, conceded that "the present situation in Arab countries is not favorable for the emergence of a Communist system."

2d Soviet Loan for Aswan Dam

Letters exchanged by UAR Pres. Nasser and Soviet Premier Khrushchev and made public in Cairo Jan. 18, 1960 confirmed that the USSR had agreed to finance the 2d stage of the Aswan High Dam project "on the same basis as . . . the first stage." The announcement was made after Nasser had met Jan. 17 with Soviet Electric Power Station Construction Min. Ignati T. Novikov.

Nasser had set off a 10-ton dynamite explosion Jan. 9 at Aswan to open a diversion canal and formally inaugurate the construction of the project. Speaking at ceremonies attended by Moroccan King Muhammad V, Soviet Electric Power Station Construction Min. Novikov, ex-Syrian Pres. Shukri al-Kuwatly and Ivan V. Komzin, Soviet chief engineer for the project, Nasser hailed the dam as a reminder that "small nations can always undertake the greatest construction works and can . . . bore their way through rocks, even with their fingernails and their blood." The USSR's 400 million-ruble

($93 million) loan toward the construction of the project's first stage was "absolutely sincere aid without conditions and even without cumbersome terms," he said. (Nasser Jan. 10 opened Egypt's first hydroelectric plant, a 2 billion-kwh.-annual-capacity project attached to the existing Aswan Dam, 5 miles below the site of the high dam.)

The 2d-stage agreement, providing for 900 million rubles ($225 million at official rates) in long-term Soviet credits to build the 2d stage of the Aswan project, was signed in Moscow Aug. 27 by UAR Public Works Min. Moussa Arafa and Deputy Chairman Ivan Arkhipov of the Soviet State Committee for Foreign Economic Relations. The credit was to pay for Soviet materials and personnel used in erecting the main dam for the project.

A number of other economic aid developments took place at about this time. Among them:

- A contract for Soviet construction of a shipyard in Alexandria was signed in Moscow Aug. 23 by Syrian Vice Pres. Nureddin Kuhala. (Kuhala had been appointed July 19 to succeed Baathist leader Akram Hourani.)
- The delivery to the UAR of 1,000,000 tons of U.S. surplus wheat and flour during 1961 was provided for in agreements announced in Cairo Aug. 1 and Washington Aug. 9. Egypt was to receive $58,200,000 worth of grain under the Aug. 1 accord, and Syria was to get $17 million worth under the Aug. 9 pact. Both were local currency sales repayable over 30 years. The U.S. agreed Sept. 19 to sell Syria an additional $1,600,000 worth of barley.
- A $17 million U.S. loan agreement signed in Cairo July 5 provided funds for the construction of a sugar refinery in Edfu, central Upper Egypt, and other projects. The loan was in local currency from sales in the UAR of U.S. surplus food.
- The U.S. Development Loan Fund Aug. 2 signed a $7 million loan for the Egyptian Industrial Bank's small and medium industry development program.

Soviet-UAR Quarrel Renewed

After 5 months of increasingly rancorous attacks on the UAR by the Soviet press and radio and by Communist newspapers in Rome, Prague and Beirut, UAR newspapers began June 5, 1961 to strike back. The UAR government-owned Middle East News Agency said in an article in 3 Cairo newspapers June 5 that the Soviet campaign "could no longer be tolerated."

The Soviet press had accused the UAR of persecuting Communists. The Soviet party daily *Pravda* June 6 repeated its charge of the previous week that the Lebanese Communist Party leader Farajallah al-Hilw had been tortured to death in a Damascus prison in the UAR's Syrian Region. Moscow Radio had charged that another Lebanese Communist leader–Riad el-Turk–had been killed in a Damascus jail. The UAR's Middle East News Agency retorted June 6 that the UAR had informed the USSR 2 weeks previously that Turk was alive. The article said Turk had met newsmen in his prison in Damascus June 5. The agency said that the UAR had denied the Hilw charge and had informed the Soviet Union that it had no knowledge of Hilw being in a Syrian prison. The Cairo newspaper *Al Gomhouria* June 6 accused the Soviet Union of attempting "to exert pressure" on the UAR. It said the USSR had been under a "misconception" by "interpret[ing] our positive neutralism as some sort of alignment with the camp they represent."

The Cairo newspaper *Al-Ahram* reported June 9 that Soviet Premier Khrushchev had assailed UAR Pres. Nasser May 3 for suppressing communism. It said that Khrushchev, speaking before a visiting UAR parliamentary delegation in Moscow, had predicted that Nasser would be overthrown unless he embraced communism.

Pravda June 17 attributed the "intensified" "spread of anti-Soviet leaflets" in the UAR to the U.S. Information Service center in Cairo.

Nasser Bars Israeli Cargoes from Suez

A direct confrontation between Israel and the UAR had loomed in late spring 1959 as the result of Nasser's newly absolute embargo of the Canal to Israeli trade.

The owners of the Danish freighter *Inger Toft,* halted May 21 by Egyptian officials as it attempted to transit the Suez Canal with an Israeli cargo, refused June 2 to unload the ship in compliance with orders of a UAR war prize court. The vessel, under charter by a U.S. firm, was *en route* from Haifa, Israel to the Far East with a cargo of Israeli potash, cement, scrap brass and marble. UAR officials denied June 4 that the vessel would be unloaded forcibly, but they made clear that it would not be permitted to leave Port Said with the Israeli cargo.

Israeli vessels had been barred from the Suez Canal since the Arab-Israeli war in 1948. But nonmilitary Israeli cargoes carried by vessels of other nations had been permitted through the Canal until early 1959, when some were seized, others allowed to pass.

Israeli Premier David Ben-Gurion June 3 denounced the intensified Suez blockade against Israel as "a blow not only at the interests of Israel but also at the charter" of the UN "and the decisions of the Security Council."

UAR State Min. Ali Sabry said June 10 that Israeli ships and Israeli cargoes "hiding behind the standards of other nations" would not be permitted through the Suez Canal despite any action by the UN, the International Court of Justice (World Court) in Geneva or the great powers. Sabry asserted that the UAR "cannot allow Israeli shipping free passage as this would expose this vital waterway to sabotage and delay" from any "action Israel might undertake" against the UAR.

UN Secy. Gen. Dag Hammarskjöld visited Cairo June 30–July 1 in an effort to persuade UAR leaders to end or to relax their refusal to permit Israeli-owned or chartered vessels through the Canal. Hammarskjöld, who conferred July 1 with Nasser and UAR Foreign Min. Mahmoud Fawzi, was said to have urged unsuccessfully that the World Court be permitted to rule on whether the *Inger Toft* should be allowed to carry its Israeli cargo through the canal.

The Egyptian War Prize Commission, meeting in Alexandria, had decided June 25 that the UAR's seizure of another Israeli cargo from the Liberian freighter *Kapitan Manolis* was legal. It denied claims that the Ceylon-bound vessel's cargo from the Liberian freighter was Ceylonese property.

Challenges to Israel to resume its 1948 and 1956 battles with Egypt were voiced by Nasser and other UAR leaders July 23–28. Field Marshal Abdel Hakim Amer, UAR vice president and war minister, said at a Cairo military review July 23 on the 7th anniversary of the Egyptian revolution that "if Israel attacks us at any point on our borders, she must face total war." UAR weapons displayed included nearly 200 Soviet-built MiG jet fighters and light bombers.

Speaking at an Alexandria rally celebrating the 3d anniversary of the nationalization of the Suez Canal, Nasser asserted July 26 that if another Israeli-Arab conflict occurred, "this time we will exterminate Israel." Nasser, who described Israel as a "crime established by treachery and imperialism," said that "if there is a challenge, then we accept that challenge. . . . All the Arabs want a decisive battle." The UAR had "defeated Britain, France and Israel 3 years ago" when they attacked in the Suez Canal Zone, Nasser said. "We have never been defeated with arms although we were defeated now and then with treachery." Alluding to published articles by Gen. Moshe Dayan, former Israeli chief of staff who had directed Israel's successful 1956 Sinai attack, Nasser warned: "Moshe Dayan threatens to invade Sinai; let him come—we are waiting for him." (Dayan, then a candidate for the Israeli

Knesset [parliament], had urged a policy toward the UAR of "meeting hostility with hostility" but had barred as unfeasible an Israeli invasion of Sinai or the Canal Zone.)

Nasser, at July 28 land-distribution ceremonies near Alexandria, reiterated his hopes for "a decisive battle with Israel to avenge 1948." He said: "Again we tell them, welcome to the battle if they want it. In the last bout you attacked and we retreated because of England and France, but this time we will get rid of Israel and the problems of Israel." (Nasser said at a Cairo rally Aug. 8 that the UAR would not permit Israel to use the Suez Canal. He said Israel had not observed a single UN resolution "from 1948 until this day.")

Israeli Foreign Ministry spokesmen July 29 described the Nasser and Amer speeches as "another attempt to improve Egypt's standing with the other Arabs and help smooth up Nasser's . . . battered relations with them."

Israeli Foreign Min. Golda Meir Aug. 13 rejected a compromise plan for the passage of Israeli-owned cargoes through the Suez Canal in foreign-owned vessels. The proposal, evolved by Hammarskjöld in his talks with UAR leaders, would ban publicity on the sailing of any vessel carrying an Israeli cargo toward the Canal and would require Israeli cargoes to be purchased by receivers before leaving Israeli ports for the Canal. Mrs. Meir said Israel would "not accept the principle that Nasser has any right to put forward any conditions to anybody about free and innocent passage" through Suez. She conceded that Israel's rejection of the Hammarskjöld formula was "creating a deadlock," but she denied that the Suez blockade could be resolved by "giving in to demands made . . . without any legal right or moral right." She said that Israel planned to bring the Suez blockade before the UN and that "we are not ready to accept that the UN should pass over it in silence."

In a series of speeches made while touring Syria Feb. 17-25, 1960, Nasser reiterated his enmity for Israel and the West and swore to lead Arabs in liberating Palestine. Nasser said at a rally in Aleppo Feb. 17 that the UAR never would let Israeli vessels or cargoes through the Suez Canal. He charged that the U.S. had financed the right-wing Syrian National Party in a campaign of "intrigue and dissension" against the UAR. Speaking at a meeting in Hama Feb. 20, he declared that "we will shed our blood, sacrifice our lives–including myself, ministers and every citizen–for the realization of all Arab rights" and the recovery of Palestine from Israel.

A warning that the situation in the middle east was "deteriorating" and that it was time for "action which rightly belongs to the Security Council" was voiced Feb. 18 by UN Secy. Gen. Hammarskjöld. At a news conference in New York, Hammarskjöld declared that "an atmosphere of . . . mistrust" had forced the Middle East "back to a position where we have been before and from which I . . . hoped that we had departed." Hammarskjöld refused to comment on the UAR's seizure of Israeli-origin cargoes shipped via the Suez Canal, but he urged the UN "to stick to its guns" to break the "chain reaction" of Arab-Israeli clashes and reprisals.

The *N.Y. Times* reported from Cairo Feb. 23 that Soviet Amb.-to-UAR Vladimir Erofeyev and Amb.-to-Israel Mikhail F. Bodrov had conferred, respectively, with UAR Foreign Min. Mahmoud Fawzi and Israeli Foreign Min. Golda Meir in efforts to ease Arab-Israeli tension. But the Israeli Foreign Ministry denied Feb. 24 that the USSR had taken any initiative for Middle Eastern peace.

Israel protested to the UN Security Council Feb. 25 that "extensive military preparations directed against Israel" from the Egyptian and Syrian regions of the UAR were endangering peace in the Middle East. The Israeli protest came after repeated reports of UAR troop movements into the Sinai Peninsula and Gaza Strip area from Egypt and into the Israeli-Syrian border area. The reported UAR troop buildup followed a series of armed clashes on the Israeli-Syrian frontier. A note delivered to Sir Pierson Dixon of Britain, Security Council president for February, by Israeli Rep.-to-UN Joseph Tekoah, charged that Nasser had "repeatedly proclaimed his country's policy of war, blockade and boycott against Israel, threatening her with destruction in a 'sacred march.'" Tekoah, who did not ask that the Council be summoned to consider the Israeli charges, urged UN action to halt the UAR "incitement to war."

Attempt to Normalize UAR-Jordanian Ties

The reestablishment of Jordanian-UAR diplomatic relations was announced in Cairo Aug. 16, 1959 by the UAR Foreign Ministry as part of an effort by the UAR to restore its deteriorating relations with several fellow Arab states. Diplomatic ties between the 2 countries had been broken in 1958 after Jordan had accused the UAR of trying to overthrow King Hussein. Ex-Jordanian Foreign Min. Muhammad Pasha Shuraiqi was named Jordanian ambassador to the UAR, and rapid approval of a UAR envoy to Jordan was pledged. The border between Jordan and the Syrian Region of the UAR had been reopened to travel and transit trade July 30 after being closed intermittently since 1958.

The basic agreement on resuming Jordanian-UAR relations was reached in negotiations with Jordanian and UAR leaders and Arab League Secy. Gen. Abdel Khalek Hassouna of Egypt. As a further move in the UAR's rapprochement with alienated Arab states, Hassouna announced Aug. 16 that he would visit Libya and Tunisia to seek a renewal of UAR-Tunisian diplomatic ties. And King Saud of Saudi Arabia visited Cairo Aug. 31 for talks on ending Saudi-Arabian-UAR hostility. King Saud and Nasser said after meeting Sept. 1 that "full cooperation has been renewed between us regarding Arab affairs."

A year of more or less normal diplomatic UAR-Jordanian relations was broken in Aug. 1960 by the assassination of one of Hussein's major domestic supporters, Jordanian Premier

Hazza Majali. Majali, 44, was killed Aug. 29 in the explosion of a time bomb in his office in Amman. The explosion a 2d blast in the same building killed 10 other persons—among them Foreign Affairs Undersecy. Zahouddin el-Mahmoud and Tourism Department Director Assem Taji—and injured 47. (The death toll reached 12 Sept. 6 when Maj. Mamduh Ishasat, a Majali aide-de-camp, died of wounds suffered in the first explosion.)

It was not known at first whether the bombs had been set by pro-UAR opponents of Majali's neutralist regime or by revolutionaries opposed to the Jordanian monarchy. But King Hussein announced Aug. 30 that an investigation had determined the identities of 2 men, a messenger and an office cleaner, to whom all evidence pointed as those who had planted the bombs. Both had fled at once to Syria, Hussein said, and their extradition was being sought.

The Majali government had complained July 3 to the secretariat of the Arab League against what it alleged to be the UAR's instigation of attacks on Hussein's regime. Nasser had predicted in a speech June 24 that Hussein would be assassinated, as was his grandfather, King Abdullah. The 2 countries' relations had begun declining noticeably after Jordan had publicly aired its suspicions that the UAR had taken a hand in a continued attempt to disaffect the allegiance of Jordan's assimilated Palestinian refugees. Hussein had challenged Iraq and the UAR Mar. 16 to let "neutrals" conduct a plebiscite among former Palestinians living in Jordan to determine whether they supported Jordan's absorption of former Palestinian territory west of the Jordan River or favored the creation of a separate "Palestinian entity." He pledged in a statement reported from Amman Mar. 17 "to accept the results."

Secy. Gen. Abdel Khalek Hassouna of the Arab League arrived in Amman Sept. 2 to investigate Jordan's allegations of UAR complicity in the Majali assassination. Hussein charged in a radio address Sept. 5 that the assassination of

Majali was part of a plot "to destroy the Jordanian nation." Hussein had charged at an Amman news conference Aug. 30 that "responsible" UAR officials, "mainly in Syria," had known of the assassination plot. He told western newsmen Sept. 6 that he was sure that Nasser had personal knowledge of the conspiracy.

Jordanian-Iraqi border posts were reopened Oct. 17 for the first time since 1958.

EGYPTIAN-SYRIAN UNION'S FINAL YEARS (1959-61)

Domestic Developments

Under a decree issued Jan. 6, 1959 by Syrian Agrarian Reform Min. Mustafa Hamdoun, UAR officials confiscated 35,000 acres of farmland belonging to 39 large Syrian landholders. The decree, the 3d to order Syrian land seizures and the most sweeping of them, brought to more than one million acres the land confiscated under Egyptian land reform laws extended to Syria by the UAR. Compensation for the confiscated land, distributed to peasants beginning Feb. 21, was paid in 1½% government bonds in amounts equal to 10 times the annual rent of the seized parcels.

4 former members of the Syrian Baathist party resigned Dec. 30, 1959 from the UAR's central cabinet and the Syrian Regional cabinet. The resignations were linked to Nasser's reported dissatisfaction with Syrian application of UAR reform laws and Syrian opposition to the naming of Vice Pres. Abdel Hakim Amer as administrator of the Syrian Regional government. Vice Pres. Akram el-Hourani and National Guidance Min. Salah el-Bitar quit the central UAR cabinet; Social Affairs Min. Abdel Ghani Kanout and Agriculture Min. Mustafa Hamdoun resigned from the Syrian Regional cabinet. Nasser Dec. 31 named Syrian Regional Interior Min. Abdul Hamid al-Serraj to Kanout's post and Municipal & Rural Affairs Min. Toma al-Awdatullah to Hamdoun's post in addition to the positions they already held.

Nasser shifted several cabinet ministers Sept. 20, 1960 and gave others additional assignments to fill vacancies left by more resignations of Syrian Baath members. The announced appointments: Kamal el-Din Hussein, to remain education minister and become chairman of the Egyptian Region Executive Council; Abdul Hamid al-Serraj, to remain Syrian interior minister and become chairman of the Syrian Region Executive Council; Nurredin Kahala as UAR planning minister; Fakher el-Kayali as UAR justice minister; Toma al-Awdat-ullah, UAR municipal and rural affairs minister; Muhammad el-Alem, UAR communications minister; Jadou Ezeldin, Syrian public works minister; Sabet el-Ariss, UAR culture and national guidance minister.

Cairo's 4 leading newspaper and magazine publishing firms were nationalized and "reorganized" under control of the ruling National Union by decrees issued May 24, 1960. Newspapers thus placed directly under government control were the dailies *Al-Ahram* and *al-Akhbar* and the weekly *Ruz-al-Youssuf.* The decree, which said that the papers had been taken from "capitalist owners" for the "people," provided for the repayment of the owners in 3½% government bonds. The decree made all Egyptian journalists subject to National Union licensing. Nasser told Egyptian editors at a Cairo meeting May 29 that the papers had been seized because foreign embassies were trying to control them through political advertising, a common practice in Egypt.

Suez Canal operations yielded a net profit of $47,355,000 in 1959, 16½ times the amount of royalties paid to Egypt by the Universal Suez Canal Co. in 1955, the North American Newspaper Alliance (news agency) reported from Cairo Oct. 17, 1960. Secy. Gen. Abdul Hamid Abu Bakr of the UAR's Suez Canal Authority told newsmen Nov. 21 that the Canal would be able to handle vessels of 37-foot draft and 47,000-ton displacement by Jan. 1961 and that Canal tolls were expected to reach $175 million in 1961. He reported that 9,322 vessels with a total net tonnage of 91,468,465 tons had used the Canal in January-June 1960. (The *N.Y. Herald Tribune* had reported Oct. 2 that 15 foreign pilots had quit the Suez authority in a dispute over job contracts.)

Foreign Relations

Premier Amintore Fanfani of Italy ended a visit to the UAR and talks with Nasser Jan. 9, 1959 after reaching agreement on a wide range of economic matters. A joint communiqué issued Jan. 8 by Fanfani and UAR Foreign Min. Mahmoud Fawzi disclosed accords on (a) increased Italian imports of Egyptian cotton in exchange for Egypt's purchase of 130,000 tons of wheat; (b) free UAR entry and exit for Italian residents and their property up to a value of $20,000; (c) the return of Italian property sequestered by the UAR, and (d) increased Italian-UAR trade and technical cooperation. Fanfani, who flew to Athens for talks on NATO cooperation with Greek Premier Constantine Karamanlis Jan. 9–10, returned to Rome Jan. 11 and found strong criticism of the support for neutralism that he apparently indicated in his talks with Nasser.

Relations between West Germany and the United Arab Republic had been subjected to strain by the announcement Jan. 7 that the UAR had agreed to establish consular relations with the East German government. The consular pact, disclosed by East German Premier Otto Grotewohl at the end of a visit to Cairo and talks with Nasser Jan. 4–7, brought West German threats Jan. 9 of a possible rupture of West German-UAR relations and delays in planned German participation in the Aswan High Dam project. West Germany disclosed Jan. 14 that Chancellor Konrad Adenauer had been assured by Nasser that the agreement, although permitting an East German trade mission to perform consular functions, would not establish formal consular ties or imply UAR recognition of East Germany.

An accord settling British-Egyptian financial differences arising from Egypt's 1956 nationalization of the Suez Canal and the ensuing Anglo-French invasion of the Canal Zone was concluded in Cairo Jan. 17, 1959 by British and Egyptian negotiators. The agreement, reached in Cairo talks Jan. 12–16 between Sir Denis Rickett of the British Treasury and Trade & Economy Min. Abdel Moneim el-Kaissouni of the United Arab Republic, provided for (a) the release of approximately £74 million ($207.2 million) in blocked Egyptian sterling accounts in Britain; (b) the Egyptian payment of £27½ million ($68 million) for nationalized British property and the return to their owners of sequestered British holdings; (c) the Egyptian payment of an unspecified portion of £20 million ($56 million) in claims by the Royal Dutch Shell Oil Co. for losses from the sequestration and cancellation of leases. The accord reportedly omitted any settlement of conflicting war claims for the Egyptian seizure of British military bases and war material in the Suez zone and damage inflicted on Egyptian Canal installations by the Anglo-French attack of Oct.–Nov. 1956. The Cairo agreement was reached after World Bank Pres. Eugene R. Black had won British and Egyptian approval Jan. 9 for a resumption of negotiations to end the Suez zone dispute.

British requests for reestablishing diplomatic relations with the UAR were conveyed to UAR State Min. Ali Sabry Aug. 3, 1959 by Canadian Amb.-to-UAR Arnold Smith. Relations between the 2 countries were restored at the level of *chargés d'affaires*, it was announced Dec. 1.

A U.S.-UAR agreement was signed in Cairo Nov. 14, 1959 for the sale of 150,000 tons of surplus U.S. wheat and barley to the UAR's Syrian Region. The cost of the grain and transportation totalled $9.6 million and was to be paid for in local currency, of which half would be available for development loans in Syria. It was reported in dispatches from Cairo Nov. 14 that agreement had been reached on a $700,000 U.S. Development Loan Fund loan to build a Syrian textile mill. These transactions represented the first U.S. aid accepted by Syria.

Nasser in Damascus Feb. 22, 1960 denounced the U.S.-British-French Tripartite Declaration of 1950 on Middle Eastern frontiers as "dead and buried." He spoke at a military review and parade celebrating the 2d anniversary of the Egyptian-Syrian merger into the UAR. The UAR leader charged Feb. 25 in Deraa, near the Syrian-Jordan border, that the U.S., Britain and France had used the declaration to claim "guardianship over this area" and were "premeditating aggression against us." He warned the west that "the Arab people . . . will rise in arms to crush any new aggression." Dispatches from London had reported Feb. 24 that the U.S., Britain and France had reaffirmed their 1950 declaration pledging coordinated action through the UN to maintain the *status quo* in the Middle East. The British Foreign Office said Feb. 24 that the declaration remained in force.

U.S. Labor Union Boycotts Egyptian Vessel

The 8,193-gross-ton UAR cargo vessel *Cleopatra,* owned by the Khedivial Mail Line of Alexandria, Egypt, was picketed and prevented from unloading in New York Apr. 13–May 6, 1960 by Seafarers' International Union (SIU) members, whose picket lines were respected by the International Longshoremen's Association (ILA). The picketing was begun by the SIU in protest against (a) the alleged threat to U.S. seamen's jobs caused by the Arab blacklist of U.S. vessels trading with Israel and (b) alleged mistreatment of U.S. seamen in Arab ports. It was ended after the U.S. State Department pledged action in an effort to eliminate the grievances.

The State Department, urging a halt to the picketing, had declared in a statement Apr. 21 that the U.S. did not "condone the Arab boycott" of Israel but that "the picketing is regarded abroad as a political demonstration related to the . . . restrictions against Israel" and was "embarrassing" because it was "an effort by a private group to apply pressure publicly" to force "shifts in the policies of foreign governments." SIU Pres. Paul Hall replied the same day that "the source of the State Department's embarrassment should be its failure over the years to have prevented" the harassment of U.S. ships and seamen.

An application for a restraining order against the picketing had been denied to the Khedivial Mail Line Apr. 15 by Federal Judge Edward Weinfeld. The denial was upheld

Apr. 23 by Federal Judge Thomas F. Murphy. A motion for a temporary restraining order pending appeal was rejected Apr. 24 by Chief Judge J. Edward Lumbard of the U.S. 2d Circuit Court of Appeals, and an appeal against the Murphy decision was rejected May 4 by a 3-judge federal tribunal headed by Lumbard.

An Eisenhower Administration appeal for a halt in the picketing was transmitted to Pres. George Meany of the American Federation of Labor & Congress of Industrial Organizations (AFL-CIO) May 3 by Labor Secy. James P. Mitchell but was rejected by Meany the same day and by the AFL-CIO Executive Council May 4. The council, backing the SIU-ILA protest, called on the State Department to "take all appropriate action to protect . . . our shipping and seamen, now being discriminated against by the Arab boycott and blacklisting policy."

An agreement to stop picketing the *Cleopatra* was reached May 6 in Washington by State Undersecy. C. Douglas Dillon and Arthur J. Goldberg, AFL-CIO special counsel. It was based on the State Department's issuance May 6 of a statement of U.S. "foreign policy affecting the American merchant marine" that contained pledges: (a) to support freedom of the seas and Suez Canal transit rights for all nations; (b) to "investigate fully the [SIU] grievances" and "protect the interests of our shipping and seamen now being discriminated against by the Arab boycott and blacklisting policy"; (c) to seek a settlement of the Arab-Israeli conflict on every "suitable occasion"; (d) to consult with the AFL-CIO and maritime unions on future developments "affecting American vessels and seamen in the areas concerned."

Meany asked Hall May 6 to withdraw the SIU pickets on the strength of the "good-faith assurances" in the State Department declaration. Hall complied but warned that the picketing of Arab vessels would be resumed if the State Department failed "to give practical implementation to the assurances." Unloading of the *Cleopatra* began May 9.

Sen. J. William Fulbright (D., Ark.), chairman of the Senate Foreign Relations Committee, had denounced the picketing Apr. 25 as a "coercive" attempt to push U.S. foreign policy in "special-interest directions." Fulbright reiterated in the Senate Apr. 30 that the U.S.' Middle East policies were being "whipsawed by an irresponsible maritime union and by a minority pressure group." He charged that "in recent years we have seen the rise of organizations dedicated apparently not to America but to foreign states and groups." This development, he asserted, had "seriously compromised" the conduct of U.S. foreign policy. Meany, rejecting Fulbright's views, asserted May 4 that the SIU had not set up a "political picket line" but was protesting "the indignities suffered by American seamen at the hands of the United Arab Republic." State Department officials conceded May 6 that U.S. seamen had been subjected to harassment in Arab ports.

A retaliatory boycott of U.S. shipping had been begun Apr. 30 by port workers in Egypt, Syria, Iraq, Libya, Lebanon and other Arab states but was lifted May 9. The boycott, ordered Apr. 23 by the International Confederation of Arab Trade Unions, denied U.S. ships service, unloading and repairs but did not affect their use of the Suez Canal. 9 U.S. ships carrying surplus food to the UAR were diverted to other ports May 1 for the transfer of their cargoes to foreign vessels at UAR expense. Other U.S. vessels were denied facilities to unload or disembark passengers in UAR ports until the ending of the boycott.

UAR Pres. Nasser had charged May 7 that the U.S. was dominated by "Zionist-Jewish-Israeli imperialism" but that "American wheat, grain and . . . movies will never buy our freedom and nationalism" or open the Suez Canal to Israeli commerce. Addressing the opening session of an Afro-Asian Economic Conference in Cairo Apr. 30, Nasser had rebuked Pres. Eisenhower for being "slack" with the *Cleopatra* boycott and dealing "only with Israeli demands." In a reference to U.S. Senate moves to restrict aid to the UAR if if continued the boycott of Israel, Nasser declared May 8: "We have never heard one word or threat [from the USSR] to cut off economic aid. I must thank Russia for this wise and noble policy."

The anti-UAR amendment referred to by Nasser had been adopted by 45–25 Senate vote Apr. 28 after its introduction by Sen. Paul H. Douglas (D., Ill.) and 29 cosponsors. It gave the President discretionary authority to withhold aid from nations that obstructed free navigation in international waterways or engaged in economic warfare against any other nation that would benefit from the aid bill. Senate GOP leader Everett M. Dirksen (Ill.), opposing the amendment, warned that it might be considered a use of aid for political coercion.

Sen. Fulbright, introducing an amendment to neutralize the Douglas amendment, charged Apr. 29 that "the principal reason" the latter had been introduced was "because of . . . a pressure group in the United States which seeks to inject the Arab-Israeli dispute into domestic politics." He warned that Douglas' amendment could have "potentially catastrophic consequences" in the middle east, that it would not "contribute to the reopening of the Canal to Israeli shipping but . . . tend to prevent the achievement of this desirable objective." Fulbright, in his amendment, argued that the President should not "normally" apply the Douglas amendment's principles in a situation where nations getting aid "are engaged in actions detrimental to United Nations efforts to maintain peace and stability, and application of the . . . principles would in the judgment of the President constitute [U.S.] partiality . . . regarding the merits of . . . [either antagonist's] cause."

State Undersecy. C. Douglas Dillon, in a letter opposing the Douglas amendment, told the Senate May 2 that the Administration had consistently opposed the Arab boycott against Israel and supported freedom of transit through the

Canal. He warned that the amendment would "be counter-productive."

The Fulbright amendment was killed in the Senate May 2 by a 45–39 vote (31 Democrats and 14 Republicans vs. 23 Democrats and 16 Republicans) to table it.

Fulbright was greeted enthusiastically in Cairo May 11 when he arrived for talks with Nasser. Fulbright denied Nasser's contention that U.S. Zionists controlled the U.S. Senate but said that "no doubt the Zionists have great [Senate] influence." Visiting the Israeli sector of Jerusalem, Fulbright suggested May 17 that Israel permit the return to their former homes of some Arab refugees as a first move toward ending Arab-Israeli hostility.

The UAR announced Nov. 26, 1961 that 9 Frenchmen, including 4 members of the French Property Mission in Cairo, had been arrested Nov. 24 on charges of participating in a French government plot to "spy on the UAR and assassinate Pres. Nasser." The arrest of 4 Egyptians, including ex-Egyptian Amb.-to-France Adli Andrawes, as alleged collaborators of the "spy ring," was disclosed Nov. 28. The French mission members were in Cairo under a 1958 Zurich agreement to settle claims and to handle UAR payments for any French property nationalized after France's 1956 Suez invasion. The arrested mission members were mission head André Mattei, Jean Paul François Bellivier, Henri-Pierre E. Mouton and André Miquel.

Cairo newspapers Nov. 27 published photocopies of a confession Bellivier was said to have made Nov. 24–25. In it, Bellivier allegedly said that Mattei had been directed to "try to make a *coup d'ètat* against the Nasser régime." The alleged confession said that the French mission had used the Swiss embassy's diplomatic pouch in smuggling an "enormous" amount of money out of the UAR. (The embassy had handled French interests in Cairo since France and Egypt had severed diplomatic relations in 1956.) Bellivier allegedly confessed that the French mission also had used the Swiss embassy's press to print anti-Nasser leaflets. The embassy denied the smuggling and leaflet charges. The French Foreign Ministry Nov. 27 denounced the UAR charges as false and as an "attempt to justify an unprecedented violation of all the international rules."

The *N.Y. Times* Dec. 26 reported a UAR government order requiring French nationals living in the UAR to leave the country on the expiration of their resident permits. The UAR Dec. 23 had announced a ban against the entry of French nationals. The Middle East News Agency said the order was in retaliation against "maltreatment received by Egyptians at Orly Airport" in Paris.

The 4 members of the defunct French Property Mission in Cairo and 7 Egyptians were put on trial on espionage charges Jan. 14, 1962 but were released Apr. 7 as the UAR State Security Court, on the prosecution's request, suddenly ended the trial. A UAR government source said that the 4 Frenchmen had been acquitted in appreciation for the French-Algerian rebel cease-fire agreement, which had taken place Mar. 18.

Syria Secedes from UAR

Syrian army officers led a rebellion Sept. 28, 1961 against Egyptian domination of the Syrian Region of the United Arab Republic. The revolt started in Damascus, spread quickly throughout Syria and brought independence to the country before midnight, when UAR Pres. Nasser called off Egyptian resistance to the rebels.

The rebellion ended the 4-year union of Egypt and Syria. The major causes of the revolt were said to be Syrian dissatisfaction with (a) Nasser's alleged program to "Egyptianize" Syria by putting Egyptians in all controlling jobs there and (b) Nasser's nationalization and socialization program.

In line with the nationalization/socialization program, the UAR Aug. 16 had announced a government revision in which the regional cabinets for Egypt and Syria were abolished and their functions distributed among the ministries of a revised central cabinet the was to sit in Cairo. The change caused widespread dissatisfaction among Syrian leaders and in military circles in the "Northern Province," as Syria had come to be called. Prior to the revision there had been a central cabinet plus regional executive cabinets for Egypt and Syria. The expanded UAR central cabinet (membership announced Aug. 17): *Foreign*–Mahmoud Fawzi; *Economy and Treasury*–Abdel Moneim el-Kaissouni, Hassan Abbas Zaky, Akram Deiri (Syrian); *Public Health*–Dr. Nurreddin Tarraf, Shawkhat el-Kanawati (Syrian); *Agriculture* and *Land Reclamation*–Sayed Mareio Ahmed el-Haj Younis (Syrian); *State* and *Labor*–Kamal Rifaat; *Presidential Affairs*–Ali Sabry; *State* and *Planning*–Abdelwahab Homad (Syrian); *Land Reform*–Ahmed Honeidy (Syrian), Ahmed Muhammad el-Mahrouki; *Interior*–Abbas Radwan; *Religious Foundations* (*Waqfs*)–Ahmed Abdullah Toheima, Youssef Muzahim (Syrian): *Scientific Research*–Saladin Hedayat; *Supply*–Dr. Kamal Ramzy Stino, Gaml Soufi (Syrian); *Industry*–Aziz Sidky; *Communications*–Mustafa Khalil; *Public Works*–Ahmed Abdul el-Sharabasi; *Higher Education*–Amgad el-Tarabulsi (Syrian); *Housing* and *Public Services*–Toma al-Awdatullah (Syrian); *Justice*–Nihad el-Kassim (Syrian); *Culture* and *National Guidance*–Sarwat Okasha; *Local Administration*–Gadou Essedin (Syrian); *Regional Administration*–Abdelmohsin Abu el-Nour; *Aswan High Dam*–Moussa Arafa; *Social Affairs*–Sabet el-Ariss (Syrian); *State Ministers*–Abdel Kader Hatem, Ahmed Hosni, Fakher el-Kayali (Syrian).

The ministerial posts for housing and public services, Aswan High Dam, scientific research and regional administration were new, as was the division of responsibility among more than one person in 8 ministries. Another change was the creation of 4 more vice presidencies, making a total of 7; these were filled as follows: *For Defense*–War Min. Abdel Hakim Amer; *for Planning*–Abdel Latif el-Boghdadi; *for Pub-*

lic Services—Nureddin Kuhala; *for Local Government*—Kamaleddin Hussein; *for the Interior*—Col. Abdul Hamid al-Serraj; *for Nationalized Enterprises*—Zakaria Mohieddin and Hussein Shafei. (Only Kuhala and Col. Serraj were Syrian. Field Marshal Amer and Boghdadi had been vice presidents since the creation of the UAR. Sabri al-Assali had resigned his post and retired from public life 4 months after his appointment to it in 1958, and Akram al-Hourani, a Syrian, had resigned as vice president at the end of 1959 after having become an outspoken opponent of Pres. Nasser. Kuhala had been president of the UAR's Syrian Region or Northern Province.)

Serraj, who had been a powerful aide to Nasser in ruling Syria, apparently had lost out in a power struggle with Field Marshal Amer, UAR armed forces commander, shortly before the successful Syrian revolt. Serraj had been one of the secret planners of the union of Egypt and Syria and was among the last Syrians to hold an important UAR post. In the major government reform Aug. 16, Serraj lost his posts as chairman of the Syrian Executive Council and as both interior minister and information minister of the Syrian Region. After he and Amer had received 2 of the 7 newly created UAR vice presidencies, Serraj complained that in his new post he had no duties or powers. Amer, meanwhile, had the most powerful job in Syria. (Amer had been Nasser's closest friend since the early 1940s). Serraj conferred with Nasser twice in September but failed to persuade Nasser to give him more power. He then resigned Sept. 26.

Serraj, 36, frequently identified as the "strong man" of Syria after his rise in 1957, was arrested by the new, post-union Syrian régime on charges of trying to subvert the revolution. His arrest was disclosed by Premier Mahmoun al-Kuzbari Oct. 2. Al-Kuzbari charged that Serraj had been described as "chief of intelligence of what used to be the center for corruption and persecution and torturing."

The Syrian uprising started before dawn Sept. 28 when

troops, tanks and armored cars from Camp Katana, about 15 miles southeast of Damascus, were moved into the city by rebel leaders. The insurgents, acting on the orders of a so-called Higher Arab Revolutionary Command of the Armed Forces, seized the Damascus radio station and other key points. They surrounded UAR First Army headquarters and trapped Field Marshal Amer, commander-in-chief of UAR armed forces, and Gen. Gamal Feisal, First Army commander. But Amer and Feisal, both Egyptians, were permitted to fly to Cairo later Sept. 28.

Nasser's first public reaction to news of the revolt came in a Sept. 28 broadcast in which he ordered UAR forces in Syria to crush the rebellion. In a 2d Sept. 28 broadcast he called the uprising more serious thant the 1956 British-French-Israeli attack and barred any compromise. Nasser conferred with Amer, Feisal and his cabinet late Sept. 28 and then ordered an airlift of 2,000 paratroopers to the area of Latakia, Syria's chief seaport. But he changed his mind and canceled the order after the planes were in the air.

Nasser told a crowd in Cairo's Republic Square Sept. 29 that he had decided not to resist the rebels with military force "so that no Arab blood would be shed." He said: "Before midnight yesterday I ordered that planes heading to Latakia return. But the order reached them after 120 parachutists were already dropped. I ordered the forces which had landed not to shoot but to surrender." (The Syrian Revolutionary Command asserted Sept. 29 that about 120 Egyptian paratroopers had landed on the coast near Latakia and had started shooting. "Our forces were obliged to return the fire in self-defense," and the Egyptian paratroopers had been "annihilated," the Syrian statement claimed.)

Nasser charged Sept. 29 that the Syrian rebellion was reactionary, imperialistic and capitalistic. He told the Republic Square crowd that "in the last 4 years [since the Syrian-Egyptian merger], I have spent most of my time solving the problems of Syria." He said he was sure Syrians "will not give up the rights they have earned in the last 4 years." Nasser said the UAR must remain "a fortress of Arab nationalism." "Our aims are long-reaching," he declared. "They do not depend on events of the hour." Nasser, explaining the rebel's success, said at a Cairo University rally Oct. 2 that when the revolt broke out, "Egyptian officers were on the front facing Israel and doing their duty."

6 Syrian officers reported to be leaders of the revolt were dismissed by Nasser from the UAR army Sept. 28 on treason charges. Those ousted were Maj. Gen. Abdel Ghani Dhaman (commander of Camp Katana), Maj. Gen. Mofak Assafa, Col. Abdel Kerim el-Nahlawi, Col. Khedar el-Kerzi (commander of the Syrian Camel Corps), Col. Nassib Hindi and Col. Hisham Abdrabou.

Syria's Revolutionary Command Sept. 29 installed Dr. Mahmoun al-Kuzbari, 48, a conservative lawyer and law professor, as head of an all-civilian cabinet. In a broadcast the same day, Kuzbari proclaimed Syria's independence. He said that the Revolutionary Command had "finished its mission" and that its members had returned to their normal military duties. Kuzbari pledged that his interim regime would pave the way for "a true and democratic life" in Syria and would "lead the country within 4 months to a constitutional stage." Denying Nasser's charge that the break-up of the Syro-Egyptian union was an attack on Arab nationalism and unity, Kuzbari averred: "Syria again affirms to the Arabs that she is the bastion of Arabism."

Kuzbari's interim Syrian cabinet consisted of: *Premier, Foreign Affairs* and *Defense*–Kuzbari; *Finance* and *Supply*–Dr. Leon Zamaria; *Public Health*–Dr. Karhan al-Jandali; *Interior*–Dr. Adnan al-Kuwatly; *Education & National Guidance*–Dr. Izzat al-Nus; *Economy & Industry*–Dr. Awad Barakat; *Agriculture & Agrarian Reform*–Amin Nazif; *Justice* and *Charitable Works (Waqfs)*–Ahmad Sultan; *Communications* and *Public Works*–Abd al-Rahman Huriyah; *Planning* and *Municipal & Local Affairs*–

Dr. Niman Nashari; *Labor*—Fuad al-Adil; *Information & Propaganda*—Mustafa Baroody. (Gen. Abdel Karim Zahredin became commander of the Syrian army Oct. 1. Lt. Gen. Fateh Baker succeeded Lt. Gen. Muhammad el-Jarrah as Syrian police chief Sept. 30.)

Syria's interim government Sept. 30 ordered the deportation of all Egyptians, military and civilian. (An estimated 6,000 Egyptian troops, 5,000 Egyptian civilian government employes and 10,000 to 20,000 other Egyptians were in Syria.) Egyptians were directed to report to Syrian authorities by Oct. 2 for shipment to Egypt. The deportations began Oct. 2.

The interim Syrian government was recognized by Jordan and Turkey Sept. 29, by Guatemala Sept. 30, by Nationalist China Oct. 1 and by Iran Oct. 2. Nasser broke relations with Jordan and Turkey Oct. 1 for recognizing Syria. The U.S. State Department received from the UAR Oct. 2 a formal request that it refuse to recognize Syria.

Telegrams of regret over the revolt were sent to Nasser by Kin Hassan II of Morocco Sept. 28 and Presidents Tito of Yugoslavia and Habib Bourguiba of Tunisia Sept. 29. Iraqi Premier Abdul Karim el-Kassem, an old enemy of Nasser's, issued a call Sept. 29 for "our brothers in Syria and Egypt to stretch their hands together in peace and loyalty."

Syrian Premier Kuzbari told reporters Oct. 2 that his government would follow a policy of nonalignment in foreign affairs. "We are not with the West or East," he declared. "We are with every country that extends to us the hand of friendship."

Nasser, forming a new, all-Egyptian cabinet, Oct. 18 dismissed 6 ministers and appointed 4 new ones. Those dismissed: Economy and Treasury Min. Hassan Abbas Zaky; Public Health Min. Nurreddin Tarraf; Agriculture Min. Sayed Marei; Land Reform Min. Ahmed Muhammad el-Mahrouki; Religious Foundations (Waqfs) Min. Ahmed Abdullah Toheima; State Min. Ahmed Hosni. (New ministers appointed (posts in parentheses): Abdel Aziz el-Sayed (higher education); Fathi el-Sharkawi (justice); Muhammad Naguid Hashad (agriculture); Muhammad el-Nabawi el-Mohandes (public health). Vice Pres. Abdel Latif el-Boghdadi was appointed to the additional post of treasury minister. Dr. Abdel Moneim el-Kaissouni was named economy minister, and Abdelmohsin Abu el-Nour was named land reform minister.

Radio Cairo reported Nov. 4 that Nasser, apparently upset by the Syrian revolt, had promised elections in 2 months for representatives to a newly-formed National Congress of Popular Powers. The congress (apparently formed to broaden the base of political power) was to consider a new constitution to be submitted by Nasser. The new charter was to pave the way for free parliamentary elections. In a speech to the congress' 250-member preparatory committee in the National Assembly Nov. 25, Nasser empowered the committee to prepare the basis for popular elections, a constitutional assembly and a freely elected parliament. Nasser pledged a "popular" government that would improve living conditions and guarantee the "right of every individual to say 'no'". (Ex-National Assembly Speaker Anwar al-Sadat headed the committee as secretary general. Other members included vice presidents, cabinet and deputy ministers, provincial governors, editors and publishers of state-controlled newspapers, 22 workers, 36 university professors, 14 lawyers and 9 journalists and writers.)

Yemeni Ties Cut

Nasser Dec. 26, 1961 dissolved the UAR's federation with Yemen. Yemen had joined the UAR Mar. 1958 in a limited association involving only defense, economic and cultural affairs. Its ouster reduced UAR membership to only one land—Egypt. In announcing Yemen's ouster, UAR State Min. Abdel Kader Hatem declared that there was nothing common in "the nature of . . . [Egypt] and Yemen to make the federation between them an effective political instrument able to contribute positively in strengthening the Arab struggle."

Yemen, along with Jordan and Saudi Arabia, had been denounced by Nasser Dec. 23 for its opposition to his socialization program. In a broadcast from Port Said, Nasser declared that conditions in Yemen and in Saudi Arabia were contrary to the "law of justice and the law of God." He described Yemen's Imam Ahmad and King Saud of Saudi Arabia as "reactionaries." He called Islam a "Socialist religion."

UAR: '3D WORLD' CHAMPION (1961-6)

Nasser's Blueprint for the Future

Egyptian Pres. Gamal Abdel Nasser May 21, 1962 made public a Charter for National Action–a document that gave a complete, quasi-Socialist account of the Egyptian revolution as well as a blueprint for the future. The Charter was officially promulgated at the inaugural convocation of the newly elected National Congress of Popular Forces (Egypt's sole party, promised to the electorate in late 1961 and elected in Feb. 1962). 1,750 Congress members attended. The Charter's 10 sections, forming the groundwork for a future constitution, were based on the principles of "scientific socialism." It upheld the right of all Egyptians to decent medical care, education and employment opportunities and to adequate sickness, disability and old-age insurance.

The Charter was assumed to be part of a new liberalization program that Nasser offered to all Egyptians after the Syrian revolt in order to broaden his popular base. (These views gained some currency when the semi-official newspaper *Al-Ahram* Sept. 17 announced the lifting of censorship on press telegrams.) Informed foreigners, however, seemed most intrigued by the Charter's Pan-Arabist perspective in which Egypt, for example, was described as "the security" of "the Arab area." The Charter attributed to "the revolution in Egypt . . . far-reaching effects on the liberation movement in Africa, Asia and Latin America."

According to the Charter, in 1952 the Egyptian people had "begun their revolutionary march with no political organization" and "without a complete theory for the revolutionary change," excepting "the famous 6 principles": "destruction of imperialism and its stooges among Egyptian traitors"; "eradication of feudalism"; "ending monopoly and the domination of capital over the government"; "social justice"; "a powerful national army"; and "a healthy democratic system."

The Egyptian revolution, according to the Charter, had "awakened the possibilities of revolution in the entire Arab world," and "this awakening was one of the main factors leading to the success of the revolution in Egypt. . . ." The Charter said: "Revolution is the only course that the Arab struggle can take in the direction of a better future," and "the revolutionary path is the only bridge that the Arab nation can cross to reach the future to which it aspires." The "objectives of the Arab struggle" were "freedom, socialism, unity." These had "always been the slogans of the Arab struggle, but the Arab revolution now faces the responsibility of striking a new path" and "cannot afford to copy what others have achieved." "In facing . . . [the post–World War II] world the Arab revolution must have a new approach that does not shut itself up within the confines of theories, . . . although it must by no means deny itself access to the rich storehouse of experience gained by other striving peoples. . . . This, then, is the first duty of the popular revolutionary leadership in the Arab nation. It means that the greater part of the responsibility for this pioneer revolutionary action devolves upon the popular revolutionary leadership in the United Arab Republic, since natural and historical factors have made the UAR . . . the nucleus state in this endeavor to secure liberty, socialism, and unity for the Arab nation."

The Charter offered the first cohesive view of the post–World War I revolutionary movement in Egypt. It said: The "revolutionary wave "that had arisen in 1919, following the First World War, had failed for "3 obvious reasons": "The revolutionary leaderships almost completely overlooked the need for social change." "The revolutionary leaderships . . . failed to extend their vision beyond Sinai . . . [and] were unaware of the danger of the Balfour Declaration, which set up Israel as a dividing line tearing Arab territory apart," so that "the Arab struggle was deprived of the Egyptian revolutionary energy" and "the imperialist forces managed to deal with an Arab nation torn and exhausted." "The revolutionary leaderships could not adapt their methods of struggle to the methods adopted by imperialists," who were offering "formal and superficial concessions." The 1919 revolution, therefore, "ended by declaring an independence of no content and an ailing freedom under the guns of the occupation," while the Anglo-Egyptian Treaty of 1936 was "like a document of surrender to the great bluff by which the 1919 revolution was taken in."

According to the Charter: "The truly dangerous period in the long struggle of the Egyptian people" had been "that long period of deceit, namely from the setback in 1919 until the popular powers became aware of the danger threatening them. . . ." "The palace and imperialism had one and the same interest and therefore stood in one camp," and "there was a deceitful democratic facade which the defeated remnants of the 1919 revolution exploited to divert the people from their true demands." By early 1952, however, "the masses in town and country had already given adequate expression to their real will. . . . The armed forces who set out to stage . . . [the 1952 coup] were not the makers of the revolution but its popular tool." The 1952 revolt "could have ended in a mere change of cabinet or of the system of government" or "could have turned into a military dictatorship to add one more experiment to the list of Fascist experiments that had failed." These dangers were prevented because "the genuineness and strength of the revolutionary consciousness controlled the direction of events" and produced "a radical and all-embracing change."

"Democracy means the assertion of sovereignty of the people and the placing of all authority in their hands," the Charter declared. "Similarly, socialism is the true sign of the progressive nature of a revolution. . . . Democracy is political freedom while socialism is social freedom. . . . The depth of the revolutionary consciousness" had "outlined the form of the democracy of the people" in this fashion:

• "Political democracy cannot be separated from social democracy. No citizen can be regarded as free to vote unless he receives the following 3 guarantees—he should be free from exploitation in all its forms; he should enjoy an equal opportunity to have a fair share of the national wealth; [and] his mind should be free from all anxiety likely to undermine the security of his future. Only when a citizen possesses these 3 guarantees can he be said to have political freedom, and can take part by means of his vote in shaping the authority of the State he aspires to have."
• "Political democracy cannot exist under the domination of any one class. . . . The inevitable and natural class struggles cannot be ignored or denied, but their resolution must be arrived at peacefully and within the framework of national unity and by means of dissolving class distinctions. . . . The revolution should undertake to liquidate the force of reaction, . . . and prevent it from making any attempt to come back to power. . . . Because of their monopoly of wealth, reactionary interests are bound to clash with the interests of the whole people. Consequently the peaceful resolution of the class struggle cannot be achieved unless the power of reaction is first and foremost deprived of all its weapons. The removal of such clash will pave the way to peaceful solutions to class struggles. It does not remove the contradictions in the rest of the social classes, but it creates a chance for the possibility of removing them peacefully. . . ."
• After the "collaboration between the forces of reaction and of exploiting capital [collapses], . . . the road must . . . be paved for democratic interaction between the various working powers of the people, namely the farmers, workers, soldiers, intellectuals and national capital," forming "the legitimate substitute for the collaboration between feudalism and exploiting capital."
• "It is the national unity created by the cooperation between those representative powers of the people that will be able to set up the Arab Socialist Union [Nasser's first use of this name]. This union will constitute the authority representing the people, and the guardian of the values of true democracy.

"These enormous popular powers forming the Arab Socialist Union . . . make it necessary that, when dealing with the form of the political organization of the state, the new constitution of the UAR must refer to a set of necessary guarantees:

"(1) The popular and political organizations based on free and direct election must truly and fairly represent the powers forming the majority of the population. . . . The new constitution must ensure that farmers and workmen will get half the seats in political and popular organizations at all levels, including the House of Representatives, since they form the majority of the people. . . .

"(2) The authority of the elected popular councils must always be consolidated and raised above the authority of the executive machinery of the state. . . . Local government should gradually but resolutely transfer the authority of the state to the people. . . .

"(3) There is a dire need to create a new political organization, within the framework of the Arab Socialist Union, recruiting the elements fit for leadership [and] organizing their efforts. . . .

"(4) Collective leaderships are imperative in the period of the revolutionary drive. . . ."

- "Popular organizations, especially cooperatives and trade unions, can play an effective and influential role in promoting sound democracy. . . . Besides their productive role, the farmers' cooperatives are democratic organizations capable of . . . resolving the problems of the farmers. So it is high time that agricultural labor movements are established. Industrial, commercial and services trade unions were able, thanks to the July laws [of 1961, which nationalized more than 400 private firms, limited individual investments and shortened the working day from 8 hours to 7], to reach a position of leadership in the national struggle. . . . The labor forces have become masters of the production process."
- "Criticism and self-criticism are among the most important guarantees of freedom. . . . As a result of their control of economic interests, the reactionary forces controlled the press. Freedom of opinion was thus deprived of its most valuable instrument. The elimination of reaction . . . provides the surest guarantees for the freedom of assembly and . . . of discussion. The ownership of the press by the people was achieved thanks to the law of press organization, which at the same time ensured its independence of the administrative government machinery . . . and provided the surest guarantee for criticism."
- "The new revolutionary conceptions of true democracy must impose themselves upon the factors influencing the formation of the citizen—foremost among which are education and the administrative laws and regulations. . . . Thus the educational curricula in all subjects must be reconsidered according to the principles of the revolution. . . ."

"The Socialist solution to the problem of economic and social underdevelopment in Egypt . . . was never a question of free choice, [but] was a historical inevitability imposed by reality, the broad aspirations of the masses, and the changing nature of the world in the 2d part of the 20th century," the Charter declared. The achievement of progress and the expansion of national wealth could "not be left to desultory individual efforts motivated by mere selfish profit." There must be "a complete plan for production," and the "Socialist solution is the only way to economic and social progress," the Charter said. Nevertheless, "the people's control over the tools of production does not necessitate the nationalization of all means of production or the abolition of private ownership. . . . Such control can be achieved in 2 ways–first, the creation of a capable public sector that would lead progress in all domains and bear the main responsibility of the development plan; and 2d, the existence of a private sector that would, without exploitation, participate in the development within the framework of its overall plan–provided that the people's control is exercised over both sectors." The dominant position of the public sector would be assured by following these principles:

- "The major skeleton of the production operation such as railways, roads, ports, airports . . . and other public services should be within the framework of public ownership."
- Most "heavy, medium, and mining industries" should be publicly owned, and any private ownership allowed in these fields "should be controlled by the public sector." The light industries field "is open to private ownership" but "must always be beyond monopoly," and "the public sector must have a role enabling it to guide that industry."
- "Foreign trade must be under the people's full control." All import trade "must be within the framework of the public sector." Private capital should participate in the export trade, but "the public sector must have the main share in that field to preclude all possible fraudulency." "The public sector must be in charge of ¾ of [all] exports." "The public sector should within the coming 8 years . . . take charge of at least ¼ of the internal trade, with priority over private and cooperative acitivities."
- Banks should be "within the framework of public ownership," since "the role of capital . . . should not be left to speculation and adventure." Insurance companies should also "be within the same framework of public ownership for the protection of a major part of national savings and to ensure its sound orientation."
- "In the field of ownership of rural land, the agrarian reform laws [such as that of July 1961] have limited individual ownership to 100 *feddans* [about 100 acres]. Yet the spirit of the law implies that the limitation should cover the whole family–father, mother, and children under age–to avoid clustering together maximum ownerships allowing some form of feudalism. This spirit can be made to rule within the coming years provided that the families affected by that law sell the land in excess of those limits for cash to agricultural cooperative societies or to others."

The "increasing rise of the population . . . constitutes the most dangerous obstacle that faces the Egyptian people in their drive towards raising the standard of production," the Charter warned. "While the attempts at family planning . . . deserve the most sincere efforts supported by modern scientific methods, the need for the most rapid and efficient drive to increase production necessitates that this problem should be taken into consideration in the process of production, regardless of the effects which may result from the experiment of family planning. The doubling of the national income every 10 years allows for a rate of economic development which greatly exceeds the rate of increase in the population. It also provides a real opportunity for raising the standard of living, in spite of this complicated problem." The Charter listed "3 areas in which the great battle of production must take place": (1) land reclamation, (2) greater productivity, and (3) "industrialization of the countryside."

The Charter said that industry was "capable of realizing the greatest hopes in the field of social and economic evolution." It called for "special care" for "heavy industries—the bases for modern industry." It urged special attention to consumer industries, particularly as a way to save foreign exchange and provide export opportunities. The food industries, the Charter asserted, "can, more than any other [industries], consolidate rural economy and afford unlimited opportunities for markets in developed countries."

The Charter held that the importance of foreign capital in developing industry "calls for the setting up of a system of priority drawn from the essence of the national experience." First priority would go to unconditional aid from any source, 2d priority would go to unconditional loans. Finally, foreign investment could be permitted "in unavoidable circumstances, in aspects of modern evolution requiring international experience."

The Charter declared it to be "the duty of the advanced

countries to offer aid to those still struggling for development." "States with a colonialist past are, more than others, under an obligation to offer the [underdeveloped] lands . . . part of the national wealth that they sapped when that wealth was a booty for all looters," the Charter declared. Such aid was "a form of tax that must be paid by the states with a colonial past to compensate those they exploited for so long."

"Woman must be regarded as equal to man, and she must therefore shed the remaining shackles that impede her free movement," the Charter asserted. The family, as "the first cell in a society, . . . must be afforded all means of protection," and "freedom of religious belief must be regarded as sacred in our new free life."

The UAR armed forces' role in the new society was "to defend the process of social construction against external dangers," the Charter noted. The armed forces "should enjoy a decisive superiority on land, sea and air," the Charter said. They should be "capable of quick movement within the Arab area, the security of which is primarily [their] responsibility," and "must be armed in a way in keeping with modern scientific progress and possess sufficient deterring weapons to stem the greed of ambitious powers." The UAR, as "the vanguard, base, and fighting fortress of the Arab progressive struggle," was "the natural target of all the enemies of the Arab nation and its progress," the Charter warned. The aim of "the world imperialist forces and monopolies" was "to put the Arab territory extending from the [Atlantic] Ocean to the [Persian] Gulf under its military control, in order to be able to continue its exploitation." Israel had been established as "the tool of imperialism," the Charter charged. The UAR was, "both historically and actually, the only Arab nation that can assume the responsibility of building a national army capable of deterring imperialist, Zionist aggressive plans." "Science is the true weapon of the revolutionary will," and "science for society should be the motto of the cultural revolution at the present stage." The Charter said the UAR "cannot waste a moment before entering the atomic age," with the objective of "atomic energy for prosperity" and not for war. "The rallying of the popular, progressive elements in every part of the Arab nation, and the [opposite] rallying of the elements of reaction and opportunism in the Arab world, are an indication that the same social currents are sweeping over the Arab nation . . . [and are] more indicative of unity than dissension," the Charter asserted. "The concept of Arab unity no longer requires a meeting of the rulers of the Arab nation. . . . The phase of the social revolution has developed through that superficial concept . . . to a stage where unity of objective is a symbol of unity." Unity, however, "cannot be, nor should it be, imposed." Nor was it "a uniform constitutional form that must inevitably be applied" but "rather a long path with several stages." "Any nationalist government representing the will and struggle of the people within a framework of national independence is a step towards unity," and "any partial unity . . . expressing a popular will of 2 or more of the Arab peoples is an advanced step towards unity."

The Charter reported that the UAR "considers it her message to strive for complete Arab unity" and, being "firmly convinced that she is an integral part of the Arab nation, must propagate her call for unity . . . , without hesitating for one minute before the outworn argument that this would be considered an interference in the affairs of others." The UAR, however, must not become involved in local party disputes in any Arab county. "If the UAR feels that it is her bounden duty to support every popular, national movement, this support must remain within the framework of the basic principles, leaving the maneuvers of the struggle to the local elements. . . . " But the inevitable forthcoming "union between the nationalist popular progressive movements" should not "affect the existence of the Arab League." Even "if the

Arab League is not able to lead the Arab cause towards its noble and ultimate objective, it can at least lead it a few steps forward."

Egyptian-Israeli Missile Race

The jealously watched parity of arms between Israel and Egypt reached a new stage before midsummer 1962 when Egypt succeeded in launching 4 short-range jet-propelled guided missiles from a desert testing site near Cairo. The UAR then began to mass-produce the rockets, and Pres. Nasser declared July 22 that Egypt was "preparing" to oust Israel, whose principal cities reportedly lay within the missiles' reach, from "Palestine."

Israel had launched a weather research rocket to a height of 50 miles from a secret hillside site on the Mediterranean July 5, 1961 as Premier David Ben-Gurion and Israeli defense leaders and scientists watched. The ¼-ton Meteor II rocket, reportedly produced by Israeli scientists without outside help, was described as a multistage unguided rocket containing in its head sodium for ionospheric weather-testing purposes. Future rockets were to carry aloft electronic instruments for further scientific experiments, the results of which Israel would share with selected scientific institutions abroad, Israel announced. (The American foreign correspondent C. L. Sulzberger commented in the *N.Y. Times* July 29, 1961 that Israel's policy seemed to have become directed toward the acquisition or manufacture of guided missiles.)

The UAR successfully launched the 4 single-stage rockets at a Western Desert site 50 miles northeast of Cairo July 21, 1962. The semi-official Egyptian Middle East News Agency said that the first rocket had reached its target 372 miles away. Nasser, who witnessed the launchings with Marshal Abdel Hakim Amer, UAR armed forces chief, and Eastern and Western newsmen, said that the first 2 rockets–the 36-foot Al-Kahir, or Conquerer–had a 360-mile range and that the other 2–the 18-foot Al-Zafir, or Victorious–had a 220-

mile range. Nasser said that Egyptian rockets could "reach a little south of Beirut [an obvious reference to Israel]," that they were Egyptian-made, that they were in "large-scale production" and that "we are against" arming them with atomic warheads. He said that the UAR had launched rockets 14 months previously (UAR launchings had been reported in Feb. 1962 also) and had the capability of producing 2-stage rockets.

A 3-hour Cairo parade–marked by the display of 20 rockets–highlighted the UAR's celebration of the 10th anniversary of the Egyptian revolution July 23. (Soviet-made planes and tanks were also displayed. The USSR was reported July 22 to have agreed to deliver antiaircraft rockets to the UAR in a few weeks.) Nasser formally opened a new jet aircraft factory in Cairo July 25.

The Egyptian rockets reportedly had been developed by Dr. Eugen Saenger, 57, a former missile and jet expert for the Nazis and for West Germany. The Munich newspaper *Abendzeitung* reported July 23 that the 4 rockets had been bought from the U.S. and prepared by West German experts. According to *Abendzeitung*, the UAR had secretly hired about 250 West German rocket experts through Swiss firms.

The London *Times* reported July 22, 1962 that Egyptian officials had disclosed in Nov. 1961 "that experiments had been going on for 6 months, having started just before Israel launched a space rocket" July 5, 1961. The British newspaper account also said that, shortly after the Egyptian testing had begun, Saenger had "resigned as head of the Stuttgart jet-propulsion research institute" in Wurttemberg-Baden "because the West German authorities objected to his advising the UAR on rocket projects." The *Times* also noted that Egypt's latest budget showed a 12% increase over the previous year's on account of a E£50 million ($115 million) rise in defense-spending allocations.

The U.S. State Department announced Sept. 26 that the U.S. had agreed to the Israeli government's long-standing request that the U.S. sell defensive missiles to Israel. The U.S. decision reversed a Washington policy that had barred the U.S. from becoming a major source of weapons for any Middle East nation. Under an agreement made several weeks prior to the announcement, Israel was to buy an undisclosed number of 17-foot 1,275-pound solid-fuel supersonic Hawk missiles, and Israeli crews were to train in the U.S. in the operation of the missile system. The sale, which made Israel the first non-Western nation to receive such U.S.-made military equipment, was designed to end the military imbalance resulting from the earlier purchase by the UAR, Syria and Iraq of Soviet-bloc arms assumed by the U.S. to have included missiles, planes and other military supplies. U.S. officials were said to have feared that the imbalance would have encouraged either an Arab attack against Israel or a preemptive war by Israel to destroy Arab offensive power.

Israeli Finance Min. Levi Eshkol had declared in a speech in Washington Sept. 22 that when UAR Pres. Nasser "stands by Egyptian rocket launchers and boasts that they are trained in our [Israel's] direction, we dare not mistake this for an idle propaganda boast." "Like it or not," he said, "the missile race has entered the Middle East, and our only hope lies in convincing Nasser that the distance from Tel Aviv to Cairo, as the rocket flies, is the same as from Cairo to Tel Aviv."

UAR Foreign Min. Mahmoud Fawzi said Oct. 2 that the American supply of antiaircraft missiles to Israel would encourage Israeli leaders to "more aggressiveness and more hostility." The U.S.' position that its action was reasonable in view of Soviet missile shipments to the UAR and Iraq was "untenable" because it could not be justified against a neighbor that "has never committed any aggression," Fawzi said.

Syrian-Egyptian Relations Further Strained

Pro-Nasser army officers in northern Syria Mar. 31, 1962 launched a revolt against the armed forces high command, which had seized control of the government in a Mar. 28

coup. The high command reported Apr. 3 that the rebellion, led by self-proclaimed "free officers," had ended following minor skirmishes and a compromise that had been worked out at a conference in Homs Apr. 2.

The high command conferees agreed to a demand by the pro-Nasser officers that the original leaders of the Mar. 28 coup be exiled. 7 of these leaders reportedly arrived in Geneva Apr. 3. Other rebel demands included: (a) the release of Pres. Nazem el-Kodsi and other political and military leaders arrested in the Mar. 28 coup; (b) the restoration of the provisional constitution proclaimed after the Sept. 1961 coup; (c) the formation of a transitional government to supervise a referendum to determine whether Syria was to rejoin the UAR.

The Mar. 31 revolt had started in Homs, where rioters demonstrated in favor of UAR Pres. Nasser and clamored for a new Syro-Egyptian union. The revolt spread to Aleppo, Hama and Baniyas (the ancient Caesarea Philippi). Pro-high command troops moved into Aleppo and Homs to suppress the riots. 5 soldiers were killed in Aleppo in clashes between government troops and a "free officers"-led group. The rebels later gained control of the city and were reported to have complete control of northern Syria by Apr. 2.

A rebel broadcast from Aleppo Apr. 2 declared that "the armed forces of the northern area have expressed their solidarity with the officers of the southeast battle command, the middle area and coastal area in their liberal movement designed to get rid of the opportunist, exploiting clique." A high command broadcast from Damascus replied that the high command favored unity "with all liberated Arab countries, and with Egypt in particular, provided that such unity could be established on a sound basis, and on condition that it guaranteed the dignity and integrity of [Syria] . . . and provided that such conditions were presented in a free public referendum."

Government troops surrounded Damascus Apr. 2 as pro-

Nasser demonstrations broke out in the city. An 8 p.m.-to-5 a.m. curfew was imposed. The Syrian border was closed to all travelers.

The high command said Apr. 3 that it had intercepted a cable from the Syrian rebels to the UAR ambassador in Beirut, Lebanon requesting that the UAR send military aid to Aleppo. The UAR denied the Damascus report. Aleppo radio Apr. 3 broadcast a rebel appeal to the UAR to fly troops into Syria to aid the rebels. The plea was made after government planes attempted to bomb the radio station's transmitter. Cairo radio Apr. 3 broadcast an offer by Nasser to mediate the Syrian dispute. The offer went unanswered.

The rebels withdrew their plea for UAR aid after the government Apr. 3 issued an ultimatum to the rebels to surrender in 90 minutes. Shortly after the ultimatum deadline had passed, Damascus offered a truce and the rebels accepted. The Aleppo rebel commander, Col. Louai al-Attassi, who had seized control in the name of the UAR, ordered a curfew to clear the city's streets of pro-Nasser demonstrators. Damascus radio Apr. 3 broadcast a high command statement that "calm and order prevail" in Aleppo. The statement said that the rebel soldiers returned to the city's barracks after being assured that "the principles of the Homs conference" would be carried out.

The UAR government announced May 11 that Col. Abdel Hamid al-Serraj, ex-Syrian security chief and ex-UAR vice president, had arrived in Cairo after escaping from a Damascus military hospital May 5. Serraj conferred May 11 with Nasser. Serraj was accompanied by Sgt. Mansour Rawashada, chief of the Damascus hospital's guards, who had helped him escape.

Syrian Premier Bashir al-Azmah June 6 proposed a restoration of Syria's union with the UAR under which the Damascus government would retain its sovereignty. Azmah announced in a nationwide broadcast that his "government believes in the rise of such a federation and will start contacts with Egypt on this basis." But Azmah June 23 in effect withdrew his proposal. Azmah said that his June 6 statement had been misinterpreted. He explained that his government could not commit the state to any such federation because its régime was transitional and did not represent public opinion.

UAR delegate Akram Deiri walked out of an Arab League Council conference in Shtura, Lebanon Aug. 28 as the council met to take up Syrian charges of UAR interference in Syrian affairs. Before leaving the meeting, Deiri said the UAR would withdraw from the league "unless the league council immediately takes a firm stand toward the comedy of slanders staged by the Syrians." Deiri said the league had "become a humiliation to its member states" and "can do nothing for the aspirations of the Arab struggle." Khalil Kallas, deputy chairman of the Syrian delegation, reportedly asked the council to adopt a resolution condemning the UAR. The league council Aug. 31, by 10-1 vote (Syria opposed), approved a resolution saying that "it could not continue discussion of the Syrian complaint against UAR interference because the UAR had withdrawn." The council resolved to discuss Syria's complaints at its next meeting.

League Secy. Gen. Abdel Khalek Hassouna, an Egyptian, had gone to Beirut, Lebanon Aug. 28, on the league's instructions, in an unsuccessful effort to persuade Deiri and the UAR delegation to return to the Shtura conference. Deiri returned to Cairo Aug. 30. Hassouna was unanimously reelected Sept. 15 in Cairo to a 3d full 5-year term as the league's secretary-general. Nonetheless, the UAR continued its boycott of the league council's meetings in opposition to Syrian charges that the UAR was interfering in Syrian affairs.

Nasser Fails to Unite Egypt, Syria & Iraq

Egyptian Pres. Nasser July 22, 1963 renounced an agreement concluded in mid-April by the UAR, Syria and Iraq to form a new United Arab Republic merging the 3 lands. This ended Nasser's 2d attempt in as many years to reunite Egypt and Syria. (It was Cairo's last move toward multilateral Arab federation for several years.)

Nasser, speaking in Cairo in observance of the 11th anniversary of the Egyptian revolution, declared that he would continue to shun such a merger as long as the Baath party retained power in Syria.

Nasser said: "We cannot . . . have any link, any alliance, any unity or objective with a Fascist state in Syria"; "we have reached a decision that the tripartite agreement [of Apr. 17] is binding as far as the people of Syria are concerned, but not as far as the Fascist government of Damascus is concerned"; "I am most eager to maintain Arab unity, but we want a unity of the people, not of a Baathist concentration camp."

Noting that Syria's Baathists were accusing their domestic opponents of being "Nasserites," Nasser said: "None of the men accused are known to me."

Nasser's cancellation of the merger plan followed an apparently unsuccessful conference in Cairo July 18-19 with a 4-man Syrian delegation on "union affairs." The delegation was headed by Lt. Gen. Louai al-Attassi, Syria's chief of state. Commenting on the talks, Syrian Information Min. Sami el-Jundi said in Damascus July 23 that Nasser had rejected Syria's bid for unity despite Gen. Attassi's offer to reinstate "Nasserite" officers ousted from the Syrian army and to give Nasserites equal status with Baathists in the cabinet and National Revolutionary Council.

The formation of the new, 3-country United Arab Republic had first been announced in a communiqué signed in Cairo Apr. 11 by the heads of the 3 Arab governments shortly after revolts in Iraq and Syria.

Iraq had undergone a revolution early in Feb. 1963, and the Iraqi strongman, Premier Abdul Karim el-Kassem, had perished at the hands of Baathist and army rebels. An armed coup led by Syrian military elements sympathetic to Nasser had overthrown the Damascus government of Premier Khaled el-Azm Mar. 8, and had won immediate recognition from

Nasser and the Iraqi provisional administration of Pres. Abdel Salam Arif and Premier Ahmed Hassan al-Bakr. (The promise of armed support also came from Cairo, where UAR State Min. Abdel Kader Hatem announced that UAR forces had been alerted following reports of "anti-revolutionary concentrations against Syria." Hatem had declared earlier that "the UAR considers [that] any outside aggression against Syria is aggression against the UAR.")

The conclusive unity talks had started Apr. 7. The proposed federation was to take effect Sept. 28 following its expected ratification in national plebiscites Sept. 27. A 30-page communiqué outlining the structure of the new UAR was signed Apr. 11 by Nasser, Lt. Gen. Louai al-Attassi, president of the Syrian National Revolutionary Council, and Iraqi Premier Ahmed Hassan el-Bakr. The final agreement on the merger had been reached after a compromise on the principal obstacle—the composition of the governing Federal Presidential Council. Nasser had insisted that at least half of the council members be Egyptians on the ground that Egypt, with a population of 27 million, had more than twice the population of Syria (about 4 million) and Iraq (about 7 million) combined. Syria and Iraq had demanded that all 3 nations have equal representation. The eventual compromise provided for equal representation but gave veto power to the council president, who was expected to be Nasser.

The federation was to be governed by a constitution (to be drawn up in 5 months) for a transitional period of 20 months after the plebiscite. During this transitional period, the presidential council was to have executive and legislative powers. The constitution provided for the unification of the Egyptian, Syrian and Iraqi armies. The federal government was to conduct the foreign affairs of the 3 states, but the federation's individual members were to direct most of their own internal affairs and to elect their own parliaments.

The Cairo agreement also called for linking the parties of the 3 regions into a single political command: Egypt was to be represented by its only political party, the Arab Socialist Union; Syria was to be represented by its Arab Union Front, which had been formed Apr. 5 to unite the country's 3 conflicting political groups—the nationalist Baath party, the pro-Nasser Arab Nationalist Movement and the Socialist Union Front; Iraq was to be represented by its National Front, comprising the Baath party, the Arab Nationalist Movement and the Istiqlal party headed by Siddik Shanshal.

Other details of the federation plan: Nasser's UAR was to resume its previous name of Egypt; a customs union was to be established to permit the free flow of goods among the 3 states; the 3 states were to share common finances, including a common currency, treasury, budget, bond issue and loan agency; among agencies to be established were a supreme economic council, a supreme planning council for agriculture and transport, a Federal Ministry for Cultural Development & Information and a federal justice department to codify a system of federal laws; the 3 states were to share federal education and scientific planning.

Syria's course toward the new federation project had been much more difficult than Iraq's, according to the available information on the matter. UAR-Syrian differences over the proposed new union were heightened with the return to Cairo Mar. 14 of 12 high-ranking Syrian exiles who had been refused entry in Damascus Mar. 13. The Syrians had taken up residence in Cairo after Syria had seceded from the UAR in Sept. 1961. On their arrival in Damascus, Syrian War Min. Muhammad el-Soufi boarded their plane (which also carried back Iraqi Foreign Min. Taleb Hussein Shabib from talks with Nasser) and told them: "Do not debark now for the sake of unity and country. The time is not ripe." The exiles were permitted to phone Lt. Gen. Attassi, the pro-Nasser Syrian military commander, for permission to remain, but Attassi rejected their appeal. The Syrian exiles included 4 ex-ambassadors and these 5 former ministers:

Akram Deiri, Jadu Izzidin, Jamal Soufi, Ahmad Huneidi, Tohme Oudetallah.

Meanwhile, the negotiations delegation of Syrians and Iraqis had arrived in Cairo Mar. 14 following an announcement by Damascus radio that they had been sent to "begin the unification of the UAR, Syria and Iraq." Preliminary discussions had been conducted 3 days previously by Shabib, who met first with Syrian officials in Damascus and then for 2 days with Nasser in Cairo.

(The Syrians and Iraqis had originally proposed a 5-state federation that would have included Algeria and Yemen. The idea was shelved, largely because of Algeria's reluctance to join. Yemeni Pres. Abdullah al-Salal had said in Sana Mar. 16 that he was ready to join a federation. Cairo sources reported that Salal had cabled Nasser that he was also prepared to "leave the matter [of Yemen's entry] in the hands of" Nasser.)

A Syrian cabinet statement Mar. 14 had expressed opposition to a UAR proposal that the projected 3-country merger be preceded by the restoration of the UAR-Syrian union, followed by Iraqi membership. The Syrian statement, issued after consultation with Iraqi officials, declared Syrian support for Iraq and said: ". . . Syria realize[s] that the new unity this time will stand on studied and clear foundations. . . . Syria realize[s] also that unity among the 3 Arab states will benefit from experience of the previous union between Egypt and Syria." The Syrian cabinet suggested that the Cairo conference delegates not make decisions themselves on unity but submit their proposals to their governments and that their citizens approve or reject them in referendums.

The Syrian cabinet statement overrode demands from the cabinet's pro-Nasser ministers for immediate union with the UAR. The Nasserites then issued a statement of their own, but it was censored in the Mar. 15 edition of *Al Wanda*, the Arab nationalist newspaper in Damascus. The newspaper *Al Baath* asserted that "union between Syria and Egypt only is wrong and harmful" and was "surrender to the emotionalism of the masses." The pro-Nasser Syrians' statement was published in Cairo Mar. 17. It said: Egyptian-Syrian unity should be restored "without loss of time and vain formalities"; a tribunal should be established to punish "traitors and separatists"; there should be a "prohibition of political activities not in line with the Arab national cause in its broad meaning."

Syria's ruling Revolutionary Command Council decreed a state of emergency Apr. 1 to curb pro-Nasser demonstrations and appointed Lt. Gen. Amin al-Hafez as deputy military governor with the power to enforce the state of emergency. Hafez immediately announced an 18-hour (6 p.m.–12 noon) curfew in Damascus. The Nasserites, demanding an immediate Syrian-UAR union, had carried pictures of Nasser and chanted his name before the official guest house, where Algerian Defense Min. Houari Boumedienne had arrived on a state visit from Cairo Mar. 31.

The demonstrations were believed linked to an anti-Baathist article that had appeared Mar. 31 in the Cairo newspaper *Al-Ahram*. The article, written by editor Muhammad Hassanein Heikal, an associate of Nasser, had charged that Syrian Premier Salah el-Bitar, leader of Syria's ruling Baathist party, and Michel Aflaq, the party's secretary general, were responsible for articles in the party's newspaper "that do not inspire enough confidence to make us turn to a new page in the relations between the UAR and the party." Heikal's article said: In the past 2 weeks the Baathist newspaper *Al Baath* had published statements blaming Nasser for the "mistakes" of the 1958–61 UAR-Syrian union; *Al Baath* unfairly criticized Nasser for abolishing the Baath party in Syria and Egypt during the union; Baath leaders had assisted in the "infiltration of opportunists" who had blocked Nasser's Socialist and nationalist programs and finally had wrecked the Syrian-Egyptian union in 1961; the ex-Syrian Baath party leader Akram el-Hourani had supported "secessionists" in Syria prior to the coup; Bitar had cooperated with Syrian regime established after the 1961 coup.

Al-Ahram's attacks on the Baathists followed talks held in Cairo Mar. 19-21 by Nasser, Bitar, Aflaq and Lt. Gen. Attassi of Syria. The purpose of the conference was to consider the problem of relations between the Baathists and Nasserites in any future UAR-Syrian union. A joint communiqué issued Mar. 21 said: Both sides favored "an equal federal union" available to every "liberated Arab country"; Syria and the UAR had agreed on the "inevitability that all revolutionary unionist forces in the UAR, Syria and Iraq should . . . jointly bear their full responsibilities in leading and building up a unionist revolution"; Syria and the UAR agreed not to repeat the mistakes of their former union.

Heikal disclosed Mar. 22 that Nasser had told the Syrian leaders that the Baath party and the Nasserites must form "one single front" before the UAR could join the proposed Arab federation, including Syria and Iraq. Heikal said that Nasser had insisted that a united political front, such as Egypt's Arab Socialist Union, must precede the holding of a plebiscite (to approve the proposed federation) as advocated by the Syrian Baathists.

After 5 members of Syria's 3 pro-Nasser parties resigned from the cabinet and National Revolutionary Council May 2, the Baathist party became Syria's sole ruling force, and Nasser's plans for a renascence of the former union of Egypt with Syria were shelved indefinitely. Compounding the Nasserite political collapse in Syria, 2 high-ranking military officials resigned in support of the pro-Nasser ministers: Lt. Gen. Muhammad el-Soufi, defense minister, and Gen. Rashed Katinin, deputy chief of the general staff. Both had been leaders of the Mar. 8 coup that overthrew Pres. Nazem el-Kodsi. The ministers who resigned: Deputy Premier

Nihad el-Kassim; Finance Min. Abdel Wahhab Homad; Planning Min. Hani el-Hindi; Communications Min. Johad Dahi; Supply Min. Sami Soufan.

The resignations followed a deadlock in negotiations on forming a single National Front of the Baathists and the 3 pro-Nasser parties—the Arab Nationalist Movement, the Socialist Union Front and the Arab Union Front (originally formed Apr. 5 as a coalition grouping of Baathists and the pro-Nasser parties). The Nasserites had demanded equal representation with the Baathists in the cabinet and council. The Baathists, insisting on majority representation, claimed that they had the organizational structure to run the government and that their party had a greater following than the 3 rival parties combined.

The Baathist-Nasserite dispute had flared earlier in the week as 47 pro-Nasser officers were dismissed or pensioned off following reports of a Nasserite attempt to oust the Baathists. Reports from Beirut, Lebanon May 3 said that a plot had been discovered to assassinate Lt. Gen. Louai al-Attassi, the National Revolutionary Council president. Among the 47 officers dismissed was Lt. Col. Fawwaz Mohares, a Revolutionary Council member.

Cairo reported May 4 an indefinite postponement of military unity talks among the UAR, Iraq and Syria. The talks were to have started May 12. Meanwhile, Algerian Premier Ahmed Ben Bella May 4 welcomed the visiting UAR Pres. Nasser in Algiers with a declaration that Algeria hoped to join Egypt, Syria and Iraq in the emerging new United Arab Republic.

As a "first step" toward Arab unity, Ben Bella suggested a union of the North African countries of Algeria, Morocco and Tunisia. As for the projected new UAR merger, Ben Bella said: "We welcome this unity. And we hope that very soon we shall be within that union. Our brothers in North Africa should understand its meaning." Ben Bella called on

Syria and Iraq to stay united and "beware of Israel, our common enemy."

Nasser left Algeria May 8. Prior to his departure, he and Ben Bella had issued a joint communiqué which said: "Socialism" was the "only way to the establishment of healthy democracy"; Arab unity must be based on a "unity of objectives" and on "national unity in each country"; there must be a "liberation" of Palestine (Israel) and the recovery of "all the rights of the Palestinian Arab Republic."

Israel Apr. 29 had submitted to the UN Security Council a letter protesting the threats to Israel's existence in the Apr. 17 declaration by Egypt, Syria and Iraq on their proposed federation. "This declaration," the letter said, "states the following among the principles and objectives of the new federation": "Unity is a revolution especially because it is strongly connected with the question of Palestine and the national duty to liberate it." "The establishment of a military unity capable of liberating the Arab homeland from the dangers of Zionism. . . ."

"The expression 'liberation of Palestine' signifies nothing else than the aim to destroy Israel," the Israeli letter charged. "These statements must be taken against the background of the proclaimed policies of the 3 countries concerned. The policies of these states are manifested by a complete refusal to recognize the right of Israel's existence, an unrelenting attitude of belligerency towards Israel, an obstinate opposition to settling outstanding issues by peaceful means and making any advance towards the establishment of permanent peace in the Middle East, and the accelerated accumulation of offensive armaments for the declared purpose of attacking Israel when the time comes, as stated by Pres. Nasser on Dec. 23, 1962. The statements appearing in the joint declaration of Apr. 17, 1963 repeat in solemn and constitutional terms what has been said in innumerable declarations made by the leaders of these countries in the past. They were further elaborated in public statements made by the governments signatory to the joint declaration, when introducing the declaration to their own peoples. It is unprecedented for a constitutional document of member-states of the United Nations to proclaim the destruction of another member-state—which is one of the avowed aims of the new federation. Such a declaration is incompatible with the obligation of all members of the United Nations to refrain in their international relations from the threat or use of force against the territorial integrity or political independence of any state."

In Iraq, the pro-Nasser premier, Brig. Bakr, tendered his resignation to Pres. Abdel Salam Arif May 11. 2 Nasserites, the ministers of housing and finance, were dismissed and replaced by Baathists. The National Council of the Revolutionary Command reported May 25 that it had smashed a conspiracy to arrest Arif and destroy the 40,000-man Baathist militia. 4 Nasserite political parties were implicated. Between May 25 and July 10, 56 alleged conspirators were shot in Baghdad.

The Syrian army July 18 crushed an armed attempt by pro-Nasser elements to overthrow the Baathist government. 40 to 70 persons were killed and 300 injured in the fighting in Damascus. Several hundred persons were arrested, and 27 were executed. Warrants were issued for the arrest of 9 suspected plot leaders and 58 accomplices. A 10 a.m.–6 p.m. curfew was imposed throughout Syria. A communiqué issued by Maj. Gen. Amin el-Hafez, defense minister and army chief, said: "A small group of civilians backed by some cashiered officers attempted this morning to disturb the peace. But their attempt was nipped in the bud [after a 3½-hour battle]." The ruling National Revolutionary Council July 19 gave this account of the attempted revolt: A former intelligence officer and several civilians secured arms from the military public works section; they distributed the arms to hundreds of military men and civilians who had surrounded the army's general headquarters and the radio station; with elements of the Signal Corps joining the plotters and assisted by 4 jet fighters, the insurgents attacked the headquarters but were quickly defeated by a guards regiment and a tank corps; a group of discharged pro-Nasser officers had entered 2 military camps in Damascus but were surrounded and arrested.

The government reportedly had advance knowledge that the uprising would occur July 18. In a move to counter the plot, the government July 17 had transferred a group of officers suspected of planning to join the revolt. The principal leader of the attempted coup was identified as Lt. Col. Jasm Alwan, a Nasserite who had led an abortive uprising at Aleppo Mar. 28, 1962 in an attempt to restore the Syrian-Egyptian union. The Revolutionary Council July 18 charged that Abdul Hamid al-Serraj, vice president and interior minister during the Syrian-Egyptain union, also was behind the plot.

The 8 other suspected coup leaders named were Youssef Muzahim, religious affairs minister in the union government; Muhammad Jarrah, deputy security chief in the union regime; Akram Safadi, ex-aide to Pres. Nasser; Abdo Hakim, deputy intelligence chief in the union government; Raef Maari; Talaat Sidky; Munir Brikkan; Naithan Ayoubi. Among the 58 accomplices named were Abdel Wahab Homad, a leader of the Arab Union Front and an ex-union government minister; Hani el-Hindi, a leader of the Arab Nationalist Movement; Socialist Unionist leader Sami Soufan; Johad Bahi, a minister in the first cabinet after the Mar. 8 coup; Maj. Gen. Rashed Katinin, who had resigned in May as deputy chief of the general staff in protest against the dismissal of Nasserite officers.

20 soldiers and civilians were executed by firing squad July 19 after a Damascus military court had convicted them of participating in the uprising. Among those shot was Col. Hisham Shabib, Syria's army signal corps commander.

5 soldiers and 2 civilians were executed July 21; 3 persons were acquitted.

Egypt displayed new military weapons in an 11th anniversary parade in Cairo July 23. The new equipment included 2 new-type rockets: one was a Soviet-made SA-2 ground-to-air weapon recently tested near Cairo; the other, the first 2-stage missle (Pioneer) developed in the UAR, was said to have a range "exceeding 360 miles" but was untested. Other weapons displayed included long-range field rocket launchers and MG-21 supersonic jet fighters. Field Marshal Abdel Hakim Amer, armed forces deputy commander, announced in an address before the parade that the UAR had developed "the first Arab submarine, which will be tested at sea within 15 days." The UAR had 9 Soviet-built submarines.

Arab Summit Meeting

The chiefs of state of the 13 Arab League† countries conferred in Cairo Jan. 13–17, 1964 and agreed to the establishment of a unified military command for possible use against Israel. The conference, which had been called by UAR Pres. Nasser, also devised an undisclosed plan to counteract Israel's project to divert Jordan River waters to irrigate its arid Negev desert.

The agreement on the establishment of a joint military command was announced at the Jan. 15 meeting. The joint command was to have a permanent headquarters and "financial capabilities." Lt. Gen. Abdel Hakim Amer, the UAR's chief of staff, was named chief of the proposed

---

†Participants: UAR Pres. Nasser; Maj. Gen. Amin el-Hafez, president of Syria's National Revolutionary Council; Prime Min. Sheik Abdullah al-Salim al-Sabbah of Kuwait; Pres. Abdel Salam Arif of Iraq; Crown Prince Hassan el-Rida el-Senussi of Libya (representing his father, King Idris I); Pres. Ahmed Ben Bella of Algeria; King Saud of Saudi Arabia; King Hussein of Jordan; King Hassan II of Morocco; Pres. Habib Bourguiba of Tunisia; Pres. Abdullah al-Salal of Yemen; Pres. Fuad Chehab of Lebanon; Premier Ibrahim Abboud of the Sudan.

command Jan. 17. In another accord announced Jan. 15, Jordan and the UAR agreed to resume diplomatic relations. The UAR had severed relations with Jordan in Sept. 1961 after the Amman government recognized a Syrian revolutionary regime that had seceded from the UAR union with Egypt.

A final communiqué issued at the conclusion of the Arab summit meeting Jan. 17 announced the 13 leaders' accord on the "necessary practical resolutions" to frustrate Israel's plan for diversion of the waters of the Jordan. Although the communiqué did not say what specific measures were envisaged, it was believed that the Arab counter-plan called for the building of dams in Syria and Lebanon to drain off the headwaters of the Jordan River before they reached the portion of the river flowing through Israel.

(Gen. Hafez of Syria reportedly had been rebuffed at the Jan. 13 meeting when he demanded an immediate military blow against Israel to thwart its irrigation plans. Opposition to this stand was said to have been expressed by Nasser, Pres. Bourguiba and King Hussein. In arguing for a more moderate approach, the 3 leaders were said to have reasoned that before attacking Israel, the Arab states should develop strength and unity and press their own reclamation plans.)

Other league resolutions dealing with Israel were equally vague. The meeting's final communiqué said that the conference had reached decisions on opposing the "Zionist danger" and on "organizing the Palestine Arab people to enable it to play its role in liberating its country and and determining its future." The conferees expressed hope for Afro-Asian support of the Arab struggle against "Zionist-imperialist dangers." The communiqué denounced Israel's "aggression since its emergence as an imperialist force occupying . . . [Arab] land and practicing racial discrimination against the Arab minority." Other points of the communiqué included these: (a) the Arab League states agreed to end their political differences and halt propaganda campaigns heretofore directed against each other; (b) they agreed to support anti-colonial revolutions in Angola and South Africa and in "every other place in the world"; (c) another Arab summit meeting would be held in August in Alexandria, and the Arab chiefs of state would meet in the future at least once yearly.

Israel's official reaction to the Arab League meeting was voiced by Premier Levi Eshkol Jan. 20. In a statement to the Knesset (parliament), Eshkol warned that Israel would "oppose unilateral and illegal measures by the Arab states" and would "protect her vital rights." The premier charged that the Cairo conference had "proclaimed a plan of sabotage . . . based entirely on negation and envy, violation of law and deliberate aggression."

In defending Israel's Jordan River project, Eshkol said that his country would not use more water than alloted to it under the plan proposed in 1953 by Eric Johnston, Pres. Eisenhower's special envoy for a U.S.-backed scheme for joint Arab-Israeli development of the Jordan River Valley. The plan, accepted by Israel but rejected by the Arabs, would have permitted Syria, Jordan and Lebanon to use all the Jordan River waters they needed for irrigation, with the remainder (about 40%) going to Israel. Israel had argued that its current project was not a river diversion because despite the fact that part of the waters of the Jordan River and the Sea of Galilee were to be pumped away, their course would remain unchanged, although their flow would be reduced. Israel also recalled that Syria and Lebanon were using Jordan headwaters rising in their territories, and Jordan was diverting the Yarmuk River, a tributary of the Jordan that entered the river south of the Sea of Galilee.

(A UAR air force pilot defected and landed his Czech-made Yak-11 training plane at an undisclosed point in Israel Jan. 19. The flier, identifying himself as Lt. Mahmoud Hilmi Abbas Hilmi, 26, said he had taken the plane from a training base at Bilbeis, near Cairo, and had fled to Israel "for political reasons." A government spokesman in Cairo Jan. 19 reported a training plane missing because of atmospheric conditions.)

UAR & Iraq Form Joint Command

UAR Pres. Nasser and Iraqi Pres Abdel Salam Arif in Cairo May 26, 1964 signed an agreement to set up a joint Egyptian-Iraqi military command in time of war and to appoint immediately a joint presidential council to explore means of unifying the 2 governments. (The agreement was subject to ratification by both legislative assemblies.) Nasser said that the agreement also opened the door for the "Syrian people" to join in this "first step toward full Arab unity."

Arif May 3 had proclaimed a provisional constitution "purposely patterned after the United Arab Republic constitution in preparation for the forthcoming union." The 105-article constitution described Iraq as a democratic Socialist state seeking unity among Arabs.

The text of the agreement to establish a joint presidential council:

PREAMBLE

Believing in the unity of the Arab nation as a unity springing from the common language and history and from the common Arab struggle and destiny, and realizing the forgery of the artificial scheme reflected in the current political divisions on the Arab soil and which had been imposed by colonialism in accordance with its interests in exploitation and domination, the Arab nation finds itself bound by its unity stemming from historical facts and from experience. The aspirations of the Arab nation were embodied in a pioneering experience, namely that of the rise of the United Arab Republic between Syria and Egypt, to prove to the whole world that the slogan of unity was not a hope difficult to achieve but a fact which can be established in reality.

The elements of evil in cooperation with imperialism and reaction carried out the crime of secession. But the lesson of secession left behind a rich experience which in itself constitutes a shield protecting the future of and boosting the vigilance over unity. The banners of unity continued to rise, and the unity slogans continued to be repeated in the heart of every Arab in spite of the rash attempts to obstruct them. Then came the agreement of Apr. 17, 1963, to fulfil the unity between Syria, Egypt and Iraq. However, the lack of goodwill on the part of some also destroyed this attempt and the experience proved that the mere slogans of unity are not enough for the fulfilment of unity itself. Popular organizations aware of unity must be founded. Popular organizations must be united on the national level so they may have common and clear concepts. Unity of mind leads to unity of action, which must be based on realism and carried out in a revolutionary manner so it may render a chance for fulfilment of an all-embracing unity.

The revolutionary concept of unity is based on unity of peoples, unity of the working popular forces which have the interest and right in revolution. It is the unity of the Arab Socialist society, the society of sufficiency and justice which seeks Arab social struggle so Arab unity may have a social framework to go hand in hand with its political framework, in expression of the Arab people's determination to establish a new and free tomorrow for the free Arab human being.

Moving from these principles, and on behalf of the people and Governments of the UAR and Iraqi Republic, Pres. Abdel Salam Muhammad Arif, president of the Iraqi Republic, and Pres. Gamal Abdel Nasser, president of the United Arab Republic, have agreed on the following:

AGREEMENT

Article 1. A Joint Presidency Council of the United Arab Republic and the Iraqi Republic shall be formed of the president of the United Arab Republic, the president of the Iraqi Republic and a number of members.

Article 2. (a) The Council shall meet once every 3 months, and shall also meet under necessary circumstances as per agreement of the presidents of the signatory countries. (b) Cairo is the center of the Joint Presidency Council; the Council can be invited to meet somewhere else by the agreement of the 2 Presidents.

Article 3. Resolutions of the Joint Presidency Council are binding and shall be in effect on ratification by the Council; this excludes the resolutions which require issuance of laws; this shall be carried out after their ratification in accordance with the constitutional procedures applied in each one of the 2 countries.

Article 4. Action in the Presidency Council shall be in accordance with the by-laws to be laid down by the Council and which shall be in effect upon ratification by the Council.

Article 5. The Presidency Council shall: (a) Study and carry out the necessary steps for the establishment of unity between the 2 countries. (b) Plan and coordinate policy of the 2 countries in the political, military, economic, social and cultural affairs and in the field of information. (c) Fulfill unity of thought between the peoples of the United Arab Republic and the Iraqi Republic through the 2 popular organizations inside the 2 countries, and seek unity of the 2 organizations in future.

Article 6. (a) Each government shall appoint its representatives in the Presidency Council according to the following manner: (1) 3 full-time members with the ranks of minister; (2) 3 attending members from members of the government. (b) Full-time members shall follow-up the implementation of resolutions of the Presidency Council, shall coordinate work of the joint committees and shall submit studies and recommendations to the Presidency Council when it meets. (c) The Presidency Council or the joint committees can invite technicians from both countries to attend the meetings if this is deemed necessary.

Article 7. The following organizations shall be established: (a) The Political Committee, (b) The Military Command, (c) The Economic Committee, (d) The Cultural and Information Committee, (e) Committee for Socialist Thought, (f) The Committee for Popular Organization, (g) Other committees the establishments of which may be deemed necessary. These committees shall study and prepare the various subjects for the purpose of fulfilment of this agreement, and shall also study the subjects referred to them by the Presidency Council.

Article 8. (a) The Joint Military Command shall coordinate armament, training and equipping the armed forces of the 2 countries, and shall lay down operation plans and movement of the armed forces, and shall assume their command in time of war. (b) The Joint Command shall take the necessary measures to face a state of war or danger of war, and any aggression or threat of aggression against either one of the countries is directed against the other.

Article 9. The Presidency Council shall have a secretariat-general with headquarters in Cairo. It shall be headed by a secretary-general with the rank of minister, and shall practice the following: (a) Issue invitations for meetings of Presidency Council; (b) Prepare subjects for discussion by the Council; (c) Register minutes of meetings of the Presidency Council and the joint committees, and publish the resolutions after their ratification according to procedures in practice in both countries; (d) Prepare budgets of the Presidency Council, the secretariat-general, and the joint committees listed in Article 7.

Article 10. (a) Budget of the Presidency Council and the joint committees shall be shared equally by the 2 countries. (b) Each country shall alone bear the salaries and remunerations of members and officials appointed by it, in accordance with its own fiscal regulations.

Article 11. There is nothing in rules of this agreement that infringe on rights and obligations borne by the 2 states under the UN Charter, nor do the aforementioned rules violate rules of any agreement signed within the framework of the Arab League.

Article 12. This agreement shall remain in effect until the necessary arrangements have been made to establish the union.

Article 13. This agreement shall be considered standing when ratified in accordance with the constitutional procedures in practice in both countries.

Hamid Fathy el-Deeb of the UAR was named secretary general of the Council, with headquarters in Cairo. The other UAR members were Pres. Nasser, Kamaleddin el-Hennawi, Sharawai Gomaa and Ali el-Said Ali. The Iraqi members were Pres. Arif, Gen. Naji Taleeb, Adeb al-Jadir and Abdel Satar al-Hussein.

The UAR and Yemen agreed July 13 to set up a coordinating council, somewhat like the UAR-Iraqi presidential council, with each side having 3 permanent and 3 part-time members. The council was to coordinate UAR and Yemeni policies in the spheres of politics, information, economic, social, cultural and military affairs. The UAR agreed to pay 90% of all costs.

Khrushchev Visits UAR

Soviet Premier Nikita S. Khrushchev paid a 16-day visit to the UAR May 9–25, 1964 in connection with celebrations marking the completion of the first stage of the Soviet-aided Aswan High Dam project.

Khrushchev landed in Alexandria May 9 from the Soviet liner *Armenia.* He was accompanied by a 100-member delegation that included his wife, Nina Petrovna Khrushchev, his son, Sergei, his son-in-law and daughter, Aleksei I. and Rada Adzhubei, Foreign Min. Andrei A. Gromyko, Foreign Ministry press chief Leonid Zamyatin and Pavel Satyukov, editor of the Soviet Communist Party newspaper *Pravda*.

Khrushchev, welcomed by UAR Pres. Nasser, noted that it was "the first time I have ever set foot on the African continent." He said that he was proud to participate in the celebrations for the initiation of the construction of the Aswan Dam's 2d stage. Khrushchev and Nasser then entered an open car for a drive through streets thronged by tumultuous Alexandria crowds to the railway station, where they boarded a train for Cairo. The enthusiastic popular reception accorded Khrushchev was repeated on his arrival in Cairo later that day and as his motorcade drove to the capital's Kubbah Palace, where the Soviet visitors were housed. Khrushchev conferred with Nasser later May 9 at his Cairo home and was his guest at a state dinner.

(Western newsmen reported from Cairo and Alexandria that the enthusiastic public reception given Khrushchev contrasted sharply with the warm but restrained welcome given Chinese Premier Chou En-lai on his 10-day visit to the UAR in mid-Dec. 1963—a period of international unease shortly after the sudden change of administrations in Washington on the assassination of Pres. John F. Kennedy. The Nasser government had made elaborate preparations for Khrushchev's visit, and it was believed that more than one million Egyptians turned out to see him in his first 3 days in the UAR.)

Khrushchev, accompanied by Nasser, toured Cairo museums May 10 and then spoke at a rally attended by an estimated 100,000 young Egyptians. He hailed Nasser as a "great leader" of the forces of "liberation" and asserted that the UAR and USSR were working "together for the complete eradication of imperialism."

Addressing the UAR National Assembly May 11, Khrushchev expressed total support for the Arab states in their dispute with the "imperialist" powers and with Israel, which he termed a "stooge of the imperialists." He denounced Israel for its projected diversion of Jordan River waters to irrigate the Negev Desert; he said the project had "robbed Arabs of their own sources of water." He added that the USSR supported the "just demands of the Arab countries that Israel should implement the United Nations resolutions on Palestine." He demanded that Britain withdraw its troops and military bases from the middle east, and he emphasized that "our [Soviet] armaments will always be available to those struggling for independence and liberty."

Khrushchev, visiting a Soviet-built pharmaceutical plant near Cairo May 12, declared: "In the name of the Soviet

Union, we shall not be neutral [in disputes between Arabs and imperialist nations]." He added that the USSR had not been neutral when ex-British Prime Min. Anthony Eden had informed him that Britain would "fight by every means to preserve its oil interests" in the Middle East. Imperialism was not invincible, Khrushchev declared: "You in Egypt were able to twist the British lion's tail." (Sen. Ernest Gruening [D., Alaska] charged in the U.S. Senate May 12 that Khrushchev's visit to the UAR had been planned as part of a Soviet effort to seize control of Middle East oil resources. Gruening said Nasser had served as the USSR's "stooge" in this campaign. He called on Pres. Lyndon B. Johnson and the State Department to take steps to prevent further Soviet penetration of the Middle East and to give Israel treaty protection against an attack by the Arab states.)

Khrushchev visited Aswan May 13-16 to inspect the high dam project and the surrounding area. Khrushchev and Nasser May 14 set off an explosive charge to open a diversionary channel for the Nile River; this completed the first stage of the $1 billion project, about $^{2}/_{5}$ of which was being financed by the USSR. In a speech at a gathering of 5,000 government officials, diplomats and construction workers, Khrushchev called the project a "symbol of peaceful cooperation" in which "the Russian experts worked here hand-in-hand with 30,000 Egyptians." Khrushchev then named Nasser a "Hero of the Soviet Union" for having started construction on "the greatest dam on the African continent" and awarded him the Order of Lenin. Khrushchev later May 14 held a private conference with Nasser and 3 visiting Arab leaders: Algerian Pres. Ahmed Ben Bella, Iraqi Pres. Abdel Salam Arif and Yemeni Pres. Abdullah al-Salal.

Khrushchev declared in a speech in Aswan May 16 that Arab leaders were overemphasizing "Arab unity and nationalism" instead of stressing "unity with workers of all nations." "To me," Khrushchev said, "an Arab worker is closer than a capitalist in Russia." "You speak only of Arab unity.

Does that mean we Russians should go home? We are not Arabs." Khrushchev's speech was in apparent reply to a preceding address in which Arif had urged a union of all Arab nations and had lauded Nasser as an Arab nationalist leader.

Speaking at Port Said May 19, Khrushchev praised its "valiant citizens" for their defense against the 1956 Anglo-French-Israeli attacks on the Suez Canal. Recalling Soviet support of the UAR at the time, Khrushchev pledged that Moscow "will always be at your side in times of crisis and difficulty."

UAR-Soviet differences over Arab unity were again underscored in speeches made by Nasser and Khrushchev at a meeting of Arab labor organizations in Cairo May 20. Nasser said Arab unity was a "sacred goal" representing "one physical entity, one conscience and one mind." This position, Nasser emphasized, was not in conflict with the Arabs' sympathy with revolutionary movements in Asia, Africa and Latin America and with the USSR's "Socialist camp." Khrushchev said "Russians understand the question of unity in a broader fashion–not based on a concept of nationalism but on the basis of the power of the working forces."

Khrushchev and UAR Premier Ali Sabry in Moscow Sept. 22 signed 2 agreements covering the previously promised Soviet loan to the UAR of 252 million rubles ($280 million) for the construction of industrial plants under a 2d 5-year plan and for technical assistance in developing new agricultural areas. The loan was announced by Nasser at a farewell dinner for Khrushchev in Cairo May 24. The funds would finance about 10% of the 5-year plan, beginning in 1965. According to Khrushchev, the USSR also planned to give the UAR a steel plant with a capacity of one million tons annually and a 10,000-acre model farm for desert reclamation.

In a joint communiqué signed by Khrushchev and Nasser May 24: the Soviet premier assailed U.S. surveillance flights over Cuba; Nasser supported Moscow's stand on "peaceful co-existence"; both leaders scored "attempts to torpedo the Geneva agreement of 1962 with regard to Laos"; the USSR supported the Arab states in their dispute with Israel.

Khrushchev flew back to Moscow May 25.

Other Developments

The Libyan government announced Feb. 23, 1964 that it would not renew or extend the leases of the U.S. and British military bases in Libya on their expiration. (The lease of the U.S.' Wheelus Air Force Base near Tripoli was scheduled to expire in 1971. Britain operated 8 military bases in exchange for financial aid under a 20-year treaty signed in 1953.) The Libyan statement was made in reply to a major policy speech by UAR Pres. Nasser Feb. 22. Charging that foreign bases in Cyprus and Libya "form a serious threat against the Arab world." Nasser had urged the Arab states to "work for the liquidation of these bases." "What guarantees are there for us that American and British bases in Libya will not be used against the Arabs in the event of a clash with Israel?" Nasser asked. Libya's formal assurance that it would not renew the foreign base agreements was delivered to Nasser Feb. 24 by Libyan Amb.-to-UAR Tahrir Bekir.

Ambassadors and chargés d'affaires of 13 Arab states met with U.S. State Secy. Dean Rusk May 25 to express concern over a scheduled visit to Washington of Israeli Premier Levi Eshkol. After the meeting UAR Amb. Mostafa Kamel said the envoys had told Rusk of their fears that Eshkol would try to "destroy Arab-American relations in order to have liberty of aggression in the Middle East." A joint statement issued June 1 by the press attachés of the 13 Arab embassies in Washington had warned that Eshkol's visit might have "serious implications for the future of Arab-American relations." The statement said Eshkol had come to Washington to "ask the United States for arms and the conclusion of a bilateral security treaty." U.S. State Undersecy.

George W. Ball called the 13 Arab envoys to his office June 2 and reportedly reprimanded them for the statement of their press attachés. Ball was said to have called the statement an unwarranted intrusion in U.S. affairs and offensive to the Administration because of its timing.

Eshkol arrived in Washington June 1 as the first Israeli premier to pay an official visit to the U.S., and he stayed until June 11. Pres. Lyndon B. Johnson and Eshkol conferred privately later June 1 and met again June 2. A joint communiqué issued at the conclusion of their talks said that the President had reaffirmed U.S. "support for the territorial integrity and political independence of all countries in the Near East and reaffirmed the firm opposition of the United States to aggression and the use of force against any country." The communiqué also said that the U.S. and Israel had agreed to joint studies of desalination and the pertinent information would be made "available to all countries with water deficiencies."

The UAR June 14 raised Suez Canal ship tolls a minimum of 1%, effective June 29. The increase was higher for bigger ships. Canal Authority Chairman Mahmoud Yunis said that rising costs and a desire to have larger ships pay a proportionately larger share of Canal improvement costs necessitated the increase. He estimated that the toll increases would yield an annual extra revenue of $3½ million in addition to the current $150 million. It was the first toll increase since Egypt nationalized the Canal in 1956.

New Government, Parliament & Constitution

In a series of top personnel shifts, Field Marshal Abdel Hakim Amer, 45, was sworn in as UAR first vice president in Heliopolis Mar. 25, 1964, and Zakaria Mohieddin, Hussein el-Shafei and Hassan Ibrahim were simultaneously sworn in as vice presidents.

Pres. Nasser the same day named Ali Sabry as premier and created 11 deputy premierships in the cabinet. He made these appointments of deputy premiers: *Financial & Economic Affairs*—Dr. Abdel Moneim el-Kaissouni (also foreign trade minister); *Industry & Mineral Wealth*—Dr. Aziz Sidky (also petroleum & light industries minister); *Culture, Tourism & National Guidance*—Dr. Abdel Kader Hatem; *Scientific Affairs*—Kamal Rifaat; *Local Administration & Services*—Abbas Radwan; *Justice, Labor & Youth*—Dr. Nurreddin Tarraf; *Religious Affairs*—Ahmed Abdul el-Sharabasi; *Supply & Internal Trade*—Dr. Kamal Ramzy Stino; *Communications*—Dr. Mustafa Khalil; *Agriculture*—Abdelmohsin Abu el-Nour (also agrarian reform & land reclamation minister). Foreign Min. Mahmoud Fawzi became a deputy premier, and Amb.-to-UN Mahmoud Riad was named foreign minister.

The new cabinet also included these ministers (* denotes holdover): *Defense*—Abdel Wahab el-Bishri*; *Interior*—Abdel Azim Fahmi*; *Justice*—Badawi Hammooda; *Finance*—Dr. Nazih Deif; *Foreign Cultural & Technical Relations*—Hussein Khallaf; *Labor*—Anwar Salamaa*; *Planning*—Dr. Muhammad Labib Shukeir; *Aswan High Dam*—Sidki Soliman*; *Agriculture*—Dr. Shafiq el-Kheshen; *Irrigation*—Dr. Hassan Zaky*; *Heavy Industries*—Samir Helmi; *Electric Power*—Dr. Muhammad Ezzat Salamaa; *Transport*—Mahmoud Abdel Salam; *Telecommunications*—Dr. Mahmoud Riad (also foreign minister); *Scientific Research*—Dr. Riad Turki; *Higher Education*—Dr. Abdel Aziz el-Sayed*; *Education*—Said Youssuf*; *Youth*—Talaat Khairy*; *Social Affairs*—Mrs. Hekmat Abu Zeid*; *Public Health*—Dr. Muhammad el-Nabawi el-Mohandes*; *Housing*—Muhammad Abu Nossier; *Atomic Energy Organization*—Saladin Hedayat (chairman with the rank of minister). Ex-Economy Min. Ahmed Zendo became chairman of Egypt's Central Bank; ex-Deputy Foreign Min. Hussein Zulfikar Sabry became presidential adviser to Nasser.

The cabinet appointments followed general elections Mar. 10 and Mar. 19 for a new 350-member Egyptian National Assembly to succeed the one dissolved in Oct. 1961. Only 82 former deputies were elected; 8 women were also elected.

108 smallhold farmers and 71 workers were elected to the new parliament. (Pres. Nasser later exercised his privilege under Egypt's new provisional constitution and appointed 10 deputies himself.)

Nasser proclaimed the new, 7-chapter state constitution Mar. 23 as Egypt's fundamental law until the new National Assembly could draft a permanent charter and the people could approve it in a plebiscite. The constitution extended Nasser's current term as president for another 7 years. The provisional charter's first 10 articles dealt with the state and society. *The constitution's major provisions:*

Article 1. The United Arab Republic is "a democratic, Socialist state based on the alliance of the working powers of the people," who are "part of the Arab nation.

Article 3. "National unity is achieved by the alliance of the people's powers, comprising the working people–the farmers, workers, soldiers, intellectuals–and national capital, and is embodied in the Arab Socialist Union as the representative power of the people. . . ."

Article 5. Islam is the religion of the state and Arabic is its official language.

The Fundamental Elements of Society: *Articles 6-8.* "Social solidarity is the basis of Egyptian society," and "the family is the basis of society founded on religion, patroiotism and morality."

Article 9. "The state guarantees equality of opportunity to all Egyptians." "The state's economic foundation is the Socialist system, which prohibits any form of exploitation."

Article 10. The entire national economy is "directed in accordance with the development plan laid down by the state." The country's natural wealth, resources and energy are the property of the state, and the people "control all the means of production and direct their surplus in accordance with the development plan. . . ."

"Ownership takes one of the following forms: (a) State ownership: which is the ownership of the people and is achieved by creating a strong and effective public sector leading to progress in all fields and shouldering the main responsibility in the development plan. (b) Cooperative ownership: which is the ownership of all those participating in cooperatives. (c) Private ownership: which implies the private sector partaking in development within the framework of the development plan without exploitation. All 3 sectors should be under the people's control.

"Private ownership is protected; its social function is to be stipulated by law. Ownership is not to be expropriated except for public interest and in return for an equitable compensation as stipulated by the law. The law defines the maximum limit of land ownership. . . . The state encourages cooperation. . . . in all their forms. The state ensures, in conformity with the law, the protection of the family. The state ensures all social insurance services. Egyptians have a right to aid in old age, sickness, incapacity for work or unemployment.

"Work in the UAR is the right, duty and honor of every able-bodied citizen. . . . Government officials in the performance of their work should have the service of the people as their aim. The armed forces of the UAR belong to the people. Their mission is to protect the Socialist gains of the people's struggle, to protect the country, the safety of its land and its security.

"*Public Rights & Duties*: Egyptians are equal before the law, being equal with regard to rights and public obligations without any distinction in that respect with regard to race, origin, language, religion or belief. No criminal indictment or punishment is valid except in conformity with the provisions of the law, nor is punishment permissible except for offenses committed after the issue of the law incriminating such acts. No person shall be liable to arrest or imprisonment except in conformity with the provisions of the law. The right of defense by the person himself or by proxy is guaranteed by law. An Egyptian shall not be deported from the country or banned from returning thereto. An Egyptian shall not be forbidden residence in any locality or forced to live in any specific place except in respect of conditions set forth by the law. The extradition of political refugees is prohibited. The sanctity of a home is inviolable nor can it be entered except in the circumstances [and manner] specified by law. . . .

"Freedom of belief is absolute, the state ensuring the free practice of religious rites, in conformity with establishing customs, provided such practice does not violate public order or morals. Freedom of opinion and of scientific research is guaranteed, every individual having the right to express his opinion and diffuse it by written, oral or any other means within the limits of the law. The freedom of the press, printing and publicity is guaranteed within the limits of the law. Egyptians have the right of assembly without giving advance notice provided they observe calm and carry no firearms.

"All Egyptians are entitled to education to be provided by the state. . . . The state shall exercise control over public education, to be regulated by law and to be free in all its stages in schools and universities. The state ensures Egyptians equitable treatment in accordance with the work they perform, fixes working hours and rates of wages, providing social insurance, health insurance, insurance against unemployment and leaves of absence. The establishment of professional and labor unions is a guaranteed right. . . . Medical care is a right to be enjoyed by all Egyptians, through state action by the establishment and expansion of all kinds of hospitals and sanatoria. . . . [Military service is] compulsory in conformity with the provisions of the law. . . . Voting is a right for all Egyptians in the manner specified by law. . . .

System of Government: Section I–Head of the State. The head of the state is the president of the republic and exercises his prerogatives in the manner prescribed in this constitution.

Section II–The Legislative Authority. The National Assembly is the authority which exercises the legislative authority in the manner prescribed in this constitution. It shall exercise control over the activities of the executive authority in the manner prescribed in this constitution. It shall be formed of members to be chosen by general secret elections. . . . The president of the republic has the right to appoint a number of members not exceeding 10. . . . At least half of the number of members of the National Assembly should be workers and farmers. . . . The term of the National Assembly shall be 5 years from the date of its first meeting. Elections for the renewal of the Assembly shall take place during the 60 days preceding the end of its term. . . . The president of the republic shall convene the National Assembly and terminate its session. The National Assembly shall be situated in the city of Cairo . . . [and shall] convene for its annual session before the 2d Thursday in November. . . . The ordinary session shall be 7 months at least. It cannot be terminated before approving the budget. The president of the republic shall convene the National Assembly to an extraordinary session in case of necessity or on a request to this effect signed by a majority of the members of the National Assembly. . . .

"It shall be the duty of the National Assembly to decide on the validity of the membership of its members. A Supreme Court to be appointed by law shall be concerned with making investigation into the authenticity of the protests submitted to the National Assembly upon the request of its speaker. The result of the investigation is to be submitted to the National Assembly for it to take a definite decision on the protest. . . . The sittings of National Assembly shall be open sittings. However, it will be possible to hold meetings *in camera* upon the request of the president of the republic, the government, the speaker of the Assembly, or 20 of the members of the National Assembly. . . .

"The National Assembly shall not take any decisions unless the meeting is attended by the majority of its members or in cases where no particular majority is required. The decisions shall be issued according to the absolute majority of those present. When votes are equal, the subject of the debate shall be considered as rejected. Every draft law shall be referred to one of the Assembly's committees for examination and submission of a report on it. No law shall be issued unless it is approved by the National Assembly. . . .

"The levying of general taxes, the amendment or the cancellation of such taxes, shall only be effected by means of a law. Nobody shall be exempted from paying taxes except in the cases indicated in the law.

No one shall be asked to pay additional taxes and duties except within the limits of the law.

"The government shall not conclude any agreement for loans and shall not commit itself to any project entailing the expenditure of state funds in a future year or years, without the approval of the National Assembly.

"The general budget estimates shall be submitted to the National Assembly at least 2 months prior to the end of the fiscal year for discussion and approval. . . . The National Assembly shall not make any amendment to the budget estimates except by the approval of the government. . . .

"After its appointment, the government shall submit its program to the National Assembly for approval. The National Assembly shall supervise the work performed by the government. The government and its members shall be held responsible for their work to the National Assembly. . . .

"The National Assembly shall have the right to withdraw confidence from the government or any of its members.

"The premier and the ministers shall have the right to address the National Assembly or its committees whenever they wish to do so. . . . The vote of any minister shall not be counted when any subject is put to the vote, unless the minister is a member. Every member of the National Assembly shall have the right to direct questions or interpellations to the premier or the ministers with regard to any question within their jurisdiction. The premier and the ministers must give answers to members' questions. Any interpellation shall be debated at least 7 days after the date of its submission except in urgent cases and with the agreement of the government. 2 members of the National Assembly shall have the right to ask for a debate on a general subject. . . . The premier shall have the right to ask the National Assembly for a vote of confidence in the government on the occasion of submitting his program, or on the occasion of submitting any government statement dealing with the general policy of the country. The premier shall have to submit the resignation of the government to the president of the republic in case the National Assembly withdraws confidence from it. If the National Assembly decides to withdraw confidence from any minister, he shall have to resign.

"The president of the republic shall have the right to dissolve the Assembly. Any decision in this respect shall call the electors to hold new elections within a maximum period of 60 days, and shall fix a date for the meeting of the new Assembly within the 10 days following the completion of the elections.

"With exception for the instance of *flagrante delicto*, no criminal action may be taken against any member of the Assembly, when it is in session, except with permission of the Assembly. . . . No action may be taken against members of the National Assembly for the views and opinions they express while carrying out their duties in the Assembly or in its committees. Membership can be withdrawn only by a decision of a 2/3 majority and at the request of 20 members if a member has lost the confidence of the Assembly or his civil status, has failed to carry out the duties of his membership, has lost the status of worker or farmer on the basis of which he was elected, or has not attended regularly the meetings of the National Assembly or its committees.

"No member of the National Assembly may at the same time assume a public position in the government or the units of local administration. . . . No member of the National Assembly may be appointed to an organization or a company during the term of his membership except in the cases defined by law. No member of the National Assembly, during the term of his membership, may buy or rent any state property or sell, lease or barter to the state any of his property.

"*Sub-Section I–President of the Republic.* . . . The person who is to be elected president of the Republic should be Egyptian of Egyptian parents, enjoying his civil and political rights and of an age not less than 35 calendar years. The National Assembly shall nominate the president of the republic and the nomination shall be submitted to the country for referendum. The referendum shall be held in the National Assembly for the position of the president of the republic upon the proposal of 1/3 of its members at least. The candidate obtaining a 2/3 majority of the members of the Assembly shall be introduced to the country for a referendum. Should no candidate obtain the majority referred to, the nomination is to be repeated after 2 days from the date of the first voting. The candidate shall be considered president of the republic by obtaining the absolute majority of those who cast their votes in the referendum. If the candidate has not obtained this majority another candidate is to be nominated by the Assembly and the same method is to be adopted in this respect.

"The term of the presidency is 6 calendar years beginning from the date of the announcement of the result of the referendum. . . .

"The law shall fix the salary of the president of the republic. . . . The president of the republic is not to receive any other salary or remuneration. During his term of presidency, the president of the republic shall not be allowed to exercise any liberal profession, any commercial, financial or industrial work, purchase or hire any state property, or rent, sell or barter such property to the state.

"The president of the republic shall have the right to appoint one or more vice presidents, and also to dismiss them.

"The measures for the election of a new president of the republic shall be started 60 days before the expiration of the term of the president of the republic. The election of the new president will have to be made at least a week before the expiration of the term of the president. If the term expires before the election of the new president for one reason or another, the former president shall continue to exercise the duties of his post until a successor is elected. If any temporary bar should prevent the president of the republic from exercising his duties, he shall delegate the vice president to assume his jurisdiction. In case of the resignation of the president, his permanent disability or death, the first vice president of the republic shall take over temporarily. The National Assembly, by the majority of ⅔ of its members, shall decide that the post of the president is vacant. The choice of the new president of the republic shall be completed within a maximum period of 60 days from the date when the post falls vacant. . . .

"Charging the president of the republic with high treason or disloyalty to the republican system shall be effected in accordance with a proposal submitted by at least ⅓ of the members of the National Assembly. The bill of indictment shall only be issued by the majority of votes of the members of the Assembly. The president shall cease to perform his duties immediately after the issuance of the bill of indictment. The first vice president of the republic shall take over temporarily. The president shall be referred for trial before a special court appointed by law. If he should be condemned, the president shall be dismissed without prejudice to other punishments.

"The president of the republic in collaboration with the government draws up the general policy of the state as regards all the political, economic, social and administrative aspects, and supervises its execution. The president appoints and relieves the premier of his office. The president also appoints and relieves cabinet ministers of their office. The same rules apply to the appointment of deputy premiers, ministers of state and deputy ministers. The president of the republic has the right to call for the meeting of the cabinet, to attend its meetings and preside over the meetings he attends. Also he has the right to ask for reports to be submitted by the government and cabinet ministers.

"The president of the republic has the right to suggest, issue and protest against laws. If the president of the republic objects to a bill, he returns it to the National Assembly within 30 days from the date of its notification to him. If the bill is not returned within that period, the bill is considered law and is promulgated. If the bill is returned to the Assembly within the above-mentioned period and is again supported by ⅔ of the members, it is considered law and is issued.

"If during the recess of the National Assembly or when it is dissolved anything happens that necessitates immediate action, the president of the republic is allowed to issue decisions having the force of law. These decisions must be submitted to the National Assembly within 15 days of their issue if the Assembly still stands; or at its first meeting if the Assembly has been dissolved. If these decisions are not submitted to the Assembly, they shall retroactively lose their power as law. . . . In the event of the decisions being submitted to and rejected by the Assembly, they shall lose their power as law. . . . The president of the republic, in exceptional circumstances, upon the mandate of the

National Assembly has the right to issue decisions having the force of law. The mandate should be for a limited period; the subjects and bases of these decisions have to be determined.

"The president of the republic issues all security regulations and the procedure for enforcing the laws. The president of the republic is *ex officio* the supreme commander of the armed forces. The president of the republic declares war after approval by the National Assembly. The president of the republic ratifies treaties and refers them to the National Assembly with any appropriate comment. They shall have the power of law after their adoption, ratification and publication in conformity with established usage. However, treaties of peace, alliance, trade, navigation, as well as all treaties involving modification in the territory of the state, relating to sovereignty rights or entailing financial expenditure not allocated by the state budget, shall not be valid if not adopted by the National Assembly.

"The president of the republic has the right to commute a penalty or reduce it; but a full pardon is not granted except by the issue of a law. . . . The president may order a plebiscite in order to consult the people on important issues involving the higher interests of the state. . . .

"*Sub-Section II–The Government.* The government consists of the premier, the deputy premiers and the ministers. The premier administers government affairs and presides at the meetings of the Council of Ministers. The government exercises the following functions: (1) Guiding, coordinating and revising the Ministers' work as well as that of the general organizations and authorities. (2) Issuing the administrative and executive decisions . . . and checking their implementation. (3) Preparing draft laws and resolutions. (4) Appointing and dismissing employes. . . . (5) Preparing the draft of the general budget of the state. (6) Preparing the draft of the state's general plan for the development of the national economy and taking all necessary measures to ensure its execution. (7) Supervising the organization and administration of the currency and credit systems, and of insurance operations. (8) Contracting and extending loans. . . . (9) Supervising all the general organizations. (10) Supervising the enforcement of laws, preserving the security of the state and protecting the rights of the citizens and the interests of the state.

"The government controls the work of the ministries, as well as that of the local and general departments and authorities. It has the right to cancel or modify decisions which prove to be unsuitable in the light of the law. The control and inspection authorities are directly responsible to the premier.

"Anyone who is to be appointed as minister must be an Egyptian who is at least 30 years of age and who enjoys all civil and political rights.

"The president and the National Assembly have the right to put a minister on trial for any offenses he may commit while conducting his duties. A National Assembly decision to level an accusation against a minister should be at the request of at least 5 members. The accusation decision is not to be passed unless it obtains the support of 2/3 of the Assembly's members. . . .

"*Sub-Section III–National Defense.* (a) *Council of National Defense:* A council shall be set up to be called Council of National Defense. The president of the republic shall assume its command. The Council of National Defense is concerned with considering affairs relating to the means of safeguarding the country and its safety. . . . (b) *The Armed Forces:* It is the state that raises the armed forces. No body or group is permitted to form any military or quasi-military formations.

"*Sub-Section IV–Local Administration.* The United Arab Republic is divided into administrative units. It is permissible for each or some of them to have corporate personality in compliance with the law.

"The bodies representing the administrative units participate in the implementation of the general plan of the state. They are entitled to establish and administer public utilities and economic, social and health projects as prescribed by the law.

"*The Judicial Authority:* Judges are independent, with no power above them in making judgments except the law. It is not permissible for any authority to interfere in cases or in the affairs of justice. The court sittings are public unless the court decides to make them closed in the interests of public order and morality.

"Judges are not subject to dismissal except as prescribed in the law. The law organizes the function and jurisdiction of the public prosecution and its relation with the judiciary. . . . The law organizes the arrangement of the state security courts, and determines their jurisdiction and the qualifications of those who sit in judgment in these courts.

"*General Provisions:* "The City of Cairo is the capital of the United Arab Republic. . . .

"The provisions of laws shall be applicable from the dates of their enforcement, and shall not be effective with respect to acts having taken place prior to these dates. However, in non-criminal provisions, laws may stipulate otherwise with the approval of the majority of the National Assembly members. Laws shall be published in the *Official Journal* within 2 weeks from the day of their promulgation.

"The president of the republic and the National Assembly shall have the power to demand the amendment of one or more articles of the constitution. . . . In the case of the demand for amendment being made by the National Assembly, it shall be signed by at least 1/3 of the members of the Assembly. In all cases, the Assembly shall debate the principle of the amendment, passing its decision by a majority of votes. If the demand is rejected, another demand for the amendment of the same articles may not be put forward before the lapse of one year following the rejection. If the National Assembly approves the principle of the amendment, it shall, after 2 months of the approval, debate the articles required to be amended. The amendment shall become effective if 2/3 of the members of the Assembly approve it. . . .

"*Transitional Provisions:* The term of office of the present president of the republic shall end on Mar. 26, 1971.

"The application of the provisional constitution issued on Mar. 5, 1958, and the constitutional declaration on the political organization of the higher authorities of the state, issued on Sept. 27, 1962, shall lapse."

Cypriot Seeks Nasser's Support

Nasser's prestige in the 3d world was enhanced by the alacrity with which he responded to a plea from Archbishop Makarios, president of Cyprus, for military support.

A Turkish threat of military intervention in the island republic of Cyprus had been carried out Aug. 7, 1964. Determined to protect the Turkish Cypriot minority involved in fresh communal fighting, Turkey sent military planes to bomb and strafe positions of the Greek Cypriots, who form the majority of the islanders. [See the Interim History book *Cyprus 1946–68.*] The air attacks killed at least 100 Greek Cypriots and wounded 200 before the aerial and ground fighting was halted by a UN Security Council cease-fire Aug. 9. Turkey had come under strong international pressure to cease its aerial operations there, and the Cypriot government had been subjected to similar demands to halt its military activities against the Turkish Cypriots. Prior to the outbreak of the fighting, new mediation efforts had been started in Geneva in July in a search of a political solution to the quarrel between Cyprus' 2 ethnic groups. The discussions were conducted by UN political mediator Sakari S. Tuomioja and were attended by Greek and Turkish representatives and by ex-State Secy. Dean Acheson as an informal U.S. observer.

Makarios warned Aug. 9 that Greek Cypriots would carry out full-scale attacks on Turkish Cypriot villages unless Turkey halted its air raids. Makarios said he had appealed for foreign medical aid for the air raid victims. He said he also had called on the USSR, Syria and the United Arab Republic for military assistance. In a reply by Nasser, made public by Nicosia Aug. 11, Nasser said the UAR was ready to give Cyprus all the help it needed. The Soviet Union promised Cyprus Aug. 15 that it would "defend" the island's "freedom and independence from a foreign invasion." In the Russian statement, published by Tass, Moscow said it was "prepared to begin negotiations on this matter right now." Soviet Premier Khrushchev charged Aug. 16 that Turkey's air attacks had been part of a U.S.-British "imperialist plot" aimed at the Cyprus government. Speaking at Frunze, Kirghizia, Khrushchev warned Turkey that the USSR could "not remain indifferent to the threat of an armed conflict" near the Soviet Union's southern frontier.

Makarios visited Nasser in Alexandria Aug. 29-31 to inform him of the critical Cyprus situation and to negotiate for possible military and political support. At the conclusion of the talks, Nasser declared in a communiqué Aug. 31 that the UAR would provide "all possible assistance to the Cyprus government's efforts to defend its country against foreign intervention." Nasser also pledged "support for Cyprus' "struggle" for "independence, territorial integrity and the right of self-determination." On his arrival, Makarios, accompanied by Foreign Min. Spyros A. Kyprianou, had said to Nasser in an airport statement that Turkey and "certain other countries, serving their own sinister interests, are trying to impose" an unfavorable solution on Cyprus. In his talks with Nasser Aug. 30, Makarios was quoted as having said that Greek Cypriots "want unity with Greece, not unity with NATO [the Western powers' North Atlantic Treaty Organization]." After the conclusion of the talks, Makarios said at a news conference Aug. 31: Cyprus did "not want to have any foreign bases"—"Greek bases, Turkish bases, British bases, NATO bases, any bases. We want Cyprus demilitarized." While in Egypt, Makarios implied that the U.S. and Britain were responsible for the Turkish air raids on Cyprus. A Cairo report said that Makarios, replying to a shout from an audience he was addressing in Alexandria that the raid was the work of "the Anglo-Americans," had said: "I do not wish to deny this." Kyprianou Sept. 2 repeated the charge that Turkey's air attacks had been carried out "with the tolerance" of the U.S. and Britain. Kyprianou said that the U.S. and Britain had refused "even after the events to condemn this barbarous attack on a noncombatant population."

Nasser Vs. Tshombé

Egypt and Nasser were hosts at a major conference of the Organization of African States July 17-21, 1964 when representatives of 34 African countries met in Cairo for the first Assembly of Heads of State & Government.

The troubled situation in the former Belgian Congo was a principal topic of concern—but not action—at this OAU meeting, which took place less than 2 weeks after Moïse Tshombé, from his exile in Spain July 5, had accepted appointment to the Congolese premiership. Many African leaders had opposed Tshombé on the ground that he had allegedly been in league with whites during his secessionist activities in the Congo's Katanga Province. Jon Woronoff wrote in 1970 in *Organizing African Unity*: "[Congolese] Pres. [Joseph] Kasavubu had been invited by the Egyptian government [to the OAU meeting], but there was a minor tempest when the delegates learned that he would be accompanied by Tshombé. Certain African leaders bitterly regretted . . . [Tshombé's] appointment as . . . [premier] and protested against his appearing at the Assembly. Although it would be quite normal for Tshombé to attend as head of government, there was considerable relief when he responded to the criticism by boycotting the conference." Kasavubu also cancelled his trip to Cairo.

In his welcoming address, Nasser July 17 urged the African leaders to bury their differences in order to achieve a "real spirit of understanding" and "constitutional unity." At the meeting, speakers and resolutions called for action against South African *apartheid*, the white Rhodesian government and Portuguese colonialism in Africa. Kwame Nkrumah of Ghana, who was said to share Nasser's ambitions for "3d-world" leadership, called again for the creation of a pan-African federal union.

Leaders of 47 neutralist nations and observers from 10 other nonaligned countries* met in Cairo Oct. 5-11, 1964 to discuss such world issues as the promotion of disarmament, peaceful coexistence, Western colonialism and the economic development of emerging nations. It was the 2d such meeting of neutralist nations; the first had been held in Belgrade in 1961. But the Cairo meeting was overshadowed by the conferees' refusal to permit Congolese Premier Tshombé to attend and a subsequent UAR-Congolese dispute that involved Tshombé's detention in Cairo for 3 days.

A majority of delegates of the nonaligned countries' political committee had agreed at a pre-conference meeting in Cairo Oct. 3 to a resolution barring Tshombé from parley. The move to deprive Tshombé of a conference seat had been initiated by Algerian Pres. Ahmed Ben Bella and Yugoslav Pres. Tito at a meeting Oct. 2 with UAR Pres. Nasser. In a message sent to Léopoldville Oct. 4, Nasser informed Congolese Pres. Kasavubu that the delegates believed Tshombé's presence at the conference would have an "undesirable effect." Nasser suggested that Kasavubu head his

---

*Participating members: Afghanistan, Algeria, Angola (rebel government in exile), Burma, Burundi, Cambodia, Cameroon, Ceylon, Chad, Congo (Brazzaville), Congo (Léopoldville), Cuba, Cyprus, Dahomey, Ethiopia, Ghana, Guinea, India, Indonesia, Iraq, Jordan, Kenya, Kuwait, Laos, Lebanon, Liberia, Libya, Malawi, Mali, Mauritania, Morocco, Nepal, Nigeria, Saudi Arabia, Northern Rhodesia, Senegal, Sierra Leone, Somalia, Sudan, Syria, Togo, Tunisia, Uganda, UAR, United Republic of Tanganyika & Zanzibar, Yemen and Yugoslavia. Observer nations: Argentina, Bolivia, Brazil, Chile, Finland, Jamaica, Mexico, Trinidad & Tobago, Uruguay and Venezuela.

country's delegation instead. (Nasser reportedly ignored Kasavubu's reply that only the Congo had the right to choose its representatives to the conference and that other countries had no right to interfere.)

Tshombé defied the ban against him and attempted Oct. 5 to land in Cairo by plane with a 50-member Congolese delegation. UAR authorities, however, refused to grant landing rights; they said the airport's runways were in bad condition (but the planes of other delegates landed on the runways without difficulty). Tshombé's plane was diverted to Athens. Tshombé and his staff then left Athens for Cairo aboard an Ethiopian airliner Oct. 6, and this time landing permission was granted. The Congolese premier was quartered in a palatial guest house, where he was placed under virtual detention to prevent his attending the conference. Troops and police surrounded the house, blocking Tshombé's departure. Tshombé managed to release to the press a statement in which he assailed the conference's decision to bar him. He said Nasser's message to Kasavubu "divided the Congolese government into 2 personalities." Tshombé said he was prepared "to leave Cairo immediately and return to the Congo."

In retaliation for Tshombé's detention, the Congolese government Oct. 6 sealed off the UAR and Algerian embassies in Léopoldville. Troops surrounded the 2 buildings and prevented the embassy staffs from leaving. In a counteraction, the UAR Oct. 7 barred Tshombé from leaving Cairo until the Congolese government lifted its blockade of the UAR and Algerian embassies. 28 African delegates to the conference wired Kasavubu to protest the restrictions against the 2 embassies. In a letter to the conference delegates, Tshombé denounced his detention, charging that since his arrival "we were forbidden all movement, forbidden telephones and cut off all contact with the outside world."

The UAR-Congo dispute was resolved Oct. 8 with the Congo lifting restrictions against the UAR and Algerian embassies and Nasser permitting Tshombé to leave the UAR. Tshombé, by phone to his cabinet, ordered the release of UAR Amb. Mostafa Kamel and Algerian Amb. Abdel Hamid Hadjali and their staffs and permitted them to go across the Congo River to Brazzaville, capital of the Congo Republic. Both ambassadors said in Brazzaville Oct. 10 that their departure from the Congo meant that diplomatic relations between their countries and the Congo had been suspended, not broken.

Tshombé left Cairo Oct. 9 and flew to Paris. Assailing the actions taken against him by the Nasser government, Tshombé charged that the UAR "wants a weak and chaotic Congo," not "a strong Congo which might diminish Nasser's chance for leadership." Nasser, Tshombé asserted, sought "to dominate the African continent." Tshombé charged that Nasser had ordered his detention in the hope of provoking the Congo into severing diplomatic relations with the UAR "so that he could recognize the [Congolese] rebel regime in Stanleyville," capital of the country's Eastern Province. (The rebels were led by ex-Vice Premier Christophe Gbenye, founder and head of the National Liberation Committee and a follower of the late Premier Patrice Lumumba.)

Tshombé returned to Léopoldville Oct. 13 and received a tumultuous welcome by thousands of Congolese. Hundreds of persons carried placards denouncing Nasser, Ben Bella, the Arabs and Ghanian Pres. Kwame Nkrumah. Ben Bella and Nkrumah had tacitly supported the Congolese rebels. Tshombé charged in a Léopoldville speech Oct. 17 that the UAR, Algeria and Mali had plotted to kill Congolese leaders by means of assassins from the neighboring Congo Republic. Speaking to 50,000 persons at the city's football stadium, Tshombé said the plot had been arranged by UAR Pres. Nasser, Algerian Pres. Ben Bella and Malian Pres. Modibo Keita at a meeting in Cairo following the conference of non-aligned countries. Because of this, Tshombé demanded that "all Egyptians and Algerian citizens . . . leave the Congo as soon as possible." Tshombé then modified the expulsion order to exempt the nationals of those 2 countries who worked in the Congo with the UN and other international organizations.

In a radio appeal to 5 other African states Oct. 28, the Congolese rebel leader Christophe Gbenye said that he would "adopt a scorched earth policy, and thus the Americans and Belgians will find only a desert," if the African states did not help the rebels counter U.S. and Belgian "bombardments"—apparently a reference confusing the counterinsurgent activities of white mercenaries with U.S. and Belgian airborne rescue missions. Gbenye's "final appeal, in the name of Lumumba," was directed to Presidents Nasser of the UAR, Ben Bella of Algeria, Sékou Touré of Guinea, Modibo Keita of Mali and Kwame Nkrumah of Ghana. Tshombé charged that since the Congo's independence, the UAR, Algeria, Communist China "and other countries have never stopped encouraging disorder and provoking anarchy in the Congo." "These countries," he asserted, "bear responsibility for thefts, rapes and massacres committed by outlaws."

It was reported from Cairo Dec. 6 that the USSR had agreed to finance and supply a UAR-Algerian military airlift to the Congolese rebels. Algerian and Egyptian Soviet-built AN-12 turbojet military transports were said to be flying USSR-made arms and ammunition from Algeria and the UAR to the Congolese insurgents via the Sudan. Ghana was also reported to be shipping arms to the rebels by this route. The arms airlift was said to have been negotiated the previous week at a meeting in Cairo of Soviet Amb.-to-UAR Vladimir Y. Yerofeyev and Gaston Soumialot, the rebels' defense minister. Soumialot also was said to have conferred with UAR Pres. Nasser and with Algerian Pres. Ben Bella in Algiers. Under the agreement, the Soviet Union was to replace the Algerian and UAR arms sent to the rebels. The Sudanese government was said to have granted Soumialot's request that the Algerian and UAR planes be permitted to land the supplies at airfields in Khartoum and in Juba, near the Congolese border. It was believed that the equipment was then transshipped by truck from Juba to the insurgent stronghold of Aba in the Congo, 128 miles to the south. Despite a denial Dec. 5 by Sudanese Foreign Min. Muhammad Mahgoub, at least 12 Algerian and UAR transport planes carrying supplies for the rebels were said to have landed in Khartoum since Soumialot's visit to Cairo. Tshombé Dec. 7 reiterated charges that Algeria, the UAR and the Sudan were aiding the rebels. Tshombé said his government had filed a complaint to that effect with the UN Security Council.

Nasser Dec. 23 admitted for the first time that his government was shipping military equipment to the Congolese rebels. In a speech in Port Said, Nasser said: "Our policy is clear and we say it openly. We say that we sent arms to the Congolese people, and we shall keep sending arms to the Congo."

An estimated 300 million tons of military equipment, supplied largely by Algeria and the UAR, were funneled through the Sudan to the Congolese rebels between Nov. 1964 and mid-Jan. 1965. (A report from Léopoldville Jan. 30, 1965 said that the Sudan had barred the use of its territory for the transshipment of arms to the Congolese rebels for fear that the equipment would be captured by Sudanese insurgents in the south. Most of the Sudanese rebels were Azande tribe members opposed to the Congolese rebels. The Azandes, many of whom also lived in the northeastern Congo bordering the Sudan, reportedly were angered at the Congolese rebel practice of turning oppositionist southern Sudanese refugees over to Khartoum in exchange for weapons.)

The UAR Jan. 30, 1965 ordered the closing of the Congolese embassy in Cairo and directed the 3-member mission to leave the country. The embassy staff members, including Chargé d'Affaires René Bavassa, left for Léopoldville Feb. 3. UAR officials said that the ouster did not constitute a break in UAR-Congolese diplomatic relations but only a severance in ties with Tshombé's government.

U.S.-UAR Friction

Important segements of public opinion in the U.S. were reported to have become increasingly indignant at the employment of German scientists, several of them ex-Nazis, on military projects in Egypt. At least some of this U.S. opposition to the actions of the UAR was attributed by some sources to the influence of the American Jewish community. There was an increasing demand in the U.S. for the withdrawal of economic aid to Egypt unless the German scientists left UAR soil.

A crowd of about 200 people, mostly Africans and including some Egyptians, attacked the U.S. embassy in Cairo Nov. 26, 1964 and burned both the U.S. Information Service's John F. Kennedy Memorial Library in the embassy compound and the Marine guards' building. The incident took place during a protest–one of several in African and east European capitals–against a U.S.-Belgian rescue mission begun Nov. 24 to recover white hostages from Congolese rebel strongholds. The demonstrators attempted unsuccessfully to break into the embassy building. Police said they had seized 41 demonstrators. U.S. Amb. Lucius D. Battle protested to the UAR government and demanded compensation for damage. Deputy Premier (for foreign affairs) Mahmoud Fawzi, after delaying for 2 days, apologized to Battle Nov. 28 and agreed in principle to negotiate on restitution.

U.S.-UAR relations were strained further after a U.S. oil company plane was shot down Dec. 19 by 2 UAR air force jet planes 30 miles south of Alexandria. The plane's U.S. pilot and Swedish copilot were killed. The aircraft, a 2-seater propeller-driven Fairchild, was owned by the John W. Mecom Oil Co. of Houston, Tex. It was on a routine flight from Amman, Jordan to Benghazi, Libya.

Cairo authorities contended Dec. 20 that the plane did not have clearance to fly over UAR territory. They claimed that the plane had been shot down only after it had ignored ground instructions and warning shots by the Egyptian jets to land. But a company official insisted Dec. 20 that the plane had advance clearance for the flight. The U.S. State Department Dec. 22 disclosed information from the Jordanian Civil Air Authority that supported the company's contention.

U.S. Amb. Battle Dec. 24 delivered on oral protest to UAR Deputy Premier Fawzi. A UAR Foreign Ministry communiqué issued after the meeting said the UAR "denied any responsibility" for the plane attack. The communiqué said Fawzi had told Battle that the "UAR used its legitimate rights and fulfilled its duty for the security of the nation and therefore we cannot accept this protest."

U.S. expressions of displeasure over the plane incident and Washington's previous criticism of the mob assault on the U.S. embassy in Cairo Nov. 26 had prompted UAR Pres. Nasser Dec. 23 to deliver a general attack on U.S. foreign policy. In a speech at Port Said marking the 8th anniversary of the Suez invasion, Nasser said that Battle had discussed the plane incident with a UAR official Dec. 22 but "was so upset over Egyptian conduct, he stayed only 2 minutes." If Battle did not approve of UAR behavior, Nasser said, he could "drink from the sea [Egyptian slang equivalent to 'jump in the lake']." (In this speech, Nasser upheld his government's support of the Congolese rebels.)

In Sept. 1964 Cairo had asked the U.S. for $35 million worth of corn, meat and chicken to alleviate a food shortage. Prior to Nasser's speech Battle had informed the UAR supply minister that it would be inappropriate to discuss the request in view of the shooting down of the U.S. plane. According to a report from Washington Dec. 28, U.S. officials, angered at Nasser's anti-American stand, had decided to delay consideration of the grant of food until 1965. The U.S. House of Representatives Jan. 26, 1965 approved an amendment, proposed by Rep. Robert H. Michel (R., Ill.), to bar any use of the funds to finance food exports to the UAR. Supporters of the ban cited such incidents as the burning of the U.S. library in Cairo, the downing of the U.S. plane and Nasser's speech. (The U.S. State Department announced June 22, 1965 the Presidential reauthorization of surplus food shipment to the UAR under a contract due to expire June 30. The announcement said that there had been "a definite improvement" in U.S. relations with the UAR and that the UAR had promised compensation for the burning of the library. The Administration action was assailed by Sen. Jacob K. Javits [R., N.Y.] in a speech before the Zionist Organization of America in New York July 1. Javits said the UAR was getting U.S. wheat "at bargain prices and then selling their rice to Communist countries" and was thus enabled to get Communist arms. The Soviet Union June 26 announced the diversion of an Australian wheat shipment from Russia to Cairo, an action hailed by the Egyptian press as a rescue from U.S. "imperialist pressures." UAR wheat stocks reportedly had dwindled to about a 3 weeks' supply.)

Cairo-Bonn-Pankow-Jerusalem Dispute

The UAR and 9 other Arab countries broke off diplomatic relations with West Germany in mid-May 1965–2 months after West Germany and Israel had agreed to establish diplomatic relations. The Arab move came as the climax of a series of developments that arose from a deterioration in relations between the UAR and West Germany. Animosity had begun to grow between the 2 countries after it became known that West Germany, for some time, had been sending arms to Israel. Events had assumed the aspect to Egyptian leaders of a deliberate West German change in course when the Bonn government stated late in Oct. 1964 that the more than 300 West German experts employed in the UAR's armaments industry were there without their government's permission or approval.

A distinct dispute erupted between the UAR and West Germany with the announcement by Cairo that East-German Chief of State Walter Ulbricht had been invited to visit the UAR Feb. 24, 1965. West German Amb.-to-UAR Georg Federer, meeting with UAR Pres. Nasser Jan. 31, expressed "serious concern" over Ulbricht's projected visit. Nasser then restated the UAR's intention to invite Ulbricht but assured Federer that "no decision to recognize East Germany is now before me." But Nasser repeated the warning that his government would recognize East Germany if West German arms shipments to Israel did not cease. West Germany recalled Federer to Bonn Feb. 1 to report on the situation.

West German press chief Karl-Günther von Hase warned at a news conference Feb. 1 that "if Ulbricht, the arch-enemy of German unity and a satellite of Moscow, goes to Cairo, one must expect that far-reaching changes" in Bonn-Cairo relations "would follow."

The Marquis de Nerva, a Spanish Foreign Ministry official, with Bonn's and Cairo's consent, started mediation efforts Feb. 5 in an effort to prevent a break in UAR-West German ties. De Nerva announced Feb. 10 that under a compromise plan, Bonn had agreed to stop sending arms to Israel and Cairo had "reciprocated with several good-will gestures" to West Germany. De Nerva filed his mediation report with the West German Foreign Ministry Feb. 12, and von Hase announced the same day that de Nerva's mediation services were "over."

West German Chancellor Ludwig Erhard confirmed Feb. 12 that his government had suspended arms shipments to Israel. The suspension followed a fresh UAR warning Feb. 7 and 8 that Cairo would end diplomatic relations with West Germany and recognize East Germany if Bonn continued its arms deliveries to Israel. By this time West Germany reportedly had fulfilled about 80% of an $80 million military aid program it had contracted with Israel; the arms shipments had started in Oct. 1964.

West German Foreign Min. Gerhard Schröder warned the UAR ambassador in Bonn Feb. 15 that if Cairo did not withdraw its invitation to Ulbricht, West Germany would cut off economic aid to the UAR (about $190 million worth had already been given) and "reappraise" its diplomatic relations with Cairo. A government spokesman said West Germany might also enlist its industrialists in an economic boycott of the UAR.

The Israeli Knesset (parliament) Feb. 15 approved by 54-26 vote a parliamentary statement made earlier by Premier Levi Eshkol on the West German arms suspension. In opening debate on Israeli-West German relations, Eshkol described the arms delivery halt as Bonn's "surrender to blackmail" by the UAR. Eshkol insisted that West Germany "continue to observe its obligation to Israel in the spirit and the letter." "Germany's duty," he said, "is to help Israel with the equipment necessary for her security." Eshkol rejected West German offers of financial assistance to compensate for "the cancellation of the promised security aid."

In parliamentary debate on West Germany's Middle East policy, Chancellor Erhard said Feb. 17 that Nasser's invitation to Ulbricht was "a hostile act." Accusing Nasser of "meddling" with West Germany's vital interests, Erhard said the Egyptian leader associated himself "with those who divide the German state." Erhard made it clear that his régime would adhere to the "Hallstein doctrine," which provided for the severance of diplomatic relations with any country that recognized East Germany, with the exception of the Soviet Union. In reply to Erhard, Nasser Feb. 18 spurned West German assistance. Speaking at Aswan, Nasser said: "We can build our own future with our sweat, with our blood if necessary and with our own money. . . . There are other sources where we can get loans." Ulbricht's visit "ultimately has to do with Egypt's independent policy, and nobody can dictate our policy." In a Feb. 27 interview with Mrs. Katharine Graham (president of the Washington Post Co.) and *Newsweek* editor Osborn Elliott, Nasser warned that West Germany "would be punishing herself, not us," if it "stopped any contract she signed with us." In the interview, published by the Cairo newspaper *Al Ahram* Mar. 2, Nasser said that West German failure to ship any items it had agreed to ship would be "considered a breach" of contracts and would relieve the UAR of the need to "stick to our commitments" to repay West Germany the £40 million ($112 million) the UAR owed it. He added that the UAR also had arrangements, which he implied also would not be fulfilled, to pay in sterling £30 million owed to West Germany as a result of the UAR-Bonn trade balance surplus in favor of West Germany.

Ulbricht arrived in Alexandria Feb. 24, and West Germany halted all economic aid to the UAR the same day. Bonn's aid cut-off included the stoppage of additional expenditures under current programs and the withdrawal of government underwriting of capital export projects. (The U.S. State Department said Feb. 24 that it also opposed Ulbricht's visit to Cairo "for the good reason that we support the Federal Republic of Germany as the representative of the German people.")

In a welcoming speech for Ulbricht at a Cairo banquet, Nasser had said Feb. 24 that Egyptians "know how to appreciate our friends and to express our appreciation." As for UAR relations with West Germany, Nasser said his government was "still exerting . . . maximum . . . efforts so that matters do not deteriorate any further." Nasser attributed the strained Bonn-Cairo ties to a "stab in the back"—West Germany's (since-suspended) arms agreement with Israel. Nasser and Ulbricht held held their first formal talks Feb. 25. Subjects discussed included Israel and Cairo's relations with East and West Germany. (In a National Assembly speech following his talks with Ulbricht, Nasser restated his régime's opposition to communism. He said: "Our differences with communism are radical. We believe in religion and we reject the dictatorship of any class. . . . We do not liquidate any class by use of violence. But we do liquidate privileges enjoyed by any class.")

While Ulbricht was touring the Egyptian countryside Mar. 1, a 3-part $100 million aid agreement was formally signed in Cairo by East German Foreign Min. Lothar Bolz and UAR Deputy Premier (for industry and mining) Aziz Sidky. (The pact had first been initialed Jan. 31.) The agreement provided for (a) a $70 million East German long-term credit to finance Cairo's 2d 5-year plan (the loan originally had been for $47,600,000, but Ulbricht had agreed Feb. 28, at a meeting with Nasser, to expand it); (b) a $30,800,000 short-term industrial credit from East German trade organizations (guaranteed by the East German government); and (c) an East German-Egyptian scientific and technical cooperation exchange.

A joint East German-UAR communiqué Mar. 1 based on the Ulbricht-Nasser talks: (a) pledged closer economic relations between the 2 countries; (b) announced the acceptance by Nasser of an invitation to visit East Germany; (c) condemned the "aggressive schemes of imperialism, which created Israel to serve its end as a spearhead directed against the rights of the Arab people and their struggle for liberation and progress."

In a departing statement in Port Said Mar. 2 Ulbricht assailed West Germany's policies toward the Arab states and condemned the presence of U.S., British and French troops in West Berlin.

Bonn had been unwilling to see its relations with the Arab world jeopardized further without some public confirmation of its private contention to Arab diplomats that it had supplied arms to Israel under diplomatic pressures analogous to constraint. The U.S., Feb. 17, 1965, therefore, admitted openly for the first time that it had approved in advance West German shipment of U.S.-made M-48 tanks to Israel in 1964. Unofficial sources said the U.S. actually had persuaded Bonn to make the shipments. The tanks were sent under the $80 million Bonn-Jerusalem arms pact that West Germany had canceled earlier in February under UAR pressure. State Department spokesman Robert J. McCloskey said the U.S. had not been consulted by Bonn about the arms delivery halt. But he said the U.S. "would give sympathetic consideration" to any West German request "for our good offices" in mediating "in their behalf in the Middle East" in Bonn's dispute with the UAR.

West German press chief Karl-Günther von Hase said Feb. 19 that the reluctant U.S. statement of support for Bonn "was only gradually wrung out of the American government." Von Hase deplored a decision by some U.S. businessmen to boycott West German goods in protest against Bonn's withdrawal of military aid to Israel. "So forceful a reaction," he said, "is all the more disappointing when it is recalled that respect for public opinion in America was a factor in the Federal Republic's long and continuing concern for good relations with Israel." These 3 U.S. firms had instituted the boycott: Botany Industries, Inc. (textiles); Phillips-Van Heusen Corp. (shirts); Philip Rothenberg & Co. (men's wear). Phillips-Van Heusen Executive Vice Pres. Lawrence Phillips said Feb. 12 that his firm had canceled all orders for German piece goods, finished goods and machinery. Philip Rothenberg Pres. Harvey Rothenberg disclosed Feb. 12 that his company had canceled more than $50,000 worth of orders for cotton flannels from 2 West German firms. Botany Pres. Michael Daroff said Feb. 16 that his company's buyers had been told not to buy West German sportswear.

A State Department statement Feb. 18 criticized the boycott. It said: "As a matter of principle, we do not favor private boycotts as a measure of retaliation. This policy applies no matter what the reason or inspiration for such a boycott." West German Amb. Heinrich Knappstein expressed his government's concern over the boycott at a meeting with State Secy. Dean Rusk Feb. 18.

State Secy. Rusk explained at a news conference Feb. 25

that the U.S. had encouraged West German arms shipments to Israel and approved the sending of the U.S.-made tanks there in line with Washington's Middle East policy of maintaining a military balance between Israel and the Arab states. Rusk also supported Bonn's opposition to the visit to Cairo of East German Pres. Ulbricht. Rusk said: The U.S. does "not look with favor upon any action that would seem to reinforce the division of Germany or to undermine the authority of the Bonn government as spokesman for all the German people in international affairs."

U.S. Amb.-at-Large W. Averell Harriman discussed the deteriorating Middle East situation with Israeli officials in Jerusalem Feb. 25–Mar. 1. No communiqué was issued at the end of the talks, and the exact nature of the discussions was not disclosed. Among those who conferred with Harriman were Premier Levi Eshkol and Foreign Min. Golda Meir.

The UAR Feb. 27 announced the arrest of 4 West Germans as members of a spy ring. They were charged Mar. 4 with spying for Israel and conducting a terrorist campaign against West German rocket and aircraft experts in the UAR. Johann Wolfgang Sigmund Lotz, alleged ex-Nazi, was named as the leader of the spy ring. He and his wife were arrested Feb. 22. The other defendants were Franz William Kiesow and his Egyptian wife, Nadya Muhammad Hamdy.

After a 4-day West German cabinet debate on the government's Middle Eastern policy, Chancellor Erhard decided Mar. 7, 1965 to establish diplomatic relations with Israel. (West Germany had agreed late in 1952 to pay Israel 3 billion Deutschmark [$715 million] worth of goods and services as reparations for Nazi crimes against Jews, and Israel in late Dec. 1957 had sent Shimon Peres of the Israeli Defense Ministry to Bonn on an unsuccessful arms-purchasing mission. Before Mar. 1965, however, the 2 countries had maintained no formal diplomatic missions in each other's capitals. Currently, Israel's only formal contact with West Germany was a trade mission that had been established in Cologne in

1955 to buy German products with West German restitution payments.) A West German government statement Mar. 7 included the declaration that Bonn's move was "directed against no Arab state." It warned that the government would tolerate no interference by any party to the middle east dispute in an effort to influence Bonn's policy, "particularly with respect to the formation of relations with Israel." The announcement said East German Chief of State Ulbricht's visit to Cairo had been properly "answered" by Bonn's halting of economic aid to the UAR. The statement warned Cairo that "an upgrading of this terror régime [East Germany] will be regarded by" West Germany "as an unfriendly act and answered in each case by appropriate measures."

When he started the cabinet discussions Mar. 4, Erhard reportedly had been determined to sever diplomatic relations with the UAR in retaliation for the Ulbricht visit. But the chancellor was said to have changed his mind after being cautioned against such action in a meeting Mar. 5 with the U.S., British and French ambassadors. U.S. Amb. George C. McGhee, supported by Sir Frank Roberts of Britain and Roger Seydoux of France, was said to have warned Erhard that Bonn's ending of ties with Cairo would hasten a military clash between Israel and the Arab states. Erhard's initial position was said to have been backed by about 6 cabinet ministers. A more moderate stand was advocated by Foreign Min. Gerhard Schröder and 4 or 5 other ministers. Schröder was said to have argued that if Bonn ended relations with the UAR, at least 5 Arab states would join Cairo in recognizing East Germany.

Preliminary talks on the proposed Israeli-West German relations were held in Jerusalem Mar. 8-10 by Israeli Premier Levi Eshkol and Kurt Birrenbach, a member of the West German Bundestag's foreign affairs committee acting as Erhard's personal representative.

10 of the 13 Arab League foreign ministers, spurred by

Nasser, voted in Cairo Mar. 15 to sever diplomatic relations with West Germany if it recognized Israel. As a warning to Bonn, the league countries ordered the immediate withdrawal of their ambassadors from the West German capital. (These league states were no longer to be represented in Bonn and were to sever their relations either through ambassadorial recalls or formal withdrawals: the UAR, the Sudan, Saudi Arabia, Morocco, Iraq, Syria and Yemen.) The representatives of 3 league members–Morocco, Tunisia and Libya–reserved decision on severing relations pending the approval of their heads of state. The action had previously been approved at a meeting of lesser Arab League delegates in Cairo Mar. 9. The ministers failed to reach agreement on 2 other UAR-sponsored proposals, and these were not mentioned in the final announcement. In the debate, which had started Mar. 14, only Yemen and Iraq were said to have favored Nasser's suggestion of severing economic relations with West Germany. The 2d Nasser proposal, calling for recognition of East Germany, was supported only by Algeria, Kuwait, the Sudan, Iraq and Yemen.

Nasser had made these proposals Mar. 10 in a speech in Shibin el-Kom, 50 miles north of Cairo. In addition to threatening to recognize East Germany, Nasser also said Mar. 10 that the UAR would "seize all German property and German schools, and we shall put all German funds under sequestration" if Bonn established diplomatic relations with Israel. Asserting that "30% of West Germany's trade is with Arab countries," Nasser declared that "if we boycott West Germany economically, we shall deprive her of 30% of her trade." (According to a Bonn spokesman, Arab states accounted for only 3% of all West German exports and only 1.8% of the total West German trade.)

The West German decision to establish diplomatic relations with Israel provoked anti-German riots in Iraq and Lebanon Mar. 16 and in Yemen Mar. 17.

The Israeli Knesset Mar. 16, by 66-29 vote (10 abstentions), had approved a Mar. 14 cabinet decision to accept the West German offer of diplomatic relations. The 29 Knesset members who voted against diplomatic ties with Bonn were members of the Mapam (left-wing), Herut (right-wing) and Communist parties. In the parliamentary debate prior to the vote, Premier Eshkol had argued that "in the balance of emotion and reason," the need to strengthen Israel's security "must tip the scale" in favor of reason. Opposing ties with West Germany, Herut leader Menahem Begin recalled that the Nazis had "destroyed 1/3 of your people." "The least you can do," he said "is not to be friendly with the German generation of the destruction." 16 Israeli cabinet members had supported diplomatic relations with Bonn at a cabinet meeting Mar. 14, and 2 ministers reserved decision.

Israeli authorities had denied reports from Bonn that Israel's acceptance of the West German offer to exchange envoys was preconditioned on German agreement to certain demands, regarded as unacceptable by Chancellor Erhard's government. The demands were said to include the completion of West German arms shipments to Israel, suspended because of UAR pressure, and a German guarantee of Israel's security. A government spokesman said after the Mar. 14 cabinet meeting that Eshkol had told his ministers that he had "grounds to assume" that "an agreement" would be reached with Bonn on "controversial" matters. The other questions regarded as a source of German-Israeli friction were the presence of West German scientists in the UAR and the proposed extension of the statute of limitations to permit Bonn to prosecute Nazi war criminals.

Israel's agreement to the appointment of Dr. Rolf Pauls, 50, as West German ambassador to Jerusalem and Bonn's approval of the designation of Ascher Ben-Nathan as Israeli ambassador to West Germany were disclosed July 7 by the West German Foreign Ministry.

Nasser Reelected President, Mohieddin Becomes Premier

Gamal Abdel Nasser was reelected Mar. 16, 1965 to another 6-year term as president of the United Arab Republic. Nasser, the only candidate, received 6,950,652 votes: 65 ballots were cast against him, and 479 were voided.

Ali Sabry resigned Sept. 29, 1965 as UAR premier. Zakaria Mohieddin, a UAR vice president, formed a new cabinet Oct. 3. He took the post of interior minister as well as premier. Sabry was appointed a vice president and designated secretary general of the Arab Socialist Union, the nation's only political party.

The new cabinet: *Deputy Premier for Foreign Affairs*—Dr. Mahmoud Fawzi (a holdover from the Sabry cabinet); *Foreign Affairs*—Mahmoud Riad (another holdover); *Deputy Premier for Economic Affairs*—Abdel Moneim el-Kaissuni; *Economy*—Muhammad Labib Shukeir; *Deputy Premier for National Guidance*—Abdel Kader Halem; *Health*—Muhammad el-Nabawi el-Mohandes; *Labor*—Anwar Salamaa; *War*—Abdel Wahab el-Bishry; *Education*—Muhammed Youssef; *Youth*—Talaat Khairy; *Justice*—Issameddin Hassouna.

Decrees issued July 14 by Premier Sabry had ended the installment buying of cars, TV sets, refrigerators and other household supplies and had raised prices on such items by 20%. The decrees were part of a government drive to discourage consumer spending in favor of savings. The UAR's cost of living index was reported to have risen by 14% in the period Feb. 1964–Feb. 1965. Retail prices were said to have gone up by 30% in the past 2 years.

Nasser Seeks Stronger Foreign Ties

At least partly in response to the Vietnam War, Nasser devoted considerable effort in early 1965 to solidifying his ties with leaders of the so-called "nonaligned" or "3d-world" countries. These efforts included UAR attendance at the

10th Anniversary Bandung Conference in Jakarta Apr. 17-25, 2 meetings with Yugoslav Pres. Tito, and a conference with Guinean Pres. Sêkou Touré. Nasser also visited the Soviet Union in late August. Nasser lost an ally, however, when Algerian Pres. Ahmed Ben Bella was deposed.

The UAR was among the states rejecting the idea enunciated by Indonesian Pres. Sukarno at the Bandung anniversary conference Apr. 17 that nonalignment was outdated. Sukarno declared that there could be no coexistence in the world until its "Old Established Forces" had been crushed and its "New Emerging Forces," surviving such a development, could rearrange the international order. (The only states supporting Sukarno in this view were Communist China, North Korea and North Vietnam.)

UAR and Communist Chinese representatives in Cairo Jan. 13 had signed an agreement providing for an exchange of scientists and students and a joint scientific board to coordinate mutual research exchanges. It was reported in Cairo Jan. 31 that the UAR had accepted a Chinese request to represent Peking's interests in Burundi.

Charles de Gaulle's French government, whose policies were increasingly tending toward nonalignment and closer contacts with the 3d world, agreed to assist Egypt in its economic development. (France and the UAR had reestablished diplomatic relations Apr. 4, 1963.) A communiqué issued in Cairo Mar. 7, 1965, after 8 days of talks between Egyptian officials and a French economic delegation, disclosed that France had become the first major Western power to pledge aid for the UAR's 2d 5-year plan. A trade protocol was signed under which Paris would "furnish equipment" (reported to include fishing equipment but not industrial equipment) to Cairo, promote the UAR's development plan, buy Egyptian farm products and sell corn to the UAR.

Exiled Congolese rebel leaders were reported Apr. 26 to have formed a 20-member Supreme Council of Revolution in Cairo. The new body was established earlier in April at a meeting in Cairo of what a council spokesman described as "all fighting forces of the Congo." The council was designed to broaden the base of the rebel regime under the leadership of Pres. Christophe Gbenye. The council president was Gaston-Emile Soumialot, who had relinquished his post as rebel defense minister. But the UAR had been reported Apr. 23 to have ended all military assistance to the rebels for fear that its aid weapons would be captured by Congolese government troops.

Nasser and Tito called Apr. 30 for a halt in U.S. air raids on North Vietnam and immediate negotiations "between the parties concerned" to end the Vietnam fighting. The appeal was made in a joint communiqué issued at the conclusion of talks held by the 2 leaders in Cairo Apr. 26-30. Tito and Nasser also condemned "the imperialist powers" for "stepping up the arming of Israel."

UAR First Vice Pres. Abdel Hakim Amer conferred with the new Algerian leaders in Algiers June 20-21. The Cairo newspaper *Al Goumhouria* said June 21 that Nasser had sent Amer to Algiers in an appeal against the possible execution of ex-Algerian Pres. Ben Bella. Ben Bella, 48, had been deposed and arrested in a bloodless *coup d'ètat* staged in Algiers June 19 by the National Liberation Army. The coup was led by Col. Houari Boumedienne, 40, defense minister and vice president.

A new plea for a halt in the U.S. air attacks on North Vietnamese targets and an all-out drive for peace was urged in a communiqué issued Aug. 6 by Nasser and Guinean Pres. Touré. The joint statement was issued at the end of a 2-day visit by Touré to Cairo following similar state visits to the USSR and Yugoslavia.

Nasser visited Moscow Aug. 27-Sept. 1 and conferred with Soviet Communist Party First Secy. Leonid I. Brezhnev, Premier Aleksei N. Kosygin, Pres. Anastas Mikoyan, Foreign Min. Andrei A. Gromyko and Defense Min. Marshall Rodion Y. Malinovsky. It was Nasser's first trip to the USSR in 7 years and his first meeting with the Soviet leadership that had deposed Nikita S. Khrushchev in 1964. In a final communiqué, released in Moscow Sept. 1, Nasser and the Soviet leaders called for the immediate end of the U.S. bombing of North Vietnam, appealed for steps to prevent the spread of nuclear weapons and announced UAR support for Soviet participation in the next conference of Afro-Asian states, scheduled for Nov. 5 in Algiers. (Communist China opposed Soviet participation in the conference.)

At a Kremlin reception Aug. 27 Nasser had charged the U.S. with "aggression [in North Vietnam] that arouses the indignation of world opinion...." Mikoyan said after an Aug. 28 meeting with Nasser: "We highly appreciate the UAR policy aimed at uniting all anti-imperialistic forces, ... for the struggle against aggressive actions of imperialism and colonialism."

Tass, the Soviet press agency, reported Aug. 30 that the USSR and the UAR had signed a contract under which the Soviets would supply equipment for a high-tension electricity line from the Aswan High Dam to Cairo. The transmission line, Tass said, would carry most of the power produced by the dam after its completion in 1967. (The Cairo newspaper *Al-Ahram* had reported June 25 that the USSR had agreed to send the UAR 300,000 tons of wheat. Kosygin was said to have informed Nasser of the Russian decision in a note delivered June 24.)

Nasser left Moscow and arrived in Belgrade Sept. 1 for fresh talks with Tito. They conferred Sept. 2 and issued a joint appeal to India and Pakistan Sept. 3 for a cease-fire in their fighting over Kashmir. The 2 heads of state offered their good offices in mediating the dispute.

Although Nasser joined with 3d-world and foreign Communist leaders in frequent denunciations of Western "imperialism," he appeared to stop short of equating anti-imperialism with communism in the UAR. The dissolution of the Egyptian Communist Party had been announced Apr. 25

in a communiqué issued by the party's Central Committee and published in the semi-official *Al-Ahram.* The decision appeared to be a response to Nasser's threats to arrest Communist leaders. The party was believed to have only some 600 official members and about 2,000 party-line followers without official status. The communiqué said that Nasser's Arab Socialist Union was the only organization capable of "shouldering the responsibility of carrying on the revolution in all national fields." According to Egyptian sources, the dissolution indicated a Communist decision to increase its infiltration of Nasser's party.

Egyptian Editor Convicted as U.S. Spy

Mustafa Amin, founder and currently an editor of *Al-Akhbar*, one of the Middle East's most prominent newspapers, was arrested in Alexandria July 20, 1965. The UAR's semiofficial Middle East News Agency said July 21 that Amin had been caught transmitting UAR security information to Taylor Odell, an officer of the U.S. embassy in Cairo. Amin was found guilty a year later and given a life term.

Odell was also arrested but was released after establishing his diplomatic identity; he left Cairo for Washington July 25. The incident precipitated a barrage of anti-U.S. editorials in the UAR press.

According to the Middle East News Agency, Amin had been recruited "a long time ago by the CIA." He had been apprehended, it said, "while giving a weekly report [to Odell] at the request of the CIA." The report "contains questions from the CIA in the handwriting of . . . Odell and . . . Amin's answers, which contained political and military information harmful to the security and safety of the nation."

Egyptian officials said July 27 that Amin had confessed to working for the CIA and had implicated his twin brother, Ali Amin, London correspondent for the newspaper *Al-*

Ahram, in his activities. According to the reported confession, Mustafa had been paying half the CIA money he received to his brother; the last sum allegedly transferred to Ali in London was $56,000.

Al Gomhouria, a government newspaper, charged July 29 that the CIA's "major dream" was to bring down the Nasser government and replace it "with a stooge and traitor régime." The CIA, it said, wanted to destroy the leadership "by any means even if that involves resorting to assassination."

U.S. State Department press officer Marshall Wright had denied July 23 that Odell was a CIA employe or had received security information from Mustafa Amin. The U.S. embassy in Cairo said July 25 that Odell had returned to Washington that day "for consultations." (Odell had arrived in Cairo in Aug. 1964.)

The UAR's Supreme State Security Court Aug. 20, 1966 convicted Mustafa Amin, then 53, of being a CIA spy and sentenced him to life imprisonment at hard labor.

Opposition to the U.S.

Nasser's public statements appeared to grow stridently more anti-U.S. during 1966. Nasser Feb. 22 denounced the U.S.' admitted sale of U.S. made M-48 Patton tanks to Israel. The M-48 was a 49-ton tank armed with a 90-millimeter gun. In a speech delivered at Cairo University on the anniversary of Egypt's 1958 union with Syria (severed in 1961), Nasser said: The sale "shows a policy antagonistic to the Arab Nation and the Arab people." The U.S. and Britain had meddled in Arab affairs by supporting rightwing Islamic elements led by King Faisal of Saudi Arabia and Shah Muhammad Riza Pahlevi of Iran. The U.S. and Britain were attempting to foster "right-wing liberations movements, conspiring against the Arab people and placing them within spheres of Western influence."

The U.S. State Department Feb. 5 had acknowledged the

sale of the U.S. M-48 tanks to Israel. The sale reportedly covered 200 tanks West Germany had agreed to ship under a contract negotiated in Oct. 1964. The U.S. assumed responsibility for delivering the tanks after West Germany's Feb. 1965 cancellation of the deal under Egyptian pressure. Israel had applied to the U.S. for the weapons after West Germany canceled delivery of the M-48.

The State Department Feb. 5 released a statement in which it declared that U.S. policy was to maintain arms "stabilization" in the Middle East. The statement said: The U.S. "has made over the years repeated quiet efforts to encourage limitations on arms buildups in the [Middle East] area. . . . [But the U.S.] cannot be indifferent to the potentially destabilizing effect of massive Soviet sales of arms to the area. Over the years, to meet modernization requirements, we have sold . . . Israel . . . military equipment to help it meet its own defense and internal security requirements. . . . We and the British recently have agreed to provide an air defense system to Saudi Arabia, the United States component being Hawk missiles. Similarly, in 1962, we sold the Hawk missile to Israel to provide the basis for an air defense system. We have furnished . . . military equipment and services, including Patton tanks."

The official UAR Middle East News Agency Feb. 20 had released a warning, made by Nasser before a group of Iraqi newsmen, that if Israel began to make nuclear weapons, the "only answer" would be a "preventive war" to "wipe out all that enables Israel to produce an atomic bomb." The *N.Y. Times* had reported from Cairo Feb. 4 that in Dec. 1965 a Soviet delegation to Cairo headed by First Deputy Defense Min. Andrei A. Grechko had refused to sell atomic weapons to the UAR but had offered a guarantee of nuclear protection if Israel developed or bought nuclear weapons. (Israeli Premier Levi Eshkol told the Israeli Knesset May 18 that Nasser had revealed in a May 8 interview "that he now intends to begin developing nuclear arms." Eshkol declared that Israel "has no atomic arms and will not be the first to introduce them into our region.")

Soviet Premier Aleksei N. Kosygin paid a state visit to the UAR May 10-18, 1966. He was accompanied by Foreign Min. Andrei A. Gromyko and Adm. Sergei G. Gorshkov. Throughout Kosygin's visit, Nasser and the UAR press took a strong anti-U.S. line. In an interview May 9 with an Indian journalist, Nasser compared U.S. "aggression" in Vietnam to the British-French-Israeli action against Egypt during the 1956 Suez crisis. The U.S., he said, was responsible for Communist China's militancy.

With Kosygin at the Aswan Dam May 12, Nasser paid tribute to the USSR "for making the miracle of Aswan possible." Kosygin said the dam was an example of Communist aid, which, he said, unlike aid from Western nations, was given without strings attached. (The pro-government Cairo newspaper *Al-Ahram* charged May 13 that the U.S. was attempting to develop Saudi Arabia as a "counterpoise" to the UAR in the Middle East.) In Port Said May 15, Nasser and Kosygin laid wreaths on memorials to Egyptian soldiers killed in the 1956 Suez War.

Visiting Cairo University May 16, Kosygin described U.S. policy in Vietnam as "Hitlerite" and accused the U.S. of forcing South Korea to send troops to South Vietnam. In response to the Cairo University remarks, U.S. Amb.-to-UAR Lucius D. Battle boycotted Kosygin's May 17 speech to the National Assembly and his departure May 18 from Cairo airport. U.S. State Secy. Dean Rusk said in Washington May 17 that the anti-U.S. statements made in the UAR press had made the U.S. pause in its consideration of continuing shipment of surplus food to the UAR.

A communiqué on the Kosygin-Nasser talks, published May 18 in Cairo following Kosygin's departure for Moscow, called for a cessation of U.S. bombing of North Vietnam and for a U.S. troop withdrawal from South Vietnam. The communiqué attacked the West's policy toward Rhodesia and the

Federation of South Arabia (later Southern Yemen) and assailed "colonialist subversion" in Africa. It said that the USSR supported the "legitimate and inalienable rights of the Palestinian Arabs," but it made no mention of Yemen, where the UAR supported republicans against royalists backed by Saudi Arabia. (Kosygin had told the UAR National Assembly May 17 that the Soviet Union supported the UAR "stand on Yemen." He also conferred May 18 in Cairo with a Yemeni republican delegation headed by Acting Pres. Hassan al-Amri.) The communiqué "noted with satisfaction the coincidence of [Kosygin's and Nasser's] viewpoints on the most important problems of the international situation today." It expressed the 2 leaders' conviction that a new long-term trade agreement signed in Dec. 1965 would spur trade between the 2 countries.

In what was described as a very significant result of his UAR visit, Kosygin was reported to have persuaded Nasser to improve UAR relations with Syria. (The 2 nations had not had diplomatic relations since 1961, when Syria seceded from the UAR.) Kosygin told the UAR National Assembly May 17 that the "4 progressive Arab states–Egypt [UAR], Algeria, Syria and Iraq"–should form a united front against "imperialism" and "colonialism." (A Syrian delegation had arrived in Cairo May 16 to discuss economic contacts between the 2 countries.)

Tunisia Ends Ties

Tunisia cut diplomatic relations with the United Arab Republic Oct. 3, 1966. In announcing the decision after a cabinet meeting, Tunisian Information Min. Chaldy Klibi said the "continued campaign of insults from Cairo is incompatible with any kind of diplomatic relations." Tunisia and the UAR had closed their embassies in Cairo and Tunis in 1965 after a deterioration in relations that stemmed largely from Tunisian Pres. Habib Bourguiba's suggestion that the Arab states negotiate their dispute with Israel.

Internal Developments

Egypt's Supreme State Security Court convicted 220 members of the illegal Moslem Brotherhood Aug. 20–22 and Sept. 6, 1966 against the state. They were found guilty of plotting against the Nasser regime or attempting to revive their organization. 7 were sentenced to death Aug. 21, and the others received sentences ranging from 6 months in prison to life imprisonment at hard labor.

Those sentenced to death included Sayed Kotb, 61, Muhammad Youssef Hawash, 44, Abdulfattah Ismail, 42, Aly Ahmed Abdu Ashmawy, 22, Ahmad Abdul Maguid Samei, 33, Magdy Metwally, 29, and Sabry Arafa el-Homy, 36. Kotb, Hawash and Ismail were executed by hanging Aug. 29, but the sentences of the other 4 were commuted to hard labor for life. Those sentenced to life included Zeinaz al-Ghazali, 49, head of the brotherhood's women's branch (the Moslem Ladies Society).

The group had been charged (a) with plotting to assassinate Nasser and other government officials during the annual revolutionary celebrations in July 1965 in order to seize power and establish a Moslem theocratic state, and (b) with receiving financial aid from Saudi Arabia.

(Moslem students in Karachi, Pakistan demonstrated in front of the UAR embassy Sept. 1 in protest against the executions. Communists and pro-Nasser supporters in Khartoum, Sudan demonstrated Sept. 8 in support of the executions; 20 persons were injured slightly and 8 persons were arrested as 500 members of the Moslem Brotherhood attempted to break up the Khartoum demonstration.)

The Supreme State Security Court Sept. 8 sentenced Mustafa Agha, 43, general secretary of the banned Egyptian Communist Party, to life imprisonment at hard labor. 7 other alleged Communists received sentences ranging from 5 to 15 years. 3 were acquitted. The group had been charged in Dec. 1965 with plotting to overthrow the government.

Muhammad Sidky Soliman, 47, was appointed premier by Nasser Sept. 10 in a major cabinet shakeup involving the resignation of Premier Zakaria Mohieddin Sept. 9. Soliman had been minister for the Aswan High Dam in Mohieddin's cabinet. The newly revised cabinet: *Deputy Premier* and *Culture Minister*—Sarwat Okasha (a new appointment); *War*—Shamseddin Badran (new appointment); *National Guidance*—Muhammad Fayek (new appointment); *Communications*—Kamal Henry Abadir (new appointment); *Economy & Foreign Trade*—Hassan Abbas Zaky (new appointment); *Industry*—Ahmed Tewfiq el-Bakry (new appointment); *War Production* (new post)—Abdel Aziz Wahab el-Bishri (ex-war minister); *Deputy Premier* and *Minister for Electricity & Petroleum*—Mahmoud Yunis (ex-communications minister); *Deputy Premier for Foreign Affairs*—Mahmoud Fawzi; *Deputy Premier for Agriculture, Irrigation, Agrarian Reform & Land Reclamation*—Abdelmohsin Abu el-Nour; *Planning*—Muhammad Labib Shukeir; *Agriculture*—Dr. Shafiq Ali el-Kheshen; *Irrigation*—Abdel Khalek el-Shinnawy; *Foreign Affairs*—Mahmoud Riad; *Health*—Muhammad el-Nabawi el-Mohandes; *Youth*—Muhammad Talaat Khairy; *Education*—Muhammad Said Youssef; *Higher Education*—Dr. Muhammad Ezzat Salamaa (ex-housing & utilities minister); *Justice*—Muhammad Issameddin Hassouna; *Local Administration*—Ahmed Hamdy Ebeid; *Supply & Internal Trade*—Nureddin Korra; *Labor*—Anwar Salamaa; *Transportation*—Mahmoud Abdel Salam; *Deputy Minister*—Abdel Malek Saad; *Treasury*—Nazih Ahmed Deif; *Housing, Utilities & Tourism*—Dr. Aziz Ahmed Yassin (Deputy Minister—Ibrahim Naguib); *Works & Social Affairs*—Ahmed Muhammad Khalifa; *State (chef du cabinet)*—Amin Hamed Howeidy; *Interior*—Sharawy Muhammad Gomaa (ex-minister of state) (Deputy Minister—Maj. Gen. Youssef Hafiz).

It was reported that the cabinet changes reflected a dispute over foreign economic relations and domestic economic reform. Mohieddin had pleased Nasser, it was said, by his sweeping purge and reorganization of the UAR's police and by his exposure of the Moslem Brotherhood's plans for terrorism. But he had failed to attract Western investment capital by assuring UAR fiscal responsibility (at the cost of increased taxes and prices) and establishing an industrial free zone at Port Said, and he had failed to negotiate a $70 million loan from the International Monetary Fund (IMF). The IMF was understood to have insisted on devaluation of the Egyptian pound and reduction of government borrowing. Nasser reportedly opposed such moves.

3 ministers associated with Mohieddin were removed from the cabinet: Deputy Premier for Economic Affairs Abdel Moneim el-Kaissouni, Egypt's ranking economist and the man who applied for the IMF loan; Deputy Premier for Industry, Oil & Mining Mustafa Kalil and Deputy Premier for Supply & Home Trade Kamal Ramzi Stino. Kaissouni, who had served in the cabinet 12 years, had arranged major loans and credits in the U.S. and Western Europe. The new appointees, mostly politically neutral technicians, were expected to give Nasser more control of economic policy.

UAR & Arab League Boycott 3 U.S. Firms

Egyptian authorites announced Nov. 24, 1966 that the UAR had seized the Ford assembly plant in Alexandria and the firm's 4 bank accounts pending the settlement of a $1,084,000 customs claim. But the UAR released the company's property Nov. 30 and freed the firms' financial assets Dec. 1, a company executive, Hans Stock, reported.

The Arab League's Boycott Committee had voted unanimously at a conference in Kuwait Nov. 20 to prohibit all league-member dealings with Ford Motor Co. and the Coca-Cola Co. The committee imposed a similar ban Nov. 26 on another U.S. firm, the Radio Corporation of America (RCA). Both actions were in accordance with the league's policy of boycotting companies that operated in Israel or traded with Israel.

The league penalized Ford because it had licensed Palestine Automobile Corp., Ltd., an Israeli company, to assemble British and U.S. Ford trucks and tractors for the Israeli market. (Ford dealers in Lebanon had warned the Beirut government in October that a ban on Ford would cost the jobs of 6,000 Lebanese and put Lebanese Ford agents out of business.)

The League acted against Coca-Cola because the company had issued a franchise for a bottling plant in Israel to Abraham Feinberg, a New York banker.

Muhammad Mahboub, commissioner general of the boycott committee, said Nov. 26 that the league had decided to blacklist RCA "in the light of its earlier contraventions" of the committee's rules. The committee reportedly objected to RCA's pressing of phonograph records in Israel.

Each Arab League state was to decide itself how to apply the boycott. But it was reported in Cairo Dec. 13 that the committee had agreed to permit league states to continue to bottle and sell Coca-Cola for the next 9 months. A similar 9-month grace period was to be extended to Ford and RCA, according to Cairo reports.

ADVENTURE IN YEMEN (1959-66)

By early 1963 the UAR was becoming increasingly involved in an inconclusive civil war in Yemen, where a left-wing military group had overthrown the imamate (a religio-monarchic regime) but then had become embroiled in a long, bitter struggle with the ousted imam and forces seeking to return him to the throne. The controversial UAR intervention brought Egyptian ground and air forces into combat in a country that had no borders with Egypt. It proved so costly and unproductive to the UAR that many observers began to speak of Yemen as "Egypt's [or Nasser's] Vietnam." It took until mid-1967 for the UAR to work out a satisfactory armistice and the rest of the year to extricate its armed forces.

Crisis in Yemen

The theocratic Arab monarchy of Yemen, situated in the southwestern portion of the Arabian peninsula, had negotiated a loose tie to the United Arab Republic in Mar. 1958. It began to undergo severe civil disturbances the following year due largely to the instability of the regime of the Yemeni monarch, known as the *imam* (guide)—a religious title.

The Imam Ahmad bin Yahya was notorious for a supposed profligacy and great cruelty. His reputation and his customary self-seclusion from his own countrymen made him and his royal household inviting targets for photo-journalists. Italian cameramen were reported May 5, 1959 to have clashed with armed bodyguards of the imam in their attempts to photograph 3 of the imam's wives and 30 royal concubines visiting an Italian beach resort. The imam had arrived in Italy Apr. 15 for treatment of arthritis.

During the imam's visit, rumors reached Cairo and the West of uprisings in the Yemeni royal army. Crown Prince Seif al-Islam ("Sword of the Faith") Muhammad al-Badr, the acting ruler in the imam's absence, was reported May 26 to have formed Yemen's first representative council and to have begun a widespread purge of the Yemeni government. The prince's action appeared designed to halt growing unrest reported after the suppression of a mutiny of 180 Yemeni troops May 23 in Sana, the Yemeni national capital. Travelers reported, however, that the principal army mutiny had occurred May 15 in Baidha among troops claiming that they had not been paid. Yemeni spokesmen in Cairo June 16 denounced as "lies and nonsense" Reuters dispatches from the British Protectorate of Aden June 15 that rebellious army troops had seized control of the Yemeni port of Hodeida and of Taiz, residence of the imam and the administrative capital, 85 miles northwest of the British protectorate.

The arrest of Qadi Yahya al-Emary, Yemeni director of public safety, had been announced June 8 by Yemeni spokesmen in Cairo. Emary was charged with responsibility for the mutiny of army troops in Sana.

Faced with internal dissidence, the Yemeni government accused British agents from Aden of provoking the disorders. Relations between Yemen and the nearby British colony became strained. Yemeni spokesmen in Cairo charged July 5 that British planes had bombed the Beida area of Yemen and that British-led troops had made a "heavy attack" on El Daleh, Yemen near the Aden border but had been driven off.

Imam Ahmad arrived in Hodeida Aug. 13 after 4 months in Italy and accused rebel elements of acting as "tools of alien countries" and attempting to overthrow the monarchy in his absence. It was reported Aug. 18 that more than 60 persons had been executed for the attempted revolt. Reports from Aden Aug. 24 included word that several "Christian agitators" and others had been beheaded and mutilated on the imam's orders in his zeal to uproot Prince Muhammad al-Badr's reforms. Ahmad had reportedly sworn to "behead every black and . . . white whenever a complaint is submitted to me against him."

Further violent outbreaks occurred throughout the next 2 years despite the repression, and these culminated in an assassination attack on the imam. Ahmad, 67, was shot and wounded in a shoulder Mar. 27, 1961 when an assassin fired at the royal limousine as the imam was making an inspection tour of a hospital in Hodeida. 2 members of Ahmad's bodyguard were killed and 2 of his nephews badly wounded in the attack.

The imam's Cairo office announced Apr. 8 that 5 Yemenis had been sentenced to death for taking part in the assassination plot and that a Lt. Alafi, identified as the ringleader, had shot himself.

6 months later, in what seemed to some observers as a gesture of appeasement toward Cairo, the ailing imam agreed to step down from the throne. He announced in a radio broadcast Oct. 13, 1961 his abdication in favor of his son, Premier Muhammad al-Badr. The crown prince, who also was foreign, defense and interior minister at the time, had been named premier and interior minister by his father June 25, 1961.

After the dissolution of the federation of Egypt and Syria, it was said, UAR Pres. Nasser no longer stood to gain prestige from the tie between Egypt and Yemen. In light of the increasing unpopularity of the Yemeni monarchy among Yemenis and in the Arab world, Nasser decided to sever his country's special connection with Yemen, which had renewed that tie in Nov. 1961 for another 3 years. He denounced Yemen, Jordan and Saudi Arabia Dec. 23 for their opposition to his socialization program. In a broadcast from Port Said, Nasser declared that conditions in Yemen and Saudi Arabia were contrary to the "law of justice and the law of God." He described Imam Ahmad of Yemen and King Saud of Saudi Arabia as "reactionaries" and called Islam a "Socialist religion."

Nasser Dec. 26 dissolved his government's federation with Yemen, whose common association with the UAR had involved defense, foreign, economic and cultural affairs. In announcing Yemen's ouster from the federation UAR State Min. Abdel Kader Hatem declared that there was nothing common in "the nature of the [UAR] and Yemen to make the federation between them an effective political instrument able to contribute positively in strengthening the Arab struggle."

Civil War in Yemen

During the first half of 1962, a clandestine Yemeni army group calling itself the Liberal Revolutionary Army and favoring republican principles, prepared a *coup d 'état* against the Imam Ahmad and his dynasty. Ahmad died Sept. 18 in Taiz, the royal administrative capital. The secret military faction Sept. 26 overthrew the week-old regime of the new imam, Muhammad bin Ahmad al-Badr, claimed to have killed him in his palace in Sana and proclaimed a "Free Yemeni Republic."

An announcement broadcast over the rebel-seized Sana Radio said: "The revolutionary command ordered army units to besiege the palace of the tyrant [the Imam Muhammad]"; "the tyrant resisted"; "when the . . . ultimatum expired, army artillery [began] shelling the palace until it became rubble"; "the tyrant was buried under debris"; "men of the ousted régime were arrested and a republic proclaimed."

(Reports of the imam's death were contradicted Oct. 3 by a West German, Jürgen Griesbach, who had been in or around Sana during the rebellion and then had fled to Aden. Griesbach said that the imam had escaped from the damaged palace with a few aides. The imam's family and bodyguards were said to have been allowed to leave. 3 palace-guard soldiers were said to have been killed during the shelling. Ex-Foreign Min. Ahmad al-Shami, arriving in Amman, Jordan Oct. 9, also insisted that the imam was alive.)

The rebels reported that the revolt had spread from Sana to Taiz, Yemen's other capital, and that messages of support had been received from Salef, Ibb and Hajja Provinces and from the port of Hodeida. The rebels were believed to have won complete control by Sept. 29, when most of Yemen's sheikhs and tribes reportedly proclaimed support for the new government. Radio Sana had reported Sept. 28 that the rebels that day had executed 10 officials of the imam's government, including Foreign Min. Hassan bin Ibrahim. 5 more were reported to have been put to death Sept. 29.

Col. Abdullah al-Salal (also spelled Sallal), ex-chief of the imam's palace guard, was named premier and commander-in-chief. Abdul Rahman al-Baidany, a German-educated economist, was appointed deputy premier. Mohsen al-Ainy, an exile in Baghdad, was appointed foreign minister, and Muhammad Mahmoud el-Zubeiri, an exile in Cairo, was named education minister; both reportedly were on their way back to Yemen.

The UAR recognized the new rebel regime Sept. 29. Radio Sana announced Sept. 29 that the Soviet Union also had extended recognition. Premier Nikita Khrushchev was quoted as saying that the USSR would "meet any external aggression whatsoever by any government" opposing the rebel regime.

Prince al-Hassan bin Yahya, brother of the late Imam Ahmad and uncle of the Imam Muhammad, believing his nephew to be dead, became a claimant to the throne and established headquarters in Jidda, Saudi Arabia in an apparent first step toward gaining control of the Yemeni government. Radio Mecca reported that 100,000 Yemenis in Saudi Arabia were being mobilized to join Hassan. The prince, head of Yemen's UN delegation, had left New York by plane after learning of the revolt. On a stopover in London Sept. 28, Hassan had said that he was returning to Yemen to restore order. He said that he had no official word of the imam's death. The Yemeni legation in London denounced the revolt Sept. 28 and proclaimed Hassan as the new imam.

Foreign Min. Mohsen al-Ainy, declaring that the new government was "firmly established," warned in Cairo Sept. 30 that Hassan would "surely meet the fate of [Muhammad] al-Badr and many other members of the royal family" if he attempted to return to Yemen. Ainy said: "This was not a mere army coup. We have been working for this 14 years at home and abroad. This time we have not only the intellectuals behind us, but also the tribes—tribes whose chiefs lost their heads on the order of the old imam after 1955.'

The rebel government warned Oct. 2 that it would bomb tribal villages that sheltered members of the ousted royal family or gave aid to their supporters. Deputy Premier Abdul Rahman al-Baidany had warned Saudi Arabia in a broadcast earlier Oct. 2 that Yemen was "prepared to carry the war to Saudi Arabia itself" to fight any Yemini royal force preparing to attack the rebel régime. The warning was made following reports that regular Saudi Arabian troops were massing along Yemen's border to support tribesmen loyal to Yemen's royal family.

A military struggle between forces supporting Yemen's overthrown imam, led by Prince Hassan, pretender to the throne, and the newly-established republic headed by Premier Abdullah al-Salal, was reported to have erupted Oct. 7 in northern Yemen. Saudi Arabian and Jordanian troops were said to be fighting on the side of the royalists. Conflicting reports of the fighting emanated from Cairo, sympathetic to the Salal régine, and from Saudi Arabia and Amman, Jordan.

Radio Cairo, quoting reports from Sana, announced Oct. 7 that Salal's troops were battling "Saudi Arabian infiltrators, mostly from King Saud's royal guard, [who] were attempting to reach the northern Yemeni town of Sada" about 50 miles from the Saudi Arabian frontier. Saudi Arabia's Radio Mecca later Oct. 7 denied the Cairo report of the fighting and said

Saudi Arabian troops were not massing on Yemen's northern frontier. Radio Amman reported Oct. 9 that royalist troops were "on the way to liberate Sana" after having "liberated" Sada and the town of Marib.

Salal announced in Sana Oct. 14 that his troops had recaptured Sada and Marib. Royalist sources in Amman Oct. 16 acknowledged the loss of Sada but insisted that their forces still held Marib. They contended that Salal's forces were in control only of Sada and a triangular area in the Sana-Hodeida-Taiz sector and that Yemeni tribesmen elsewhere supported the imamate.

The Yemeni republican government announced Oct. 15 that it was fighting Saudi Arabians and Jordanians in the north and other forces from the South Arabian Federation state of Beihan in the east. Radio Sana announced Oct. 17 that government troops had repelled an attack by Saudi Arabian soldiers near Sada.

Further evidence that the overthrown Imam Muhammad al-Badr had not been killed in the Sept. 26 coup was given in a report from royalist sources in Amman Oct. 16. The report said that Prince Hassan had given up his claim to the throne and recognized the imam as the monarch of Yemen; the imam had sent telegrams to all Arab chiefs of state, asking their support. One telegram, reportedly received by Jordanian King Hussein Oct. 15, said the imam had escaped from Sana, had joined loyal tribesmen and had started to suppress the "vicious rebellion engineered in Cairo." The imam was said to have sent a protest telegram to UAR Pres. Nasser and to have appealed to the Arab League to meet to consider his complaints. The Cairo newspaper *Al-Ahram* had said Oct. 15 that the Sana command "had received reports" that the imam was alive after having fled to the village of Almahabsha. The Middle East News Agency in Cairo later quoted its Sana correspondent as reporting that the imam was hospitalized with a wound in the U.S. base at Dhahran, Saudi Arabia.

The UAR had begun to give the new Yemeni régime

material support immediately after it came to power. A UAR ship carrying "technicians and medical supplies" arrived in Hodeida Oct. 5. The UAR-controlled United Arab Airlines started operations the same day between Cairo and Sana (3 flights a week); this gave Yemen its first international air service. 2 UAR government experts arrived in Yemen Oct. 13 as the vanguard of 52 specialists requested by Yemen to advise the government on matters ranging from irrigation to finance. (Iraqi recognition of the new Yemeni régime was announced in Iraqi Premier Abdul Karim el-Kassem's name in a statement read on Baghdad radio Oct. 9.)

The first public acknowledgment of the participation of UAR troops in the fighting was made Oct. 29, 1962 by Sana radio, which claimed that Yemeni troops, "reinforced by UAR troops," had repulsed "a large infiltration force" in the Beihan region bordering Aden. UAR paratroopers were said to have been sent to Yemen Oct. 19.

The British military command in Aden had announced Oct. 22 that 3 Yemeni planes had intruded into Aden that day and had "bombed and rocketed" the village of Asaylan, killing a child and destroying 2 houses. The Yemeni republican régime urged Britain Oct. 27 to force the Beihan tribal region in western Aden to end its "hostile acts" against Yemen. The request, made by Deputy Premier Baidany to Christopher Gandy, British representative in Sana, followed Yemeni charges that the Sultan of Beihan had supplied Yemeni royalist forces with arms and ammunition.

The London *Daily Telegraph* gave this account of the military situation by the end of Oct. 1962: ". . . Fighting is on a comparatively small scale. Royalist forces are not posing a real threat to the republican government's control over the main areas of the country. . . . Enough evidence has been produced in Sana during the last few days to persuade foreign journalists there that some Saudi units, probably irregulars, are supporting royalists in northern Yemen."

Republican Premier Salal was named president in a cabinet revision announced Oct. 31. Deputy Premier Abdul Rahman al-Baidany was appointed deputy army commander, deputy president and foreign minister. Ex-Foreign Min. Mohsen al-Ainy was appointed to Yemen's UN delegation.

Baidany warned Saudi Arabia Nov. 2 that the republican army and navy were ready to move north into Saudi Arabian territory "when ordered." He said such an order would be given unless Kings Saud of Saudi Arabia and Hussein of Jordan "give up their anti-Yemen aggressive attempts." Baidany issued the warning after saying that in the past few days Yemeni forces had repulsed an attempted invasion by 5,000 Saudi Arabian and Jordanian regulars. 3,000 of the invaders were put out of action, Baidany asserted.

Saudi Arabia severed diplomatic relations with the UAR Nov. 6 after announcing the same day that UAR planes and 3 UAR warships had bombed Muwassam, a Saudi Arabian port on the Red Sea near the Yemeni border, and the nearby village of Khalaf. The Saudi Arabian communiqué said the attack had resulted in "great fatal casualties and property losses." A Saudi Arabian report Nov. 10 said the bombardment had continued intermittently for 4 days, forcing thousands of villagers along the coast between Muwassam and the Yemeni border to flee to the interior. Crown Prince Faisal, the Saudi Arabian premier, had said at a news conference in Mecca Nov. 8 that the Muwassam attack had been preceded by UAR air raids in the past few weeks on Najran and 5 villages in Qizan Province.

Muhammad al-Badr, the deposed imam, appeared before newsmen at an undisclosed site in northeastern Yemen Nov. 10 to disprove claims that he had been killed. Predicting that his troops would overthrow the republican régime and restore him to his throne "in a few weeks," the imam said: "No one is really fighting me any more except the Egyptians"; his forces had captured many UAR troops, but he could not display them "because my people are so outraged that they kill all Egyptians."

The imam gave this account of recent military developments in Yemen: Royalists had won complete control of the Es-Shan area around Sada in the north, the Jawf region in the northeast and the Khawlan tribal region in the east; major towns captured by the royalists were Sada, Maaris, Harib and Haradh; royalist troops had gained control of the Hajja area 3 weeks previously, but the town's fort was still occupied by republican troops; republican troops were in control of little or no territory outside the towns of Sana, Hodeira and Taiz. The imam said his forces had neither requested nor received aid from Saudi Arabia or Jordan.

A royal communiqué broadcast by Radio Mecca Nov. 11 said that the imam's forces Nov. 10 had captured a fort at Sinwan, 60 miles northeast of Sana, killing 250 UAR soldiers and capturing 60 republican troops. Royalist losses were listed at 12 killed and 20 wounded.

The Yemeni republican régime and the UAR had signed a 5-year mutual defense pact in Sana Nov. 10. The agreement was initialed by Yemeni Pres. Abdullah al-Salal and by Lt. Col. Anwar Sadat of the UAR's Presidency Council. The pact, ratified Nov. 11 by UAR Pres. Nasser and the Presidency Council, provided that Yemen and the UAR would come to each other's aid in the event either was attacked. The pact established a joint Supreme Council to issue military planning orders and a Military Council to recommend defense planning and the "use of armed forces in joint military operations." Salal, declaring that the pact would "consolidate" the Yemeni revolution, said Yemen had "signed the agreement after patiently enduring Saudi and Jordanian aggression."

A Saudi Arabian government statement Nov. 13 denied that Saudi Arabia had "even a single soldier" in Yemen. The statement proposed that an "impartial international body" supervise the withdrawal of "all foreign forces in Yemen together with their arms and equipment."

The UAR's Middle East News Agency in Cairo reported Nov. 21 that Robert W. Stookey, U.S. chargé d'affaires in

Yemen, had informed Washington officials that the republican régime was in "full control" of the country except for some border areas.

U.S. Pres. John F. Kennedy was reported Nov. 25 to have proposed a plan to settle the Yemeni conflict. A Presidential appeal had been made the previous week in messages to 4 major participants in the dispute: Yemeni republican Pres. Salal; Crown Prince Faisal, premier of Saudi Arabia; King Hussein of Jordan and UAR Pres. Nasser. Kennedy proposed, as a preliminary step, the withdrawal from Yemen of UAR troops fighting on behalf of the Yemeni republican forces. The President's plan also called for a halt in Saudi Arabian and Jordanian material aid to Yemeni royalists fighting the republicans.

U.S. Amb.-to-Saudi Arabia William Hart, who had delivered Kennedy's message to Faisal, had said that the maintenance of a U.S. presence in Yemen had been made essential by the extent of Soviet and Chinese Communist aid to the republican régime. According to Hart, this would make it difficult for the U.S. to avoid diplomatic recognition of the republican government. The U.S. intention of maintaining its presence in Yemen was indicated in a U.S. announcement that it would continue to provide Yemen with economic aid for road construction despite the change in government.

Faisal was reported Nov. 28 to have rejected Kennedy's peace proposal on the grounds that: (a) he considered the imam and his government the legal rulers of Yemen; (b) the Yemeni people still supported the imam and his government; (c) the royalist supporters would defeat republican forces soon.

The U.S. Dec. 19, 1962 formally recognized the republican government of Yemen. A State Department announcement said that the U.S. action had been made possible because these 2 developments in the past 24 hours had fulfilled some of the goals sought by U.S. negotiators in their efforts to settle the Yemeni civil war: (1) A declaration Dec. 18 by

Yemeni Deputy Pres. and Foreign Min. Abdul Rahman al-Baidany that his government would honor the previous Yemeni régime's international obligations, including the 1934 British-Yemeni treaty on the British protectorate of Aden and a subsequent agreement signed in 1951 that had demarcated the Aden-Yemen frontier and had called on Yemenis who had temporarily migrated to Aden not to participate in any activities opposed to British rule in the protectorate; (2) a Cairo announcement Dec. 18 that the UAR would withdraw from Yemen the 12,000 UAR troops who had been assisting republican forces in their civil war against royalist units supporting the dethroned Imam Muhammad.

UAR Culture & National Guidance Min. Abdel Kadar Hatem announced Dec. 19 that the UAR troop withdrawal would start as soon as it became evident that Jordanian and Saudi Arabian forces, reputedly supporting the royalists in the Yemen fighting, had left the border regions.

Ahmad al-Shami, foreign minister of the Yemeni royal government-in-exile and head of its UN delegation, had said in New York Dec. 7 that Prince Hassan, royalist premier, had sent Pres. Kennedy Dec. 6 a message urging him not to recognize the republican government. Shami quoted Hassan as saying that U.S. recognition would amount to support of a UAR seizure of power in Yemen. The royalist delegation had circulated in the UN Nov. 27 a petition urging a UN investigation of charges of UAR aggression in Yemen. The royalist appeal said that the revolt that had overthrown the imam in September had been engineered by a small group but that UAR "intervention" had made it "impossible for the people of Yemen to act freely and express their choice." The appeal, denying UAR charges of Saudi Arabian and Jordanian intervention, called on the suggested UN inquiry commission "to find out if there does exist any Saudi Arabian or Jordanian forces in Yemen" and "to ascertain the wishes of the Yemen tribes."

Prince Hassan announced in a communiqué broadcast by

Radio Mecca Dec. 25 that royalist tribesmen had killed 264 Egyptian and republican troops Dec. 23–24 in clashes 70 miles northeast of Sana.

UAR Expands Military Role

1963 was a year of deepening Egyptian involvement in the Yemeni civil war. Cairo sources reported Jan. 4 that the UAR had reversed its decision to withdraw its troops, then estimated at 15,000, from Yemen. The decision to maintain UAR forces in Yemen was said to have been based on reports that Saudi Arabia was massing military units on Yemen's border.

A mobilization of Saudi Arabian resources against the UAR had been announced by the Mecca régime Jan. 3. Saudi Arabian Premier Prince Faisal, accusing the UAR of continuing its air and naval attacks on Saudi Arabian territory, said that he had decided to ask his country's Higher Defense Council to take all steps required to maintain national security. UAR planes had bombed the Saudi Arabian oasis town of Najran Dec. 30 and 31, 1962 and Jan. 1, 1963. Najran, near the Yemeni border, was said to be an important Saudi Arabian transit point for shipping arms to the royalists. A U.S. State Department note to Cairo Jan. 3 expressed concern over the Najran attacks, and a spokesman for the Nasser régime said the UAR government would try to prevent future attacks across Yemen's frontiers. Chairman Ali Sabry of the UAR's governing Executive Council had told U.S. Amb. John F. Badeau in Cairo Jan. 2 that the U.S. was aware of Saudi Arabia's "feverish preparation for aggressive conspiracy against Yemen since, because of its good relations with the Saudis, the U.S. had many means to learn the facts."

The U.S. State Department Jan. 8 made public a letter written to Prince Faisal Oct. 25, 1962 by Pres. Kennedy in which the President pledged "full U.S. support for the maintenance of Saudi Arabia's territorial integrity." A State Department spokesman said that Kennedy's pledge did not necessarily involve a military commitment and that its revelation did not presage a U.S. decision to withdraw its recognition of the Yemeni republican régime. The Saudi Arabian government reportedly had asked Kennedy to make public his letter to Faisal as evidence to Saudi Arabian citizens that the U.S. still supported the Saudi royal family despite its rejection of Yemen's royal family.

King Hussein of Jordan Jan. 4 had denounced the U.S. recognition of the Yemeni régime. In an Amman interview, Hussein said that the American action, in effect, had joined the U.S. with the Soviet Union and the UAR in a "competition toward the same end, designed to overthrow Yemen's legitimate government." "Even though Jordan believes Imam el-Badr is Yemen's legitimate . . . ruler, we are neither for the royalists nor republicans," Hussein said.

A Saudi Arabian plan to end the fighting was broadcast by Mecca radio Jan. 7. It called for: (a) the "withdrawal of all foreign armed forces in Yemen of any nationality" ("when they are withdrawn, all assistance, direct or indirect, is to be stopped"); (b) a guarantee that the Yemenis would have the right to determine the type government they wanted; (c) an international commission to supervise the implementation of the proposals. The Saudi Arabian peace plan, in effect, constituted an acceptance of Pres. Kennedy's Nov. 25, 1962 proposal to mediate the dispute.

The fighting, however, continued. Yemeni republican Pres. Abdullah al-Salal reported Feb. 3 that 50 Saudi Arabians and Jordanians had been killed, more than 100 wounded and 20 captured in a battle with republican forces Feb. 2 at Wadi Jawf, near the Saudi-Yemeni border. Salal made the announcement after meeting earlier Feb. 3 with Marshal Abdel Hakim Amer, UAR armed forces head, and Lt. Col. Anwar Sadat, a UAR minister in charge of Yemen affairs. Both UAR officials had arrived in Yemen Jan. 31.

Salal said Yemeni and UAR forces were in complete control of Yemeni territory.

UN authorities announced in New York Feb. 26 that Ralph Bunche, UN undersecretary for special political affairs, had been sent to Yemen in an effort to head off a possible larger crisis threatened by the continued fighting. Bunche's mission was on the initiative of UN Secy. Gen. U Thant, who had discussed the situation in New York with representatives of Saudia Arabia, the UAR and Yemen.

Abdul Rahman al-Baidany, Yemeni republican vice president and foreign minister, had said in Cairo Jan. 22 that his government would welcome a UN mission but would oppose permanent UN observers on its territory. Baidany suggested that the UN and U.S. use their "good offices, with countries [Jordan and Saudi Arabia] committing aggression against . . . Yemen with a view to stopping that aggression." Baidany said that UAR troops would remain in Yemen "as long as reactionary aggression persists on our borders."

The ouster of Baidany as vice president and foreign minister was confirmed with the Feb. 19 announcement of the formation of a new Yemeni cabinet that excluded Baidany from membership. Pres. Salal assumed the additional post of foreign minister. Baidany had arrived in Cairo Jan. 19 on an unannounced "official visit." His unexpected arrival was believed to be a "diplomatic expulsion" by Salal, whom Baidany reportedly had sought to replace as head of the republican government. Many Yemeni nationalists regarded Baidany, who had strong ties with the UAR, as a potential "puppet of Nasser."

The U.S. was not the only Western power maintaining political and trade commitments in the Arabian peninsula to clash with Yemen's new republican regime. British-Yemeni relations had been aggravated by a series of armed clashes between Yemeni forces and soldiers of the Federation of South Arabia, a British protectorate. Yemeni Pres.

Salal announced Feb. 3 that republican forces Feb. 2 had killed 10 "infiltrators" and wounded 15 others from the federation's Beihan state in a clash near Harib in Yemen. Federation forces, led by British officers, forced Yemeni republican soldiers out of a disputed wadi (dry river bed) near Harbi Feb. 26. Federation Foreign Min. Muhammad Farid al-Aulaqi had charged Jan. 30 that Yemeni republicans were responsible for a series of land-mine explosions on federation territory in the past few months. He said the blasts had killed several people and had damaged army vehicles. Aulaqi also accused Yemen of inciting a group of 100 federation residents in Yemen against the federation and of violent anti-federation broadcasts.

Britain, in response to a Yemeni government demand, closed its legation Feb. 17 in Taiz, one of Yemen's 2 capitals. A Yemeni note Feb. 10 had not specified the reason for the demand for the legation's closure, but it was believed to be in retaliation for British refusal to recognize the republican regime. British Lord Privy Seal Edward Heath had said in the British House of Commons Feb. 4 that the unclear situation in the Yemeni civil war did not justify British recognition. The British turned over their Taiz legation to U.S. Chargé d'Affaires James Cortada, who was to look after British interests in Yemen.

Yemeni republican Pres. Salal Feb. 28 sent the UN Security Council a message appealing for "immediate [UN] action" to halt what he called Britian's "flagrant aggression" in the civil war. In his message to Council Pres. Carlos Sosa Rodriguez of Venezuela, Salal said: "We are sure of the arrival of British forces in the Harib area supported by tanks. British planes also have dropped circulars on the Yemeni forces warning them to withdraw from the surroundings of the Yemeni Harib, otherwise they would be bombed by planes. This is aid from Britain to infiltrators coming from Saudi Arabia to help the dethroned imam and those surrounded in Harib."

A note protesting British "aggression on some Yemeni villages in Yemen" was handed by Salal Feb. 28 to U.S. Chargé d'Affaires Cortada for forwarding to the British Foreign Office. Britain asked the U.S. Mar. 1 to file with the Sana government a complaint charging that a Yemeni plane had machine-gunned the airstrip at a British post in Al-Ain, Aden, Feb. 27. Salal, speaking at a mass rally in Taiz Mar. 7, called on Yemen's "brothers in the south"–*i.e.*, Aden and the Federation of South Arabia–to revolt and "take revenge against the British."

UN Undersecy. Ralph Bunche conferred with Pres. Salal, witnessed a demonstration charging Britain with "aggression of Yemen airspace" and inspected the fighting front at Marib Mar. 3. Radio Sana quoted Bunche as telling 1,000 welcoming tribesmen that "if Britain continues in her aggression on Yemen then the UN must stand by you." On his return to Sana, Bunche conferred with Field Marshal Abdel Hakim Amer, deputy commander of the UAR armed forces. Bunche flew to Cairo Mar. 5 to confer with Nasser on the withdrawal of UAR troops from Yemen and to win his approval of a UN "presence" in Yemen. Bunche left Cairo for New York Mar. 7. (Saudi Arabian Premier Faisal reportedly had refused to meet Bunche.)

The U.S. was reported Mar. 7 to have cautioned Nasser that Egyptian air and naval attacks on Saudi Arabian territory were threatening U.S.-UAR relations. A note delivered by U.S. Amb. John S. Badeau to Nasser in Cairo the previous week was said to have warned that if the Egyptian bombing attacks were followed up by an invasion of Saudi Arabia, the UAR would be on "a collision course" with the U.S.

UAR warships were said to have shelled the Saudi Arabian port of Jizan Mar. 3 and 4. A Saudi Arabian communiqué Mar. 4 charged that UAR planes Mar. 3 had twice attacked the Saudi Arabian town of Dhara, causing several deaths. UAR planes in the last week of February reportedly had attacked Jizan, an airfield near Khamis

Mishayt and the administrative center of Abha, all about 60 miles north of the Yemeni frontier. Muhammad Habib, UAR press attaché in Washington, said Mar. 7 that the UAR attacks were aimed at destroying Yemeni royalist encampments and supply lines in Saudi Arabian territory, all appropriate military targets. Radio Cairo reported Mar. 7 that an Egypto-Yemeni republican force had captured the royalist-held town of Harib in Yemen. The news climaxed reports for more than a month of a republican offensive in eastern Yemen.

Morocco's recognition of the Yemeni republican regime was announced Mar. 18 and that of Libya Mar. 25. Moroccan King Hassan II reportedly took the step to put his foreign policy in greater accord than before with the other Arab countries of North Africa and fellow members of the Casablanca Group (which included Ghana, Guinea and Mali). Libya's move developed 5 days after King Idris had ordered the formation of a new cabinet.

Pres. Salal announced Yemen's first republican constitution at a mass meeting in Sana Apr. 13. Under the principal provisions of the new charter: Salal was to hold the posts of head of state, armed forces commander and chairman of a new Presidential Council (whose 18 members were to include 5 tribal sheikhs); as the supreme governing body, the council was to have jurisdication over political, economic, social and administrative matters; an Executive Council, responsible to the Presidential Council, was to draft laws and regulations, prepare a budget and be responsible for economic planning; Islam was to be Yemen's official religion; army service was compulsory. Salal Apr. 18 formally decreed the establishment of the Presidential Council, replacing the National Revolutionary Council.

UN Secy. Gen. U Thant announced Apr. 30 that the UAR and Saudi Arabia had accepted a UN plan to withdraw their forces from Yemen. Yemen also approved the agreement. Under the "disengagement" plan: (a) Saudi Arabia was to end all military backing of Yemeni tribesmen supporting ousted Imam Muhammad al-Badr; (b) the UAR, supporting republican Pres. Salal, was to withdraw its troops from Yemen and end its attacks on royalist soldiers and Saudi Arabian territory; (c) a 12-mile demilitarized zone was to be established along the Saudi-Yemeni frontier. Swedish Maj. Gen. Carl Carlsson von Horn, chief of the UN Palestine truce supervisory organization, was ordered to Yemen Apr. 30 to enforce the 3-nation agreement.

The UN peace formula was devised after a mission by ex-U.S. Amb. Ellsworth Bunker, who had visited Saudi Arabia in March and the UAR in April as a special envoy of Pres. Kennedy. Bunker had conferred in Cairo Apr. 1-2 with Nasser on withdrawing Egyptian forces from Yemen. Bunker had returned from his mission Apr. 11 and presented his recommendations to Thant Apr. 12.

Yemeni royalist forces were reported May 28 to have broken a tacit truce and to have launched an offensive against republican troops. The cease-fire had been in effect since the Apr. 30 UN agreement. The ousted Imam Muhammad al-Badr was said to have ordered the new drive after concluding that the UAR had violated the agreement by not withdrawing its soldiers. The imam's offensive, started 2 weeks previously, was aimed at the capital city of Sana, around which royalist troops established a front whose nearest point was 5 miles from the city. Royalist sources said the imam's soldiers also had captured some territory won by UAR troops in February by occupying Wadi Jawf and the towns of Marib and Harib, 110 miles northwest of Sana. Other points reported captured by the royalists: Barat and Safra, 100 miles north of Sana; Al-Batanah in the west; the desert area in Khabt in the east.

Maj. Gen. Anwar Qadi, commander of the UAR task force in Yemen, said in Cairo May 28 that "reactionaries" should not be misled into believing that the UAR "shall pull out [of Yemen] before realizing all the objectives of our mission." Estimating that this mission would take 5 years, Qadi said it would consist "first, of securing the revolution completely and, 2d of working on creating a sound Yemeni national army." Qadi accused Saudi Arabia of violating the UN disengagement agreement by sending the royalists huge shipments of arms and ammunition since Apr. 29.

Reports that the UAR was not observing its pledge to withdraw its forces from Yemen had been confirmed in a speech delivered by Nasser in Cairo May 21. In welcoming a group of Egyptian soldiers who had just returned from Yemen, Nasser declared: "You were the vanguard of those forces on the battlefield, and you finally returned with a victory. They are on the Yemeni battlefield at this moment. They will be there until it becomes certain . . . that the reaction that hates the Yemeni revolution is forced through defeat to contain that hatred in its own heart." The soldiers Nasser welcomed were believed to have been part of a 3,000-man force recalled from Yemen since the UN disengagement plan was announced. It was reported that during the same period the UAR had sent at least 2,000 other soldiers to Yemen.

4 U.S. officials met with UN Secy. Gen. U Thant May 28 and urged him to press the UN's peace efforts in Yemen to prevent the fighting there from spreading to other countries in the Middle East. Meeting with Thant were Charles W. Yost, the U.S.' deputy permanent representative at the UN; Asst. State Secy. (for international organization affairs) Harlan Cleveland; ex-Amb. Ellsworth Bunker, who had drafted the UN's Apr. 30 Yemen disengagement agreement; and Thomas A. Bartlett, political adviser to the U.S.' UN mission. After conferring with the U.S. officials, Thant said that "a small advance party could be sent to the area [Yemen] within a few days." Thant said that all sides in the Yemen dispute had "reconfirmed" their "acceptance of the terms of

disengagement" to Maj. Gen. Carl Carlsson von Horn, head of the UN's truce supervision organization in Jerusalem, who had visited Yemen earlier in May on Thant's instructions. Thant said that "UN observers in the Saudi Arabia-Yemen area are vitally necessary and could well be the decisive factor in avoiding serious trouble in that area."

The UN Security Council June 11, 1963, by 10–0 vote (one abstention: USSR), approved U Thant's plan to send a 200-man UN observation mission to Yemen to supervise the withdrawal of UAR troops and Saudi Arabian aid. The cost was to be borne by the UAR and Saudi Arabia. Thant had arranged for the UAR and Saudi Arabia to pay for the mission largely to avoid a showdown with the Soviet Union over the General Assembly's competence to provide funds for such operations. The special Council meeting had been requested June 8 by the Soviet Union on the ground that any UN peace mission, such as the Yemen operation, must be under the sponsorship of and financed by the Council rather than the General Assembly. Implementation of the peace plan, drafted by Ghana and Morocco and approved by the UAR and Saudi Arabia Apr. 29, had been delayed because of the Soviet position.

Soviet delegate Nikolai T. Fedorenko had made clear to other representatives in private talks after the first Council meeting June 10 that if the Council did not finance the Yemen mission, the USSR would denounce Saudi Arabia as the aggressor in Yemen. A Soviet Council veto of the entire plan was feared. Fedorenko's abstention in the June 11 vote represented a reversal of the Soviet position. Fedorenko said after the vote that he was satisfied with Thant's Yemen plan since it had been ordered by the Security Council, "the only organ which under the [UN] Charter . . . is competent to take decisions relating to United Nations actions for the maintenance of . . . peace. . . ." Fedorenko said that he had abstained because he believed the Yemen mission should be confined to "a limited number" of observers "for a period of 2 months." U.S. Amb. Adlai E. Stevenson said the mission should not be restricted by a time limit.

After Council approval of the resolution, Thant sent a message to Gen. von Horn to proceed with an advance party to Yemen from Jerusalem, where he headed the UN Palestine Truce Supervision Organization. Von Horn and an advance party of UN observers arrived in Sana, Yemen June 13. Thant had announced plans for sending the mission and its financial arrangement in a report to the Security Council June 7. Thant said that Saudi Arabia had "agreed orally" to pay "a proportionate share" and that the UAR had agreed "in principle to provide assistance in an amount equivalent to $200,000 for a period of 2 months, which would be roughly half the cost of the operation over that period." In a report to the Council June 3, Thant had estimated the mission's cost for a 4-month period at $807,500.

A Saudi Arabian complaint filed with U Thant June 17 charged that UAR planes had killed more than 30 persons in 5 separate raids over Saudi territory June 6–8. Saudi Arabia had charged June 9 that UAR planes from Yemen had bombed the Saudi Red Sea port of Qizan June 8. Radio Mecca reported that 30 persons were killed and 19 wounded in the air attack, which allegedly was directed against homes and the town's hospital. Saudi Arabia had charged June 7 that UAR planes had bombed the Saudi Arabian towns of Najran (a border base for shipping supplies to Yemeni royalist forces) and Khamas June 6.

The *N.Y. Times* June 16 quoted U.S. and other diplomatic sources as estimating that the number of Soviet military technicians and instructors in republican Yemen had increased in previous weeks to about 900 or 1,000. There had been about 60 Soviet technicians in Yemen in Sept. 1962 at the time of Imam Muhammad al-Badr's ouster. They had been part of a group of 150 Soviet technicians stationed in the country since 1961. According to the *Times*, the latest group of Russians had arrived in Yemen in March on the invitation of Pres. Abdullah al-Salal. Some of the Russians were said to have flown combat missions against royalist forces, presumably in Soviet-built planes brought to Yemen by the UAR.

Meanwhile, Pres. Salal had visited Cairo and Damascus to seek membership for Yemen in a proposed United Arab Republic of Egypt, Syria and Iraq. A joint communiqué issued June 13 after a 3-day visit by Salal to Damascus said that the Yemeni president had urged a meeting of Egypt, Syria and Iraq to arrange for Yemen's membership before the Arab federation's scheduled establishment in September. After Salal visited UAR Pres. Nasser, the Middle East News June 17 quoted a joint communiqué in which the Cairo government agreed to Yemen's request to join the proposed federation.

UN Secy. Gen. U Thant reported to the UN Security Council Sept. 4 that the UN Yemen Observation Mission (UNYOM) had failed thus far in its efforts to end fighting. UNYOM's work had been scheduled to end Sept. 4, but Thant announced in his report that Saudi Arabia and the UAR had given him "oral assurances" that they would continue to finance the mission's operations for another 2 months. (The Council June 11 had extended UNYOM's life until Nov. 4 on the condition that the UAR and Saudi Arabia would continue to pay its costs.)

"It cannot be said . . . that encouraging progress has been made toward effective implementation" of the UN-sponsored agreement on UAR and Saudi Arabian disengagement, Thant reported. He charged that despite reports that the UAR was withdrawing troops from Yemen, Cairo actually was sending fresh forces. An estimated 20,000 Egyptian soldiers were said to be in Yemen. (UAR Field Marshal Abdel Hakim Amer had reported to Nasser and the UAR's ruling Presidential Council Aug. 7 that the UAR had completed its military operations in Yemen. According to Amer's report, Egyptian and Yemeni troops were in "complete control of the situation.")

Thant denied charges that UNYOM's operations had been hindered by poor administration. This charge was repeated Sept. 5 by Maj. Gen. Carl Carlsson von Horn, who was reported Aug. 27 to have resigned as mission chief. (Von Horn was replaced Sept. 10 by Lt. Gen. Prem Singh Gyani of India, commander of the UN Emergency Force in Egypt.) Von Horn said that the UN had failed to support the mission in the field and that the whole field-operations system required reappraisal. Although it had been announced that he had resigned for urgent reasons largely personal "in nature," von Horn said he had quit the post in protest against the ignoring of his recommendations.

Abdul Rahman al-Baidany, republican Yemen's former vice president, foreign minister and ranking economist, was arrested in Cairo Sept. 22, 1963 on grounds of "suspicious contacts with the British authorities" during a visit to Aden from mid-August to mid-September. He later was released but put under house arrest. Baidany had gone to Aden on the pretext of canvassing financial support for the establishment of a development bank in the British protectorate. Once there, he publicly denounced the Yemeni republican regime and advocated the formation of an independent Shafii state in southern Yemen. (Yemeni Shafiis, members of one of the 4 main schools of orthodox Islam, dwelt mainly in towns and villages along Yemen's Red Sea coast and in the southern regions and traditionally had no military power. A Shafii Yemeni minority comprised half of Aden's population.) The Yemeni Presidential Council deprived Baidany Aug. 29 of his Yemeni citizenship and accused him of being a "foreign agent," of seeking to separate northern from southern Yemen and of "placing himself in the service of imperialism in Aden."

(Baidany, born in Cairo of an Egyptian mother, was a

Shafii—*i.e.*, a Sunni Moslem of the same sect as most of the Egyptian expeditionary force in Yemen. Pres. Salal, on the other hand, was a Zaidi—nominally an adherent of a sect of Shiite [heterodox] Islam that recognized a living theocratic imam in Yemen. Zaidis comprised about 55% of the people of Yemen and Shafiis 45% at the outbreak of the revolution. The more warlike, northern tribes—especially those of the Hashid and Bakil confederations—were Zaidis. After the Sept. 1962 coup, both Salal and Baidany had called for an end to the sectarian hatred between Shafiis and Zaidis. But when the republican government began wooing the support of the northern tribesmen, whom the new regime considered more dangerous, Baidany fell out with his colleagues in the leadership and went to Cairo in mid-Jan. 1963. He met with Salal in Cairo in June but did not return to Yemen, going instead to Aden in mid-August.)

Armistice

Following Egypto-Saudi Arabian agreement on a plan for phased military withdrawal from Yemen, an armistice between the Yemeni royalists and republicans was arranged Nov. 8, 1964. The principal reason for this armistice was a deadlock in the fighting. The royalist dissidents could not be dislodged from their strong points in the rugged country bordering on proroyalist Saudi Arabia. But the republicans had become stronger, too—in Sana and other urban centers.

Among the major events leading up to the armistice was a Yemeni republican accord with the Soviet Union. The USSR and Yemen had signed a 5-year friendship treaty in Moscow Mar. 21, 1964. Moscow confirmed its recognition of the "full and absolute independence of the Yemeni Arab Republic and its [the republic's] sovereignty over Yemeni territory." The treaty was signed by Soviet Pres. Leonid I. Brezhnev and Yemeni Pres. Abdullah al-Salal, who was in Moscow on a state visit. (A Yemeni-Soviet communiqué said Moscow had also agreed to give Yemen increased economic and technical assistance.)

Nasser visited the Yemeni capital of Sana for the first time Apr. 23. A communiqué at the end of his visit Apr. 29 announced the coordination of UAR and Yemen military, political and economic policies. The Yemeni government Apr. 28 had proclaimed a new constitution declaring the 19-month-old republic "an Islamic Arab state, independent and sovereign." (The constitution had been discussed at a meeting in Sana attended by all national forces.)

Cordial relations were also reinforced by the Yemeni republican regime with Communist China. Yemeni Pres. Salal visited Peking in June and signed a 10-year treaty of friendship with The Communist Chinese government June 19.

The UN's 200-man observer team began to withdraw from Yemen Sept. 4, 1964 after the failure of the 14-month mission to persuade Saudi Arabia and the UAR to disengage their forces. In disclosing the UN's withdrawal decision, UN Secy. Gen. U Thant had reported Sept. 2 to the UN Security Council that he still hoped both countries would try to settle "their needless and now senseless dispute over the Yemen of today." Reporting a net reduction of 4,000 UAR troops in Yemen in the past 2 months, Thant said that this was "a reflection of the improved military situation . . . from the point of view of the UAR and of the increased participation by Yemeni republicans [supported by Cairo]" rather than "phased withdrawal in the sense of the disengagement agreement" that had been approved by the UAR and Saudi Arabia. Thant said that during the 2-month period, the UN observers had found no evidence of Saudi Arabian military equipment sent to the royalists. He pointed out, however, that there was proof that the royalists "continued to receive military supplies from external sources."

But events in Yemen soon took a new turn. Saudi Arabia and the UAR agreed Sept. 14 to end their intervention in the Yemeni civil war and to seek a "peaceful settlement" of the conflict. The agreement was announced in a joint communiqué issued by UAR Pres. Nasser and Saudi Arabian Premier Faisal, who had been discussing the dispute since the conclusion of an Arab summit meeting in Alexandria Sept. 11. Presidents Ahmed Ben Bella of Algeria and Salam Arif of Iraq had acted as intermediaries. An immediate result of the agreement was a cease-fire by both sides in the civil war, Saudi Arabian sources reported Sept. 16. Although details of the agreement were not officially disclosed, the pact was known to have provided that:

- There was to be a 7-month armistice in the civil war; during that period Saudi Arabia would refrain from giving the rebel followers of ousted Imam Muhammad al-Badr moral and material support and the UAR would begin to withdraw its estimated 40,000 troops from the side of the republican army.
- Both countries would seek replacements for the ousted imam, who sought to regain his throne, and for Yemeni Pres. Salal. A new Yemeni government would be formed to include some royalists but no members of the imam's family.

(In a military development not connected with the civil war, tribesmen of the Shafii [Sunni Moslem] sect had been reported Sept. 5 to have seized control of Yemen's twin capital of Taiz. A Shafii spokesman said that all Shafii political prisoners in the city had been released and that a special committee had assumed control of Taiz. A broadcast Sept. 4 from Aden had reported that 30,000 Shafii tribesmen were massed outside Sana, Yemen's other capital city, poised for a possible clash with republican-sympathizing tribesmen of the Zaidi [Shiite Moslem] sect. The Shafii dissidence had followed the replacement a few days earlier of the Shafii governor in Taiz, Sheikh Abdel Wasei Noman.

(In a letter published by the London *Times* Jan. 4, 1964, British Army Lt. Col. Neil McLean had asserted that many Shafii tribes had pledged their support to the deposed Imam Muhammad al-Badr. McLean, who had made several trips to northern Yemen in 1963, also reported that some of the Hashid, the 2d largest Zaidi confederation, supported the republican side in the war.)

Yemeni republican Pres. Salal announced Nov. 8 that the cease-fire had gone into effect that day. The UAR and Saudi Arabia had announced Nov. 5 that the truce agreement had been reached in negotiations between republican and royalist representatives in Erkwit, the Sudan Oct. 29-30. UAR and Saudi officials had attended as observers. The newspaper *Al Hayat* of Jidda, Saudi Arabia had reported Nov. 3 that the 2 delegations had agreed on a plebiscite of the Yemeni people to decide the form of government in Yemen.

Sporadic clashes between Yemeni republican and royalist forces were reported in November and December despite the cease-fire. The clashes forced an apparent indefinite postponement of a peace conference that had been scheduled to open in Yemen Nov. 23. Followers of the ousted Imam Muhammad al-Badr were reported Nov. 18 to have charged that UAR planes had bombed royalist territory in northwestern Yemen with the intent to kill Badr and his premier, Prince Hassan. In denying this, republican officials said the royalist charges were a pretext to avoid the peace conference. A dispatch from Jidda, Saudi Arabia Dec. 3 supported reports that UAR planes had bombed royalist-held areas in the Razih Mountains and the section around Sheda, where Badr and his staff were quartered. The royalists were said to have recaptured almost all territory that had been occupied by UAR-republican forces since their August-September offensive. About 200 republican soldiers were said to be trapped in the Razih Mountains.

Yemen's entire 25-member republican cabinet, with the exception of Education Min. Qassem Ghaleb, was reported Dec. 27 to have resigned. Premier Hamoud al-Jaifi was said to have refused to form a new cabinet. The resignation of 3 cabinet ministers, disclosed Dec. 12, had been described as the first action of protest against Pres. Sala's rule. The ministers were Ahmad Muhammad Noman, head of the Consultative Council, and Deputy Premiers Qadi Zubeiri and Said Abdul Rahman al-Iryany. The ministers issued a statement denouncing the government as corrupt and proposing a new "interim" constitution. The cabinet resignations were said to be part of a widespread protest against Salal's rule and the continued presence in Yemen of 40,000 Egyptian troops.

It was reported from Cairo Dec. 12 that UAR and Saudi Arabian negotiators had failed to reach agreement on a transitional Yemeni regime aimed at reconciling the warring factions. Previous UAR-Saudi Arabian talks had ended in deadlock Dec. 10.

Fresh Clashes & New Negotiations

Renewed fighting in Yemen was reported in April and May 1965. Royalist forces were said to have launched heavy attacks early in April against Egyptian and republican positions on Red Mountain in the Jawf area, 90 miles east of Sana. The royalist attack was said to have severed supply roads to the Egyptian garrisons. But a further report May 29 said the Egyptians and pro-government tribesmen had repelled the royalists and reopened the roads.

The Egyptian forces, sent to aid the republicans, were reported May 29 to have suffered these setbacks: proroyalist tribesmen overran an Egyptian garrison at Sirwah, southeast of Sana; 30 Egyptian soldiers, including Brig. Gen. Muhammad Mahmoud Kassim, were killed when their convoy was ambushed near El-Hazim, about 50 miles southeast of Sana; an Egyptian outpost at El-Juba, southeast of Sana, fell to royalists; in the Harib area, further to the east, tribesmen ousted the Egyptians from a strategic mountain pass north of the town. Egypt was reported May 29 to have shipped reinforcements into Yemen, raising its force there to 50,000 to 60,000 men. 6 to 8 shiploads of Egyptian troops and supplies were said to have been landed in the previous 3 weeks at the

Red Sea port of Hodeida. The equipment was said to have consisted largely of tanks, trucks, armored cars and artillery.

Despite the reported clashes, the positions of the opposing forces remained fundamentally unchanged. Egyptian and government troops retained control of the central, southern and coastal area of Yemen, the main cities and the principal lines of communication. The pro-royalists maintained their hold on Harib, the mountain post of Razin in northwest Yemen and large mountain regions in the north and east. The Egyptian Middle East News Agency had reported from Sana May 5 that a conference in Khamer of pro-republican tribal leaders had established a committee to urge the government to seek peace with the royalists and end "tensions with neighbors." The latter phrase referred to Saudi Arabia, which supported the imam's followers in the fighting.

Meanwhile, another domestic Yemeni political shuffle had occurred, this one seeming to some observers to brighten the prospects for peace. The republican premier, Maj. Gen. Hassan al-Amri, resigned Apr. 15, and Pres. Salal asked the liberal, Baath-leaning Ahmad Muhammad Noman to succeed him. Noman, a Shafii, an intellectual and founder of the "Free Yemenis" movement while in exile in the late 1950s, was reputed to favor a peace conference and a limitation of the presidential powers. His major concern was internal stability, which he was reported to be willing to achieve on terms short of total victory over the monarchists. Noman had been responsible for the Khamer conference, which took place in a village 20 miles north of Sana in the territory of the Beni Hashid tribe. Monarchist tribesmen were invited but none accepted. Nonetheless, the republican tribesmen agreed to seek peace with the royalists and to form an 11,000-man "People's Army" to relieve the Egyptian troops. During the conference it became clear that the departure of UAR troops from Yemeni soil was one of Noman's primary objectives.

Noman opened talks May 13 with Gen. Fathi Abdel Ghani, the Egyptian chief of staff in Yemen, with the aim of facilitating the evacuation of all Egyptian troops. But Noman resigned as premier June 28 after a dispute with Salal, who wanted broader personal powers and closer Yemeni ties with the Egyptian army. Noman was succeeded by Salal as government head.

Salal suddenly left for Cairo July 9, 1965. UAR Pres. Nasser had summoned Salal to impress on him the necessity of a compromise lest Salal's popular base become too narrow. Salal July 18 reaffirmed the principles of the Khamer conference and reappointed Gen. Amri as premier. Salal also ordered the arrest of many of Noman's supporters. Noman himself had left the country.

The principal Yemeni leaders–Pres. Salal, ex-Premier Noman and Premier Amri–met with Nasser in Alexandria, the UAR Aug. 18. A heated argument took place, with Nasser accusing Noman of being anti-Egyptian and finally appearing to convince Noman of his (Nasser's) sincere desire to withdrawing Egyptian troops. After effecting this reconciliation, Nasser visited Jidda in Saudi Arabia Aug. 22. There Aug. 24 he signed with Faisal (who had succeeded his brother Saud as king Nov. 2, 1964) an agreement aimed at ending the Yemeni war.

Under the accord, negotiated by the 2 leaders in talks held Aug. 22-24: (a) the royalist forces of the deposed Imam Muhammad al-Badr and the troops of the Yemen Republic were to halt hostilities immediately; (b) Saudi Arabia was to stop providing military aid to the royalists, and the UAR was to withdraw the 60,000-man force it had sent to support the republican troops. The agreement was to be carried out in 3 stages:

(1) A caretaker Yemeni government was to be established in 3 months and was to rule for one year. Neither the imam nor Yemeni republican Pres. Salal was to be represented in the régime.

(2) Egyptian troops were to be pulled out in 10 months.

(3) Yemen was to hold a national plebiscite Nov. 23,

1966 to decide whether the country was to have a republican, monarchial or other form of government.

Details of the plebiscite and the composition of the caretaker régime were to be worked out at a meeting of reconciliation of 50 Yemeni leaders in Haradh, Yemen Nov. 23, 1965. The disengagement of military forces in Yemen was to be supervised by a joint UAR-Saudi Arabian peace committee assisted by republican and royalist observers. The Yemeni accord was the 3d arranged by Nasser and Faisal; the 2 previous ones, reached in 1963 and 1964, had not taken effect.

Royalist officials announced in Jidda Aug. 25 that their forces had received orders to halt fighting in accordance with the peace terms. Government officials in Lebanon, Iraq and Jordan Aug. 25 lauded the Nasser-Faisal agreement as "a great achievement." But Syria's official government newspaper, *Al-Thawrah*, charged that in accepting the pact Nasser had "betrayed the Yemeni revolution."

Delegates representing rival republican and royalist factions in the Yemeni war opened negotiations in Haradh, Yemen Nov. 23 in an effort to arrange a coalition government and the holding of a national plebiscite on such a régime. Sana radio reported Dec. 25 that the talks were deadlocked and had been postponed until late Feb. 1966. A Saudi Arabian observer at the talks had reported earlier in the day that the meetings had been called off indefinitely.

The conference deadlock reportedly had developed over republican opposition to a royalist proposal that the future régime receive the neutral designation of Arab or Islamic "state of Yemen." The Yemeni republican delegation insisted that the word "republican" be retained. In a letter sent to UAR Pres. Nasser and Saudi Arabian King Faisal (made public Dec. 2), Said Abdul Rahman al-Iryany, head of the republican delegation, charged that only on arriving at Haradh Nov. 23 had his group learned that the 2 leaders' Aug. 24 agreement had provided for the abolition of both the republic and the monarchy (of the ousted Imam Muhammad al-Badr) and had stipulated that the Haradh talks "choose a régime that is neither republican nor imami."

UAR Bogged Down in Yemen

The UAR's expeditionary force remained in Yemen country throughout 1966. Nasser and Saudi Arabian King Faisal reportedly reached agreement in mid-January on the interpretation of the accord they had signed at Jiddah, Saudi Arabia Aug. 24, 1965 for ending the Yemeni war. It was reported in Cairo Jan. 18 that the 2 leaders agreed that a plebiscite should be held to determine the type of government for Yemen.

The 2d round of the Yemeni peace conference had been scheduled to open in Haradh Feb. 20, but the meeting failed to take place because the royalist delegation refused to attend. A member of the Saudi Arabian observers' committee said that the royalists were still dissatisfied with the interpretation of certain provisions of the Jiddah agreement.

In a note delivered to Pres. Lyndon B. Johnson Feb. 21, Faisal appealed for U.S. diplomatic and military aid (including air support) if the UAR resumed fighting in Yemen. Faisal was reported to have warned that if the UAR-supported Yemeni republican forces broke the truce, Saudi Arabian troops might intervene directly in the conflict. Faisal also was said to have told Johnson (according to a report Mar. 8) that the Soviet Union and Communist China might be establishing bases in Yemen for subversion in the Middle East and Africa.

Faisal said to a reporter in a Mecca radio interview Feb. 21: "We . . . have stopped all assistance to the [Yemeni] royalists. Cairo should have begun to withdraw its forces in November when the peace conference began in Haradh." (Yemeni royalists and republicans had met in Nov. 1965 but had failed in efforts to set up a transitional government.)

Faisal said he would continue with plans to call an "Islamic summit conference" in 1966 for the purpose of forging "Islamic solidarity."

Nasser threatened in a speech Feb. 22 to keep 60,000 to 70,000 UAR troops in Yemen for as much as "5 years." He said the withdrawal of the troops would depend on "the settlement of the Yemeni question and the formation of a government that will conduct a plebiscite." "Unless this government is created, we shall not withdraw our troops until the Yemeni revolution is able to defend itself against the conspiracies of imperialism and reaction," he warned. The UAR might retain its troops in Yemen until Britain fulfilled its promise to grant independence to South Arabia in 1968, he said. When he met with Saudi Arabian King Faisal in Aug. 1965, he had told Faisal, Nasser asserted, of a plot sponsored by Saudi Arabia to assist the outlawed Moslem Brotherhood in an attempt to kill Nasser.

Sporadic clashes had continued to be reported in Yemen. A royalist statement issued in Aden Jan. 15, 1966 said that tribesmen supporting the ousted Imam Muhammad al-Badr had severed the Sana-Hodeida road after Egyptian planes had bombed several royalist centers.

It was reported from Yemen Feb. 22 that Egyptian planes had aided Yemeni republican forces in an attack on the royalist Beni Hashid tribe 30 miles east of Sana. A dispatch from Cairo Mar. 10 said that UAR and republican troops had fought proroyalist tribesmen in February and that "hundreds of casualties" had been inflicted. UAR planes also were said to have been active. Both UAR and Saudi Arabian authorities insisted that the new fighting was no resumption of the civil war. Authorities in Cairo called the military moves a "punitive action" against unruly tribal elements and bandits. But Yemeni royalist spokesmen in Beirut (Lebanon) and Aden said that the latest fighting was the start of a new drive and a resumption of the civil war.

Prince Abdul Rahman Ben Yahya, deputy premier of the

exile royalist (imami) government, disclosed in Beirut May 6 that royalist troops fighting Yemeni republican forces had taken over sections of the northeast Jawf area that had been evacuated by Egyptian troops in April. Abdul Rahman said that royalist administrations had been set up in the towns Humeidat and Hazm and around Sada. The Egyptians also had evacuated Sada, but a republican garrison remained there. The deputy premier said that about 30,000 Egyptian troops had been withdrawn from the Jawf area and that Cairo's troops were currently concentrated in the Hodeida-Sana-Taiz triangle in southern and central Yemen.

The Yemeni republican government had warned May 5 that it would use force to retrieve the Saudi Arabian towns of Nejran, Qizan and Asir, near the Yemeni border. The statement said the towns belonged to Yemen before they were siezed by Saudi Arabia in 1930. The republicans claimed that the Saudi Arabian areas had been used by royalist forces for training and the infiltration of Yemen.

Yemen's claim to Qizan and Najran had been upheld by UAR Pres. Nasser May 1. In a May Day address at El Mahalla el-Kubra, 65 miles north of Cairo, Nasser warned that Egyptian forces would seize the 2 towns if royalists continued to use them for "aggression or infiltration" into Yemen.

U.S. Asst. State Secy. Raymond A. Hare had discussed the Yemeni crisis in separate meetings with Saudi King Faisal in Saudi Arabia Apr. 30 and with Nasser in Cairo May 2. The U.S. had been urging the UAR and Saudi Arabia to implement their Aug. 1965 agreement on ending the Yemeni war.

UAR Wages Gas Warfare

Sporadic fighting smoldered in Yemen late in 1966, with Egyptian troops proving unable to dislodge the royalist irregulars. In apparent response to its increasing losses in guerilla ambushes, the UAR command began to make use of gas warfare.

UAR planes were reported to have killed more than 250 persons in a poison-gas attack on the pro-royalist Yemeni village of Kitaf Jan. 5, 1967. Egyptian planes also were said to have bombed the Saudi Arabian town of Najran near the Yemeni border Jan. 27 and 28. The 3 air strikes appeared to indicate that the UAR was continuing to play a major military role in the war. Reporting on the alleged gas raid, Muhammad Abdul Koddos al-Wazir, royalist Yemeni minister of state for foreign affairs, charged Jan. 13 that 9 UAR Soviet-built Ilyushin-28 jet bombers had each dropped 3 large gas bombs on Kitaf, 25 miles south of Sana. Wazir said 95% of the village's population had been killed by "asphyxiation."

A South Arabian Federal government broadcast Jan. 11 supported the charge of a gas raid on Kitaf. The government radio said that in addition to civilian casualties, many domestic animals in the village had been killed. The broadcast said UAR planes had carried out previous gas attacks on Yemen Dec. 17 and 29, 1966. In the 1966 raids, the Egyptian planes had dropped 20 bombs in the Jabal Ayal Yazid area (30 miles northwest of Sana), killing 2 persons, the broadcast said.

A former Yemeni republican official who had defected in Sept. 1966 said in Aden Jan. 11, 1967 that he had witnessed UAR gas attacks in the Jabal Ayal Yazid area Dec. 11, 1966. Muhammad al-Yazali, ex-director of press and publications in the Information Ministry, said 2 UAR Ilyushin jets had dropped 15 gas bombs on the village of Halhal (population 150), killing 2 persons and injuring 33. (Yazali had arrived in Aden Jan. 3, 1967. He said Jan. 8 that since Yemeni republican Pres. Salal had dismissed the government of Premier Hassan al-Amri Sept. 16, 1966, more than 800 Yemenis, including military and political leaders, had fled Sana. 4,880 Yemenis reportedly had been arrested in the purge that followed Amri's ouster; the prisoners were being guarded by Egyptians who had replaced Yemenis in charge of jails and detention centers.)

The UAR Jan. 31, 1967 denied that its forces had used poison gas in Yemen. An Egyptian spokesman said that Cairo and Yemen would accept a UN investigation of the civil war. A statement issued by the International Committee of the Red Cross in Geneva Jan. 31 expressed concern over "the alleged use of poisonous gas." The statement said, however, that committee representatives in Yemen and Swiss doctors who had treated victims of the Kitaf attack had not submitted positive evidence of the use of gas in the air raid. The Red Cross appealed to all sides in the Yemeni civil war to refrain from bombing civilians.

A Saudi Arabian Defense Ministry communiqué had claimed Jan. 27 that 10 UAR Ilyushin jet bombers that day had attacked the Saudi Arabian town of Najran, near the Yemen border, killing 7 persons and wounding 9. The communiqué said that buildings in Najran were destroyed but that the UAR planes had been forced "to flee, dropping their bombs at random" after being fired on by Saudi Arabian antiaircraft guns. The Saudi Arabian government Jan. 29 reported a 2d UAR air strike against Najran Jan. 28 but made no mention of casualties or damage. (Cairo regarded Najran as a staging area for Yemeni royalist forces fighting UAR troops in Yemen.) The Saudi Arabian Defense Ministry charged May 12 that UAR planes May 11 had killed 3 Saudis and wounded 4 when they bombed "civilian targets" in 3 separate raids carried out against Najran.

UAR planes were reported to have killed 70 persons Feb. 9 in a poison-gas attack on the southern Yemeni village of Beni Salamah. The attack was disclosed Feb. 15 in Riyadh, Saudi Arabia by the Yemeni royalist Premier al-Hassan bin Yahya. Hassan said that the Egyptians had carried out the air raid 3 days after a pro-royalist guerrilla force had cut the road from Sana to Taiz during clashes with the pro-UAR Yemeni republican forces. It was reported that the gas used was probably phosgene.

The Yemen Relief Committee of Britain announced in London Feb. 17 that it had sent 250 gas masks to the Yemeni royalist legation in Jidda, Saudi Arabia. The legation was to distribute the gas masks in royalist-controlled sections of Yemen. An official of the relief group, Sir Peter Agnew, said that the committee had decided to collect the gas masks after UAR planes had gassed the Yemeni villages of Kitaf Jan. 5 and Beni Salamah Feb. 9. The British relief group had been shipping medical supplies to the royalists since the civil war had started.

The International Committee of the Red Cross (ICRC) charged in a report dated May 21 (made public in Washington July 27) that UAR planes had killed 318 persons May 10, 17 and 18 in poison-gas attacks on 5 pro-royalist villages in southern Yemen. Several hundred additional Yemenis were reported killed in other UAR poison-gas attacks during May, June and July. (The charge of the gassing of Yemeni civilians was coupled with reports that part of the Egyptian military force was being evacuated from the country in the aftermath of the UAR's defeat in the Arab-Israeli war. The ICRC said that 75 persons had died in the first poison-gas raid, which had been an attack May 10 on Gahar and Gadafa. The report said ICRC medical teams and observers, responding to a rescue appeal from the 2 villages May 11, were unable to reach the scene until May 15–16 because UAR planes had bombed the 2-truck ICRC rescue convoy. (The ICRC had given the Egyptian authorities "due notice" of the convoy's "line of march and timetable.") The ICRC report said that Gadafa had come under attack again when poison-gas raids by UAR planes May 17–18 caused 243 deaths in Gadafa and the villages of Gabas, Nofal and Gadr. The gases used were reported to be mustard gas, phosgene and a gas that kills by paralyzing the central nervous system.

The ICRC had first publicly mentioned the UAR gas attacks, without giving details in a press report issued June 2. The Red Cross that day also had appealed to the Yemeni republican government, the UAR, the Yemeni royalists and Saudi Arabia "not to resort in any circumstances whatever to the use of asphyxiating gases or any other similar toxic substances" in the fighting. The ICRC disclosed June 5 that it had "made representations" to the UAR over the bombing of the Red Cross rescue convoy heading for Gahar and Gadafa.

Radio Mecca had reported June 1 that UAR jets had dropped 50 poison-gas bombs May 29 on villages in the Ben Hashish area, 12 miles from Sana. An earlier Yemeni report said 60 persons had been killed when UAR bombers had dropped poison-gas bombs and napalm on Sarawah May 28. British intelligence sources in Aden reported July 6 that UAR planes had killed 45 persons with poison-gas and bombs dropped June 2 on the Yemeni royalist-held village of Ben Sham.

Reports from Yemen said other poison-gas attacks by UAR planes had killed about 50 persons in several villages near Khaulan July 2 and 3, about 150 persons (350 wounded) in the northern town of Hajiah July 15 and about 30 persons in El-Urr and Al-Hamran July 23.

A U.S. State Department statement July 27, without mentioning Cairo by name, condemned the gas attacks on Yemeni royalists "as inhumane and entirely contrary to the laws of nations." The statement added that Washington "would support international action to deal with this problem." The department also disclosed a letter in which U.S. Amb.-to-UN Arthur J. Goldberg had expressed the Administration's "concern over the growing number of indications that gas is once again being used by the UAR air force against the local population in Yemen." Goldberg's letter was a reply to Rep. Lester L. Wolff (D., N.Y.), who had asked why the Administration had taken no action on the reported use of gas in Yemen.

Egypt Withdraws from Yemen

Israel's lightning victory over the UAR in the June 1967 war finally put an end to the question of whether Egyptian troops would remain on Yemeni soil. The maintenance of the Egyptian contingent became too expensive, and the troops were needed on the Suez front. About 40,000 men—most of the Egyptian force—were withdrawn by the end of 1967.

An Agence France-Press report from Aden June 16, 1967 had said that Egyptian troops withdrawn from Hajja had been attacked by Yemeni tribesmen as they fled to the Red Sea evacuation port of Hodeida. The tribesmen were described as neither pro-royalist nor pro-republican but just anti-Cairo. Other UAR troops were said to have been pulled out of Marib, about 80 miles east of Sana, the republican capital. Royalist sources reported June 19 that the major portion of the UAR garrison in Sana had been withdrawn and that about 300 Egyptian troops had been slain by royalist soldiers as the Egyptians were trying to make their way to Hodeida.

Aden radio reported July 30 that Cairo had threatened to withdraw all of its remaining 25,000 troops from Yemen if the republican regime did not share the cost of maintaining the UAR force there. Egypt was said to have asked the Sana regime to provide more troops to defend the towns of Maydi and Haradh, near the Saudi Arabian border, captured earlier from the royalists by Egyptian troops.

UAR Foreign Min. Mahmoud Riad Aug. 3 submitted a plan for the implementation of the Yemen cease-fire agreement signed in Aug. 1965 by King Faisal of Saudi Arabia and Pres. Nasser of the UAR. The agreement had called for a phased withdrawal of Egyptian troops from Yemen and the formation of a provisional royalist-republican coalition government pending a referendum to determine whether Yemen should have a monarchic or republican form of government. Egypt never withdrew its forces, and the fighting had continued. The new UAR proposal called for the creation of a committee of 3 Arab states to seek the implementation of the pact and an end to the war.

In a move aimed at overcoming Yemeni republican Foreign Min. Abdul Aziz Sallam's objection to the projected plebiscite, the Khartoum Conference of Arab States Aug. 5 discussed a plan for the appointment of a 3-state fact-finding commission to negotiate a settlement of the Yemeni war without reference to the 1965 agreement. The proposal, backed by Saudi Arabia failed to satisfy Sallam, who asserted Aug. 6 that the plebiscite would constitute interference in Yemen's internal affairs.

The undersecretary of the Saudi Foreign Ministry, Omar Saqqaf, had expressed a favorable initial response to the Egyptian proposal Aug. 3. But in a statement Aug. 7 over Mecca radio, Saqqaf declared that the withdrawal of Egyptian troops from Yemen remained Saudi Arabia's condition for ending the war in Yemen. Saqqaf said that if the Egyptian forces were pulled out, the Mecca government would permit the stationing of observers on Saudi Arabia's borders with Yemen to insure that the Saudis were not sending assistance to the Yemeni royalists.

Reports reaching Aden Aug. 29 said that a cease-fire arranged the previous week-end had collapsed following an Egyptian air attack on royalist-held villages in the Lower Jawf area, 45 miles northeast of Sana. The air strike was said to have led to a resumption of royalist military operations in the Sana area. A dispatch from Aden Aug. 30 said the royalist forces were only 3 miles from Sana. A combined UAR-Yemeni republican force, aided by Egyptian air strikes, killed 250 attacking anti-Egyptian tribesmen unaligned with

Yemeni royalists in a battle at Ibb, 20 miles north of Taiz, Yemen's alternate capital, it was reported from Aden Sept. 15. UAR and government troops suffered 160 casualties. The fighting was the culmination of a series of clashes in the area in previous weeks.

But a series of reports in September told of Egyptian military evacuation from Yemen under terms of an agreement reached at Khartoum Aug. 31 between Nasser and Saudi Arabian King Faisal. A spokesman in Sana said Sept. 10 that Egyptian troops had begun to move supplies and equipment to the port of Hodeida. Aden radio reported Sept. 14 that 1,500 UAR soldiers had shipped out from Hodeida Sept. 10. This was the first withdrawal as provided for by the Khartoum accord. Yemeni royalist Social Affairs Min. Hashem ben Hashem said Sept. 17 that Muhammad ben Hussein, commander of the royalist forces in Yemen, had issued orders to his troops to protect Egyptian forces as they withdrew.

Public demonstrations against the presence in Sana of a 3-man Arab peace commission that arrived in the Yemeni capital Oct. 4 forced the group to return to Cairo the same day. The commission, established at the Arab summit meeting in Khartoum Aug. 31, sought to discuss with republican leaders means of ending the conflict. The commission's members were: Sudanese Premier Muhammad Mahgoub, Iraqi Foreign Min. Ismail Kharallah and Amb. Ahmed Ben Sueida of Morocco. A statement issued by the commission on its arrival in Cairo later Oct. 4 said: The commission had decided to leave Sana "for the sake of the safety and security of the people of Yemen." Tribal leaders had been thwarted in their efforts to meet the commission "owing to the difficult circumstances and obstacles placed in the mission's way." (Before going to Sana, the 3-man Arab peace commission had conferred with Yemeni royalist leaders in Beirut, Lebanon Sept. 17–20. Royalist Foreign Min. Ahmad Shami, who met with the commission, disclosed

Sept. 20 a royalist plan for governing Yemen once Egyptian troops were withdrawn from the country and republicans and royalists agreed to a regime of national unity. Under the plan, 150 to 200 Yemenis of varied political opinion would hold a conference to select an 8-member ruling sovereignty council and establish 2 other governing bodies: a cabinet of 18 to 24 members and an 80-member parliament.)

5 Yemeni civilians and 9 Egyptian soldiers were killed Oct. 4 in the Sana rioting, in which stone-throwing mobs attempted to storm the headquarters of the Egyptian military command in the city. 7 Egyptian soldiers disappeared in the rioting. Police arrested Col. Abdul Qader al-Khatari, deputy interior minister and chief of security, on charges of having killed the 5 Yemenis by firing his revolver into the crowd. Sana radio reported Oct. 6 that Khatari had been sentenced to death by a military court.

UAR authorities in Oct. 1967 released from 13 months of detention in Cairo Ahmad Muhammad Noman, Said Abdul Rahman al-Iryan and Lt. Gen. Hassan al-Amri, all members of Yemen's republican Presidential Council at one time and all foes of Pres. Abdullah al-Salal. (Noman and Amri had also been premiers in the Yemeni republican regime.) The 3 returned to Yemen and resumed public life after Pres. Salal was overthrown early in November. Iryany became president, Noman rejoined the Presidential Council, and Amri in December became premier.

INDEX

A

ABADIR, Kamal Henry–167
ABBOUD, Ibrahim–116
ABDRABOU, Hisham–86
ABDUL Rahman Ben Yahya, Prince –204-5
ABDULLAH, King (Jordan)–71
ABENDZEITUNG (Munich newspaper)–101
ACHESON, Dean–137
ADEN–172, 178, 182, 187, 194, 211
ADENAUER, Konrad–75
ADIL, Fuad al-–87
ADZHUBEI, Aleksei I. and Rada–122
AFGHANISTAN–140
AFLAQ, Michel–23, 110
AFRICA–139-45, 165
AFRO-Asian Economic Conference –79
AGHA, Mustafa–166
AGNEW, Peter–208
AGRARIAN Reform Laws–73, 96
AHDUT Avodah–13
AHMAD bin Yahya, Imam (Yemen) –41-2, 89, 171-4
AHMED, Shardi–56
AHRAM, Al: (Cairo newspaper)–28, 65, 74, 91, 110-1, 150, 160-2, 164, 177
AINY, Mohsen al-–175-6, 179
AKHBAR, Al- (Cairo newspaper)–74, 161
AL–Names beginning with this prefix are indexed alphabetically as though the name started with the letter following the al-. For example, Ahmed Hassan al-Bakoury is indexed under 'B' thus: BAKOURY, Ahmed Hassan al-
ALA, Hussein–12
ALAFI, Lt.–173
Al-BATANAH, Yemen–189
ALEM, Muhammad el-–74
ALEPPO, Syria–23, 33, 56, 103-4
ALEXANDER the Great–2
ALEXANDRIA–64, 197
ALGERIA–109, 112, 140, 142-4, 155, 159, 165
ALI, Ali el-Said–122
ALI, Mehmet–23
ALLDYA-war, Sheik Ahmad Ajil–54
ALWAN, Jasm–115
AMER, Abdel Hakim–20-1, 29, 33, 38-9, 43, 56, 67, 73, 83-5, 100, 116, 127, 159, 187, 193-4
AMERICAN Federation of Labor & Congress of Industrial Organizations (AFL-CIO)–78
AMIN, Ali–161
AMIN, Mustafa–161-2
AMMAN, Jordan–16, 71
AMRI, Hassan al-–165, 200-1, 206, 213
ANDRAWES, Adli–81
ANGLO-Egyptian Treaty of 1936–93
ANGOLA–118, 140
AQABA, Gulf of (Israeli name: Gulf of Eilat)–20, 59
ARAB Federation of Jordan & Iraq –40-1, 50. See also IRAQ, JORDAN
ARABIC Language–129
ARAB League–53, 105, 154-5, 168-9, 177
ARAB Nationalist Movement–108, 112
ARAB Socialist Party–23
ARAB Socialist Union–94-5, 108, 157, 161
ARAB States: Meetings & agreements–53, 105-19, 197, 211. See also ARAB League, specific state
ARAB Students, Organization of–21
ARAB Union Front–108, 112

ARAFA, Moussa–64, 83
ARGENTINA–140
ARIF, Abdel Salam (or Abd-ul-Salam Muhammad Aref)–52, 107, 114, 116, 119-22, 124-5, 197
ARISS, Sabet el-–74, 83
ARKHIPOV, Ivan–64
ARMENIA (Soviet liner)–122
ARRESTS–14, 56, 81-2, 84, 153, 161-2, 194
ASHMAWY, Ahmed Abdu–166
ASSAFA, Mofak–86
ASSALI, Sabri el-–27, 38, 84
ASWAN High Dam–2, 15, 53, 63, 122, 164. Soviet aid–61-4, 124, 160
ATTASSI, Jawdat al-–17
ATTASSI, Col. Louai al-–104
ATTASSI, Lt. Gen. Louai al-–106-8, 112
ATTIA, Mrs. Rawia–15
AULAQI, Muhammad Farid al-–186
AWDATULLAH, Toma al-–73-4, 83
AYOUBI, Naithan–115
AYYOUB, Dhummoun–56
AZANDE Tribe–144
AZIZ, Muhammad Abdul–16
AZM, Khaled el-–27, 37, 39, 106
AZMAH, Bashir al-–104-5

B

BAATH, Al (Damascus newspaper) –110
BAATH (Resurrection) Party (Syria)–23-6, 35, 106, 108, 110-2, 114-6
BADEAU, John F.–183, 187
BADR, Seif al-Islam Muhammad al-–42, 171-3
BADRAN, Shamseddin–167
BAGHDAD, Iraq–56
BAGHDAD Pact–10, 31, 58
BAGDASH, Khaled–38, 54
BAHI, Johad–115
BAIDANY, Abdul Rahman al-–175-6, 178-9, 182, 185, 194-5
BAKER, Fateh–87
BAKIL Tribe–195
BAKOURY, Ahmed Hassan al-–38
BAKR, Abdul Hamid Abu–74
BAKR, Ahmed Hassan al-–107, 114
BAKRY, Ahmed Tewfiq el-–167
BALFOUR Declaration–92
BALL, George W.–127
BANDUNG Anniversary Conference–158
BANIYAS–103
BARAKAT, Awad–86
BAROODY, Mustafa–87
BARTLETT, Thomas A.–190
BATTLE, Lucius D.–145-6, 164
BAVASSA, René–144
BAYAR, Celâl–12
BEGIN, Menahem–156
BEIHAN–177-8, 186
BEKIR, Tahrir–126
BELGIAN Congo–139. See also CONGO
BELLIVIER, Jean Paul François–81
BEN Bella, Ahmed–112-3, 116, 124, 140, 142-3, 158-9, 196
BEN-Gurion, David–13, 17, 66, 100
BEN Hashish, Yemen–209
BENI, Hashid Tribe–200, 204
BENI Salamah–207-8
BEN-Nathan, Ascher–156
BEN Sham, Yemen–209
BGENYE, Christophe–143
BIRRENBACH, Kurt–154
BISHRI, Abdel Aziz Wahab el-–128, 157, 167
BITAR, Salah el-Din el-–10, 23, 35, 38, 73, 110-1
BIZRI, Afif–24, 29-30, 33, 39
BLACK, Eugene R.–76
BLITZ (Indian magazine)–59
BODROV, Mikhail F.–69
BOGHDADI, Abdel Latif el-–38, 83-4, 88
BOLIVIA–140
BOLZ, Lothar–151
BOTANY Industries, Inc.–152
BOUMEDIENNE, Houari–110, 159
BOURGUIBA, Habib–87, 116-7, 165
BOYCOTTS–77-82, 152, 168-9
BRAZIL–140
BREZHNEV, Leonid I.–159, 195
BRIKKAN, Munir–115

BRITAIN–See GREAT Britain
BULGANIN, Nikolai–30
BUNCHE, Ralph–185, 187
BUNKER, Ellsworth–189-90
BURMA–140
BURUNDI–140

C

CABINET(S)–See country
CAMBODIA–140
CAMEROON–140
CASABLANCA Group–188
CEYLON–140
CHAD–140
CHAMOUN, Camille–45-7, 49
CHARTER for National Action–91-100
CHEHAB Fuad–61, 116
CHEMICAL Warfare–205-10
CHILE–140
CHINA, People's Republic of (Communist)–143, 158, 160, 196
CHINA, Republic of (Nationalist)–87
CHOU En-Lai–123
CIA (U.S. Central Intelligence Agency)–161-2
CLEOPATRA (UAR cargo vessel)–77-82
CLEVELAND, Harlan–190
COCA-Cola Co.–168-9
COMMUNISTS & Communist Party (Egypt)–56, 156, 160-1
COMMUNISTS & Communist Party (Syria)–23-6, 38-9
CONGO, Belgian–139
CONGO (Brazzaville)–140, 142
CONGO (Léopoldville)–139, 143-4, 158-9
CONSTANTINOPLE Convention of 1888–12
CONSTITUTION (UAR)–94-5, 129-37
CORTADA, James–186-7
CUBA–140
CYPRUS–126, 137-40
CZECHOSLOVAKIA–21

D

DAHI, Johad–112
DAHOMEY–140
DAILY Telegraph (London newspaper)–178
DAMASCUS, Syria–23, 55-6, 85, 103-4, 114, 193
DAMASCUS Radio–33, 85, 104, 109
DAR el-Hana Co.–56
DAR el-Nadim Co.–56
DAROFF, Michael–152
DAYAN, Moshe–67
DEEB, Hamid Fathy el-–122
DEIF, Nazih Ahmed–128, 167
DEIRI, Akram–83, 105, 109
De GAULLE, Charles–158
De NERVA, Marquis–148
DHAHRAN (& air base)–11, 177
DHAMAN, Abdel Ghani–86
DHARA, Saudi Arabia–187
DILLON, C. Douglas–78, 80
DIN, Muhammad Salah el-–14
DIRKSEN, Sen. Everett M. (R., Ill.)–80
DIXON, Pierson–70
DOUGLAS, Sen. Paul H. (D., Ill.)–80
DULLES, John Foster–4-6, 11, 13, 25-6, 31, 34

E

EAST Germany–75, 151
EBEID, Ahmed Hamdy–167
ECONOMY–28-30, 157
EDEN, Anthony–61, 124
EGYPT–1-2, 10, 53, 67, 79, 193
    Africa–139-45
    Arms & armed forces–100-2, 116, 136; see ISRAEL for Egyptian-Israeli hostilities
    Communists & Communist Party–56, 156, 160-1
    Economy–28-30, 157
    Elections–15-6, 88, 128-9
    Foreign aid–150-1: Soviet–21-2, 61-4, 124, 160; U.S.–2, 9-10, 21, 64
    Iraq–105-16, 119-22
    Foreign policy & relations–61, 74-7; see also specific country
    Israel & Israeli hostilities–See ISRAEL
    Jordan–16-8, 71

National Assembly—36, 128-9, 133
Soviet Union—See UNION of Soviet Socialist Republics
Syria—23-43, 102-16, 116-22
U.S.—See UNITED States
Yemen—199-203, 210-3; see also under 'Y'
See also UNITED Arab Republic
EGYPTIAN Industrial Bank—64
EILAT, Gulf of—See AQABA, Gulf of
EISENHOWER, Dwight D.—3-14, 25, 46-9, 58, 62
EISENHOWER Doctrine—3-14, 20, 25-6, 29, 33-4
EL—Names beginning with this prefix are indexed alphabetically as though the name started with the letter following the el-. For example, Muhammad el-Alem is indexed under 'A' thus: ALEM, Muhammad el-
ELECTIONS (Egypt)—15-6, 88, 128-9
ELLIOTT, Osborn—150
EMARY, Qadi Yahya al-—172
ERGIM, Shemi—32
ERHARD, Ludwig—148-9, 153-4, 156
EROFEYEV, Vladimir—69
ESHKOL, Levi—102, 118, 126-7, 149, 153-4, 156, 163
ESIN, Seyfullah—32
ESPIONAGE—81-2, 153, 161-2
ESSEDIN, Gadou—83
ETHIOPIA—140
ETHNOS (Athens newspaper)—10
EZELDIN, Jadou—74

F

FAHMI, Abdel Azim—128
FAISAL ben Turki ben Abdul Aziz, Emir (Saudi Arabian crown prince until Nov. 2, 1964, king thereafter)—40-1, 162, 179, 181, 183-4, 187, 197, 201-5, 210, 212
FAMILY Planning—97
FANFANI, Amintore—74-5
FARID, Muhammad Talaat—53
FAROUK, King (Egypt)—2, 16
FAWZI, Mahmoud—38, 42, 69, 75, 83, 102, 128, 145-6, 157, 167
FAYEK, Muhammad—167
FEDERER, Georg—148
FEDORENKO, Nikolai T.—191
FEINBERG, Abraham—169
FEISAL, Gamal—85
FEISAL, King (Iraq)—17-8, 33, 50, 54
FINLAND—140
FORD Motor Co.—168-9
FRANCE—13, 18-22, 76-7, 81-2, 158
FREE Officers—2
FULBRIGHT, Sen. J. William (D., Ark.)—79-81

G

GABAS, Yemen—208
GADAFA, Yemen—208-9
GADR, Yemen—208
GAHAR, Yemen—208-9
GALILEE, Sea of (Lake Kinneret, Lake Tiberias)—118
GANDY, Christopher—178
GAS Warfare—205-10
GAZA Strip—69
GBENYE, Christophe—142, 159
GERMANY: East Germany—75, 151. West Germany—75, 147-56, 162-3
GHALEB, Qassem—198
GHANA—140, 188, 191
GHANI, Fathi Abdel—200
GHAZALI, Zeinaz al-—166
GOLDBERG, Arthur J.—78, 209
GOMAA, Muhammad—167
GOMAA, Sharawai—122
GORDON, Rep. Thomas S. (D., Ill.)—3, 7
GORSHKOV, Sergei G.—164
GOUMHOURIA, Al (Cairo newspaper)—63, 65, 159, 162
GRAHAM, Katharine—149
GREAT Britain—2, 13, 18-22, 50, 75-7, 126, 138-9, 182, 185-7, 208
GRECHKO, Andrei A.—163
GREEK Cypriots—137-9
GRIESBACH, Jürgen—174
GROMYKO, Andrei A.—27-8, 34-5, 122, 159, 164
GROTEWOHL, Otto—75

GRUENING, Sen. Ernest (D. Alaska)–124
GUATEMALA–87
GUINEA–140, 188
GYANI, Prem Singh–194

H

HABIB, Muhammad–188
HADJALI, Abdel Hamid–142
HAFEZ, Amin al-–110, 114, 116-7
HAFIZ, Youssef–167
HAJJA Province–175, 180, 210
HAKIM, Abdo–115
HALEM, Abdel Kader–157
HALHAL, Yemen–206
HALL, Paul–77-8
HALLSTEIN Doctrine–149
HAMA, Syria–103
HAMDY, Nadya Muhammad–153
HAMMOODA, Badawi–128
HAMDOUN, Mustafa–38, 73
HAMMARSKJÖLD, Dag–5, 35, 66-9
HARADH, Yemen–180, 202-3, 210
HARE, Raymond A.–205
HARIB, Yemen–180, 186, 188-9, 199-200
HARRIMAN, W. Averell–153
HART, William–181
HASHAD, Muhammad Naguid–88
HASHEM, Hashem ben–212
HASHID Tribe–195, 198
HASHIM, Ibrahim–49
HASSAN, Abdel Fattah–14
HASSAN bin Yahya, Prince al-–175-7, 182, 207
HASSAN II, King (Morocco)–87, 116, 188
HASSOUNA, Abdel Khalek–70-1, 105
HASSOUNA, Muhammad Issameddin–157, 167
HATEM, Abdel Kader–83, 88, 107, 128, 174, 182
HAWASH, Muhammad Youssef–166
HAYAT, Al (Saudi Arabia newspaper)–198
HAZM, Yemen–205
HEATH, Edward–186
HEDAYAT, Saladin–83, 128
HEIKAL, Muhammad Hassanein–110-1
HELMI, Samir–128
HENDERSON, Loy–25-7, 30
HENNAWI, Kamaleddin el-–122
HERUT Party–156
HIGHER Arab Revolutionary Command of the Armed Forces–85
HILLAL, Fuad–16-7
HILMI, Mahmoud Hilmi Abbas–118-9
HILW, Farajallah al-–65
HINDI, Hani el-–112, 115
HINDI, Nassib–86
HODEIDA, Yemen–172-3, 175, 178, 180, 200, 210, 212
HOMAD, Abdel Wahab–38, 83, 112, 115
HOMS, Syria–23, 103
HOMY, Sabry Arafa el-–166
HONEIDY, Ahmed–83
HOSNI, Ahmad–38, 83, 87
HOURANI, Akram–38, 64, 73, 84, 111
HOWEIDY, Amin Hamed–167
HUMEIDAT, Yemen–205
HUMPHREY, Sen. Hubert H. (D., Minn.)–8
HUNEIDI, Ahmad–109
HUNGARY–6
HURIYAH, Abd al-Rahman–86
HUSSEIN, King (Jordan)–12, 16-8, 33, 40, 50, 70-2, 116-7, 177, 179, 181, 184
HUSSEIN, Abdel Satar al-–122
HUSSEIN, Ahmed–9
HUSSEIN, Kamal el-Din–73, 84
HUSSEIN, Muhammad ben–212

I

IBB Province–175
IBRAHIM, Assad–39
IBRAHIM, Hassan–127
IBRAHIM, Hassan bin–42, 175
IDRIS I, King (Libya)–116, 188
ILLAH, Abdul–12
INDEPENDENT Television Authority (ITV) (Great Britain)–20
INDIA–140, 160
INDIAN Ocean–59
INDONESIA–140

INGER Toft (Danish Freighter)–66-67
INTERNATIONAL Committee of the Red Cross (ICRC)–207-9
INTERNATIONAL Confederation of Arab Trade Unions–79
INTERNATIONAL Court of Justice–66
INTERNATIONAL Longshoremen's Association (ILA)–77
INTERNATIONAL Monetary Fund (IMF)–168
IRAN–12, 58, 87
IRAQ–12, 17, 24-5, 50, 55, 58-9, 79, 102, 140, 155, 165, 178, 193, 202. Revolution–45-54, 106. UAR & Egypt–53-63, 106-8, 119-22
IRYANY, Said Abdul Rahman al-–199, 202, 213
ISHASAT, Mamduh–71
ISLAM–89, 129, 173, 194-5, 197
ISMAIL, Abdulfattah–166
ISRAEL–13, 20, 24. Arab antagonisms & hostilities–2, 69, 116-9. Armed forces & arms–100-2, 147-9, 151-2, 162-3; see also 'Arab . . . hostilities' above, 'UAR & Egyptian . . . hostilities' below. Boycotts & barring of cargoes–66-70, 168-9. UAR & Egyptian antagonisms & hostilities–2, 67-70, 100-2, 113-4, 210. U.S.–10, 102; see also UNITED States. West Germany–147-9, 151-3, 156, 162-3
ISTANBUL-Baghdad Railroad–32
ISTIQLAL Party–56, 108
ITALY: UAR relations–74-5
IZVESTIA (unofficial Soviet government newspaper)–9
IZZIDIN, Jadu–109

J

JABAL Ayal Yazid, Yemen–206
JABARRAH, Hassan–38
JADIR, Adeb al-–122
JAIFI, Hamoud al-–198
JAMAICA–140
JANDALI, Karhan al-–86
JARRAH, Muhammad el-–87, 115
JARRING, Gunnar–45
JAVITS, Sen. Jacob K. (R., N.Y.)–147
JAWAD, Hashim–56
JAWF, Yemen–180, 184, 189, 199, 205, 211
JIDDA, Saudi Arabia–175, 201-3
JIZAN, Saudi Arabia–187
JOHN W. Mecom Oil Co. (Houston, Tex.)–145
JOHNSON, Lyndon B.–124, 127, 203
JOHNSTON, Eric–118
JORDAN–10, 24-5, 33-4, 45, 50, 55, 59, 87, 140, 146, 173, 176-7, 180, 202. Egypt & UAR–16-8, 50, 70-2, 89, 117, 179
JORDAN River–117-8, 123
JUMBLATT, Kemal–45
JUNDI, Sami el-–106

K

KAHALA, Nurredin–73
KAISSOUNI, Abdel Moneim el-–28, 38, 75, 83, 88, 128, 157, 168
KALIL, Mustafa–168
KALLAS, Khalil el-–28, 38, 105
KAMEL, Mostafa–126, 142
KANAWATI, Shawkhat el-–38, 83
KANOUT, Abdel Ghani–73
KAPITAN Manolis (Liberian Freighter)–67
KARACHI, Pakistan–166
KARAMANLIS, Constantine–75
KARAME, Rashid–45
KASAVUBU, Joseph–139-41
KASHMIR–160
KASSEM, Abdul Karim el-–51-2, 54-63, 87, 106, 178
KASSIM, Muhammad Mahmoud–199
KASSIM, Nihad el-–83, 112
KATANA, Camp–85
KATANGA Province, Belgian Congo–139
KATININ, Maj. Gen. Rashed (Rashid el-Kattani)–111, 115
KAYALI, Fakher el-–38, 74, 83
KEITA, Modibo–142-3
KENNEDY, John F.–181-4, 189. Assassination–123
KENYA–140
KERIM, Ahmad Abdel–38

KERZI, Khedar el--86
KHABT, Yemen–189
KHAIRY, Muhammad Talaat–128, 157, 167
KHALIFA, Ahmed Muhammad–167
KHALIL, Mustafa–38, 83, 128
KHALLAF, Hussein–128
KHAMAS, Saudi Arabia–192
KHARALLAH, Ismail–212
KHARTOUM, Sudan–144, 166, 212
KHARTOUM Conference of Arab States–211
KHATARI, Abdul Qader al--213
KHEDIVIAL Mail Line of Alexandria–77
KHESHEN, Dr. Shafiq Ali el--128, 167
KHRUSHCHEV, Nikita S.–31, 52, 54-63, 65, 122-6, 138, 160, 175
KHRUSHCHEV, Nina Petrovna–122
KHRUSHCHEV, Sergei–122
KIESOW, Franz William–153
KINNERET, Lake (Sea of Galilee, Lake Tiberias)–118
KITAF, Yemen–206-8
KLIBI, Chaldy–165
KNAPPSTEIN, Heinrich–152
KODSI, Nazem el--103, 111
KOMZIN, Ivan V.–63
KOREA, North–158
KORRA, Nureddin–167
KOSYGIN, Aleksei N.–159-60, 164
KOTB, Sayed–166
KOTOV, V. F.–31
KUHALA, Nureddin–38, 64, 84
KUHEIMY, Sheikh Abdul Aziz–40
KURDISH Tribesmen–54
KUWAIT–59, 140, 155
KUWATLY, Adnan al--86
KUWATLY, Shukri al--10, 12, 24, 27, 36-7, 41
KUZBARI, Mahmoun al--84, 86-7
KYPRIANOU, Spyros A.–138-9

L

LAND Reform–73, 96
LAOS–140
LATAKIA, Syria–23, 31, 33, 85
LEBANON–13, 17, 23, 25, 33, 40-1, 45-53, 59, 61, 79, 112, 118, 140, 155, 169, 202
LÉOPOLDVILLE, Congo–140-1, 144
LIBERAL Revolutionary Army–174
LIBERIA–140
LIBYA–13, 17, 79, 126, 140, 155, 188
LIFE (magazine)–59
LODGE, Henry Cabot–5
LOTZ, Johann Wolfgang Sigmund–153
LUMBARD, J. Edward–78
LUMUMBA, Patrice–142-3

M

MAARI, Raef–115
MAARIS, Yemen–180
MACMILLAN, Harold–58
MAHBOUB, Muhammad–169
MAHGOUB, Muhammad Ahmed–13, 144, 212
MAHMOUD, Zahouddin el--71
MAHROUKI, Ahmed Muhammad el--83, 87
MAJALI, Hazza–71-2
MAJLIS al-Umma–15
MAKARIOS, Archbishop–137-9
MALAWI–140
MALI–140, 142, 188
MALIK, Charles–13, 33
MALINOVSKY, Rodion y.–21, 159
MANSFIELD, Sen. Mike (D., Mont.)–8
MAPAM Party–13, 156
MAREI, Sayed–38, 87
MARIB, Yemen–177, 187, 189, 210
MATTEI, André–81
MAURITANIA–140
MAYDI, Yemen–210
McGHEE, George C.–154
McLEAN, Neil–197
MEANY, George–78-9
MEIR (Myerson), Mrs. Golda–68-9, 153
MEKKAOUI, Jamil–33
MENDERES, Adnan–12, 30
METWALLY, Magdy–166
MEXICO–140

MICHEL, Rep. Robert H. (R., Ill.)—147
MIDDLE East News Agency—17, 27, 34, 57, 65, 100, 161, 163, 177, 180, 200
MIKOYAN, Anastas—159-60
MIQUEL, André—81
MISSILE Race: Egyptian-Israeli—100-2
MOHANDES, Muhammad el-Nabawi el-—88, 128, 157, 167
MOHARES, Fawwaz—112
MOHIEDDIN (Mohyeddin, Muhyl-ul-Din), Zakaria—38, 53, 84, 127, 157, 167-8
MOROCCO—112, 140, 155, 188, 191
MOSLEM Brotherhood—166, 168, 204
MOSLEM Ladies Society—166
MOSUL Uprising—54, 56
MOUTON, Henri-Pierre E.—81
MUHAMMAD bin Ahmad al-Badr, Imam (Yemen)—174-5, 177, 179-80, 182, 189, 197-8, 201, 203-4
MUHAMMAD V, King (Morocco)—63
MUNRO, Leslie—34
MURPHY, Thomas F.—78
MUTUAL Security Act of 1954—4
MUWASSAM, Saudi Arabia—179
MUZAHIM, Youssef—83, 115

N

NAGUIB, Muhammad—14
NAHAS, Mustafa el-—14
NAHLAWI, Abdel Kerim el-—86
NAJRAN, Saudi Arabia—183, 192, 206-7
NAKURI, Ain—38
NASHARI, Niman—87
NASSAR, Ahmed Atf—14
NASSER, Gamal Abdel ('Abd-ul-Nasser)—1-2, 37, 63, 157
- Aims & policies—91-100
- Arabs & Arab countries—3-22, 45-53, 71, 113, 116, 126, 201; see also specific country
- Assassination plots—39-40, 166, 204
- Aswan Dam—63; see also under 'A'
- Cabinet appointments—37-8, 73-4, 87-8, 127-29, 157, 167-8
- Communists (domestic)—56, 65
- Foreign relations & policy—16, 18-22, 61, 76-7, 79-80, 87, 137-9, 148; see also specific country or topic
- Iraq—51-63, 105-16, 119-22
- Israel—66-70, 100, 113, 117
- Politics & elections—14-6, 37, 84, 88, 157
- Soviet Union & other Communist countries—10, 18-22, 52, 54-63, 65, 122-6, 150-1, 159-60
- Syria—23-43, 82, 84-7, 104, 107
- 3d world & Africa—142-3, 157-61
- U.S.—10, 12, 28-9, 48-9, 146, 159, 162-5, 187, 189, 205
- Yemen—42-3, 88-9, 173-4, 177, 181, 189-90, 196-7, 201-5, 210-1

NATIONAL Congress of Popular Forces—88, 91
NAZIF, Amin—86
NEGEV Desert—123
NEHRU, Jawaharlal—10
NEPAL—140
'NEW Emerging Forces'—158
N.Y. HERALD Tribune (newspaper)—11, 74
N.Y. TIMES (newspaper)—4, 10, 21, 31, 58, 60, 69, 82, 100, 163, 192-3
NEWSWEEK (magazine)—149
NIGERIA—140
NILE River & Nile waters—53, 124
NKRUMAH, Kwame—140, 142-3
NOFAL, Yemen—208
NOMAN, Abdel Wasei—197
NOMAN, Ahmad Muhammad—199, 201, 213
NONALIGNED Countries—See 3d WORLD
NORTH American Newspaper Alliance (news agency)—74

NORTH Atlantic Treaty Organization (NATO)–138
NORTH Korea–158
NORTH Vietnam–158-60
NOSSEIR, Muhammad Abu–37-8, 128
NOUR, Abdelmohsin Abu el-–83, 88, 128, 167
NOVIKOV, Ignati T.–63
NURI as-Said–12, 54, 61
NUS, Izzat al-–86

O

ODELL, Taylor–161-2
OKASHA, Sarwat–83, 167
ORGANIZATION of African States –139-45
ORGANIZING African Unity (book)–139
OUDETALLAH, Tohme–109

P

PAHLEVI, Shah Muhammad Riza–162
PAKISTAN–11-2, 58, 160
PALESTINE–See ISRAEL
PALESTINE Automobile Corp., Ltd.–169
PAULS, Rolf–156
PERES, Shimon–153
PERSIAN Gulf–59
PERVUKHIN, Mikhail G.–21
PHILIP Rothenberg & Co.–152
PHILLIPS, Lawrence–152
PHILLIPS-Van Heusen Corp.–152
PORT Said–168
PRAVDA (Soviet Communist Party newspaper)–9, 65, 122
PRESS & Censorship–17-8, 56, 74, 91

Q

QADI, Anwar–189-90
QIZAN & Qizan Province, Saudi Arabia–179, 192, 205

R

RADIO Corporation of America (RCA)–168-9
RADWAN, Abbas–83, 128
RAWASHADA, Mansour–104
RAZIH & Razih Mountains, Yemen –198, 200
RED Cross–207-9
RED Mountain–199
RED Sea–179, 194
RELIGION–89, 129, 173, 194-5, 197
RESTON, James–4, 31
REVOLUTIONARY Command Council–110, 114
RHODESIA–164
RIAD, Mahmoud–128, 157, 167, 210
RICHARDS, James P.–5-6
RICKETT, Denis–75
RIDA el-Senussi, Hassan el-–116
RIFAAT, Kamal–83
RIFAI, Abdel Moneim el-–17
RIFAI, Samir el-–17, 26
RIYADH, Saudi Arabia–40
ROBERTS, Frank–154
RODRIGUEZ, Carlos Sosa–186
ROTHENBERG, Harvey–152
ROUNTREE, William M.–9, 25
ROYAL Dutch Shell Oil Co.–76
RUSK, Dean–126, 152-3, 164
RUZ-al-Youssuf (Cairo weekly magazine)–74

S

SAAD, Abdel Malek–167
SABRY, Ali–16, 38, 42, 66, 76, 83, 125, 127, 157, 183
SABRY, Hussein Zulfikar–128
SADA, Yemen–177, 180, 205
SADAT, Anwar al-–88, 180, 184
SAENGER, Eugen–101
SAFADI, Akram–115
SAID, Ahmed–62
SAKKA, Ahmed el-–14
SALAL, Abdullah al-–109, 116, 124, 175-6, 180-1, 184-9, 193, 195, 197-201, 206, 213
SALAM, Mahmoud Abdel–128, 167
SALAMAA, Anwar–128, 157, 167
SALAMAA, Muhammad Ezzat–128, 167
SALEM, Saeb–45
SALIM al-Sabbah, Sheik Abdullah al-–116
SALLAM, Abdul Aziz–211

SAMAHY, Abdulah el--42
SAMEI, Ahmad Abdul Maguid–166
SANA, Yemen–172, 175-8, 180, 183, 188-9, 192, 196-7, 200, 210-3
SAQQAF, Omar–211
SARAWAH, Yemen–209
SATYUKOV, Pavel–122
SAUD, King (Saudi Arabia)–11-2, 16, 18, 33, 35, 39-42, 70, 89, 116, 173, 179
SAUDI Arabia–10-1, 17, 35, 140, 155, 173, 179-80, 190, 192, 211. Egypt & Yemen–89, 175-7, 179, 183-4, 187-9, 196-8, 201
SAYED, Abdel Aziz el--88, 128
SCHRÖDER, Gerhard–149, 154
SEAFARERS' International Union (SIU)–77-82
SENEGAL–140
SERRAJ, Abdul Hamid al--23-4, 29, 38-9, 43, 60, 73, 84, 104, 115
SEYDOUX, Roger–154
SHAAB, Al- (Cairo newspaper)–18, 42
SHABIB, Hisham–115
SHABIB, Taleb Hussein–108-9
SHAFEI, Hussein–38, 84, 127
SHAFIIS–194-5, 197
SHAMI, Ahmad al--174, 182, 212
SHAMMAR Tribesmen–54
SHANSHAL, Siddik–108
SHARABASI, Ahmed Abdul el--38, 83, 128
SHARKAWI, Fathi el--88
SHAWAF, Col. Abdel Wahab el--54-5
SHEDA, Yemen–198
SHIHAB, Muhammad Said–55
SHIITE Islam–195, 197
SHINNAWY, Abdel Khalek el--167
SHOUKRI, Mrs. Amina–15
SHTURA, Lebanon–105
SHUKEIR, Muhammad Labib–128, 157, 167
SHURAIQI, Muhammad Pasha–70
SIDKY, Aziz–21, 38, 83, 128, 151
SIDKY, Talaat–115
SIERRA Leone–140
SINAI Peninsula: Campaign of 1956–2, 67. UAR troop movements–69
SINWAN, Yemen–180
SIRWAH, Yemen–199
SMITH, Arnold–76
SOCIALIST Union Front–108, 112
SOLH, Sami es--13, 40, 45
SOLIMAN, Muhammad Sidky–128, 167
SOMALIA–140
SOUFAN, Sami–112, 115
SOUFI, Jamal–109
SOUFI, Muhammad el--108, 111
SOUMIALOT, Gaston-Emile–143-4, 159
SOUTH Africa–118, 140
SOUTH Arabia, Federation of–165, 185-7
SOUTHERN Yemen–165
SOVIET Union–See union of Soviet Socialist Republics (USSR)
SPARKMAN, Sen. John J. (D., Ala.)–8
STEVENSON, Adlai E.–192
STINO, Kamal Ramzy–83, 128, 168
STOCK, Hans–168
STOOKEY, Robert W.–180
SUDAN–13, 17, 53, 140, 144, 155
SUEIDA, Ahmed Ben–212
SUEZ Canal–66-70, 74, 127. Crisis of 1956–1-3, 16, 23-4, 75-7, 125
SUHRAWARDY, Hussein–12
SUKARNO–158
SULTAN, Ahmad–86
SULZBERGER, C. L.–100
SUNNI Moslems–195, 197
SVOBODNY (Soviet destroyer)–31
SYRIA–55, 73, 118, 138, 140, 155, 193. Communists & Communist Party–23-6, 38-9. Egypt–33-5, 87, 102-5, 108, 165; federation–23-43, 55, 59, 82-8, 106-8. Government & politics–23-6, 86-7, 110-2. Rebellion(s)–82, 84-6, 102-5, 114-5. Soviet Union 10, 21, 24, 30-3, 64, 102, 165. Turkey–26-8, 30-5. U.S.–10, 21, 76, 79

T

TAIZ, Yemen–172, 175, 180, 186, 197, 212
TAJI, Assem–71

TALEEB, Naji–122
TANGANYIKA–140
TARABULSI, Amgad el-–83
TARRAF, Dr. Nurreddin–38, 83, 87, 128
TAXES–131-2
TEKOAH, Joseph–70
TEL Kotchek area, Syria–54-5
THANT, U–185, 188-93, 196
THAWRAH, Al- (Syria's official government newspaper)–202
3D WORLD–91-169
TIBERIAS, Lake (Sea of Galilee, Lake Kinneret)–118
TIMES (London newspaper)–40, 51, 101, 197
TITO (Josip Broz)–87, 140, 158-60
TOGO–140
TOHEIMA, Ahmed Abdullah–83, 87
TOUKAN, Suleiman–49
TOURÉ, Sékou–143, 158-9
TSHOMBÉ, Moïse–139-45
TUNISIA–17, 112, 140, 155, 165
TUOMIOJA, Sakari S.–137
TURK, Riad el-–65
TURKEY–11, 24-8, 30-5, 58, 87, 137-9
TURKI, Riad–128
TURKISH Cypriots–137-9

U

UGANDA–140
ULBRICHT, Walter–148-151, 153-4
UNION of Soviet Socialist Republics (USSR, Soviet Union)–138, 143-4, 159. Egypt (& UAR)–21-2, 45-72, 124-5, 159-60. Middle East–3, 9, 18-22, 24, 30-3, 102. Yemen–175, 192-3, 195-6
UNITED Arab Airlines–178
UNITED Arab Republic (UAR)–1, 37, 73-89
  Arms & armed forces–37, 98, 102, 118-9; for hostilities with Israel, see ISRAEL
  Boycotts–168-9
  China–See under 'C.'
  Congo–139-45
  Constitution–94-5, 129-37
  Economy–61, 63, 146-7
  Foreign relations & policy–45-72, 59-61, 74-7, 138, 158, 165; see also specific country
  Germany–145, 147-56
  Government & politics–23-43, 105-8, 127-9, 131-6, 157; cabinet–37-8, 73-4, 83-4, 87-8, 127-9, 157, 167-8
  Iraq–54-63, 119-22
  Israel–See under 'I'
  Jordan–50, 70-2, 117
  Policies & programs–37, 59-60, 73, 82-3, 91-100, 105-16
  Saudi Arabia–179, 183, 187
  Soviet Union–45-72, 102, 122-6
  Syrian secession–82-8
  3d world–91-169
  U.S.–76, 145-7, 168-9
  Yemen–41-3, 88-9, 122, 173-5, 178, 180, 183-95, 203-10
  See also EGYPT
UNITED Arab States–42-3
UNITED Nations–45, 66, 137. Palestine Truce Supervision Organization–192. Yemen–185, 188-94, 196
UNITED States–3, 21, 138-9, 152. Arms sales & aid–25, 102, 151-2, 162-3. Boycotts–79, 152, 168-9, Egypt (& UAR)–9-10, 28-9, 64-5, 76-82, 145-7, 161-5. Food shipments–9-10, 64, 76, 146-7. Eisenhower doctrine–3-14. Israel –10, 102, 151-2, 162-3. Jordan–25. Lebanon–46-9. Libya–126. Soviet Union–18-22. Syria–76. Vietnam–159-60. Yemen–181, 184
URUGUAY–140
USSR–See UNION of Soviet Socialist Republics (USSR)

V

VENEZUELA–140, 186
VIETNAM, North–158-60
VIETNAM War–157

Von HASE, Karl-Günther—148, 152
Von HORN, Carl Carlsson—189, 191-2, 194

W

WAFD & Wafdists—2, 14
WANDA, Al (Arab nationalist newspaper, Damascus)—109-10
WASHINGTON Post Co.—149
WAZIR, Muhammad Abdul Koddos al-—206
WEINFELD, Edward—77
WHEELUS Air Force Base—126
WHITE, Lincoln—9
WILEY, Sen. Alexander (R., Wis.)—8
WOLFF, Rep. Lester L. (D., N.Y.)—210
WORLD Court—66
WORLD War I—91-100
WORLD War II—2
WORONOFF, Jon—139
WRIGHT, Marshall—162

Y

YARMUK River—118
YASSIN, Aziz Ahmed—167
YAZALI, Muhammad al-—206
YEMEN—3, 13, 21, 41-3, 88-9, 109, 122, 140, 155, 165, 171-213. Armistice (cease-fire)—189, 195-9, 210-11. Egypt's withdrawal—210-3. Gas warfare—205-10
YEMEN, Southern—165
YEROFEYEV, Vladimir Y.—143
YOST, Charles W.—190
YOUNIS, Sayed Mareio Ahmed el-Haj—83
YOUSSEF, Muhammad Said—128, 157, 167
YUGOSLAVIA—140, 159
YUNIS, Ahmad Elhag—38
YUNIS, Mahmoud—127, 167

Z

ZAHREDIN, Abdel Karim—87
ZAIDI Moslems—195, 197
ZAKY, Hassan Abbas—38, 83, 87, 128, 167
ZAMARIA, Leon—86
ZAMYATIN, Leonid—122
ZANZIBAR—140
ZEID, Hekmat Abu—128
ZENDO, Ahmed—128
ZHDANOV (Soviet cruiser)—31
ZIONIST Organization of America 147
ZIONISTS—79, 81, 117
ZUBEIRI, Muhammad Mahmoud el-—175
ZUBEIRI, Qadi—199